DIVERSITY, INCLUSION, AND DECOLONIZATION

Practical Tools for Improving Teaching, Research, and Scholarship

Edited by
Abby Day, Lois Lee, Dave S.P. Thomas,
and James Spickard

BRISTOL
UNIVERSITY
PRESS

First published in Great Britain in 2024 by

Bristol University Press
University of Bristol
1-9 Old Park Hill
Bristol
BS2 8BB
UK
t: +44 (0)117 374 6645
e: bup-info@bristol.ac.uk

Details of international sales and distribution partners are available at bristoluniversitypress.co.uk

© Bristol University Press 2024

British Library Cataloguing in Publication Data
A catalogue record for this book is available from the British Library

ISBN 978-1-5292-1664-6 hardcover
ISBN 978-1-5292-1665-3 paperback
ISBN 978-1-5292-1666-0 ePub
ISBN 978-1-5292-1667-7 ePdf

Cover design: blu inc, Bristol
Front cover image: 'Mosaic' (2008) by Jim Spickard, Centred Vision
Photography, www.CentredVision.photography

Bristol University Press uses environmentally responsible print partners.

Printed in Great Britain by CPI Group (UK) Ltd, Croydon, CR0 4YY

FSC
www.fsc.org
MIX
Paper | Supporting
responsible forestry
FSC® C013604

Contents

List of Figures and Tables

Figures

Tables

Notes on Contributors

Gretchen Abuso teaches in the Sociology and Anthropology Department of Xavier University, Mindanao, Philippines. She has taught courses in sociological theories, globalization, and indigenous peoples. She is currently studying for her PhD in Sociology at the University of the Philippines.

Fabio Bolzonar is a fellow of the Cevipol at the Université de Bruxelles. He was awarded a PhD from the Department of Sociology at the University of Cambridge and he has been a visiting scholar at University of California Berkeley and a post-doctoral researcher at the School of Social Development and Public Policy of Fudan University. His principal research interests are: social theory, sociology of religion, morality politics, right-wing populism, and historical sociology.

Danny Braverman, FRSA, is Lecturer in Theatre at Goldsmiths College. Prior to his academic post, he had a 30-year career in socially engaged theatre, including as chief executive officer of the Disability Arts Centre, The Orpheus Centre, as Senior Theatre Officer at the Arts Council, and as Education Director at Theatre Royal Stratford East. As a theatre-maker, he is mostly known for his solo show *Wot? No Fish!!*, which won the Brian Way Playwriting Award (2013) and was named by *Guardian* critic Lyn Gardner as one of the top ten plays of 2014. His book, *Playing a Part: Drama and Citizenship*, was published by Trentham Books in 2002.

Samantha Brennan is Dean of the College of Arts and Professor of Philosophy at the University of Guelph, Ontario. Her main research interests lie in the area of contemporary normative ethics, applied ethics, and feminist philosophy.

Denise Buiten is Senior Lecturer in Social Justice and Sociology at the University of Notre Dame Australia. Her research focuses on gender, media, and gender-based violence. She is particularly interested in the evolving ways we understand and represent gender-based violence, and passionate about creating a learning experience for students that enables nuanced, critical, and empathic engagement with these issues.

Gwen Chapman is Provost and Vice-President (Academic) and Professor in Family Relations and Applied Nutrition at the University of Guelph, Ontario. Her research interests focus on how everyday food practices are shaped by the social, cultural, and physical environments in which people live.

Abby Day is Professor in Race, Faith and Culture in the Department of Sociology, Goldsmiths, University of London, with a background in anthropology, sociology, and publishing. Her teaching, research, writing, and supervisions cover religion, gender, media, generations, and critical criminology. She contributes regularly to media discussions on politics, gender, and equality and is active as a reviewer and member of the boards of national and international scholarly organizations, journals, and funders. Her latest book addresses key issues, opportunities, and barriers, particularly for early-career researchers, in *How to Get Research Published and Funded* (Routledge, 2022).

Sara Ewing is Lecturer in Academic Literacies in the Centre for Academic Language and Literacies at Goldsmiths, University of London, teaching critical reading, writing, and research methods across the university. She has a background in community-based organizations, with an emphasis on access to education for marginalized and stigmatized populations. Sara is currently focused on facilitating Decolonizing Academic Practices workshops and integrating decolonizing theories and praxis with discipline-specific academic skills provision.

Ellen Finlay is undertaking her PhD at the University of New South Wales. Her current research is in understanding ageing well in urban New South Wales Aboriginal and Torres Strait Islander communities. Ellen has previously researched power asymmetries in relation to gender and security and asylum seekers' access to bodily integrity.

Rosemary Hancock is a sociologist and lecturer in the Institute for Ethics and Society at the University of Notre Dame Australia and teaches in the Social Justice programme. Her research grapples with the complex and dynamic intersection of religion with politics and activism. Her previous research has explored how religion and race are co-constituted and intertwined.

Belinda Leach is Professor in Sociology and Anthropology at the University of Guelph, Ontario. Her research interests include women and work, organizational change, gender and rural livelihoods, and migration.

Lois Lee is Senior Lecturer in Religious Studies at the University of Kent. Her books include *Recognizing the Non-religious: Reimagining the Secular* (Oxford, 2015) and *Negotiating Religion: Cross-disciplinary Perspectives* (Routledge, 2017). She was founding editor of the journal *Secularism and Nonreligion* and founding director of the Nonreligion and Secularity Research Network. She is currently Principal Investigator on a multi-million-pound Templeton Foundation project, 'Understanding Unbelief'.

Lin Ma is a lecturer at the University of Bristol. Her doctoral research investigates the interface between Chinese international students and local biblical Christians in Britain. Particularly, she approaches the phenomenon of contemporary Christian conversion by including those who have had evangelical Christian encounters but do not become Christian believers. Her thesis, to be completed in 2021, examines inclusion and exclusion co-produced by international higher education and the global evangelical space.

Paige Mann is Assistant Librarian at the University of Redlands in the US. She received her Master's in Library and Information Science from San Jose State University. Her research explores equity in open access and is action oriented to mobilize librarians and faculty toward more equitable scholarly communication practices.

Ali Meghji is Assistant Professor in Social Inequalities in the Department of Sociology, University of Cambridge. He works on the intersection of decolonial thought and critical race theory, analysing the balance of racialized social systems with the colonial matrix of power.

Alexandra Rodney holds a PhD in Sociology from the University of Toronto. She is a former postdoctoral fellow at the University of Guelph, Ontario, where she worked on the organization's gender equity initiatives.

Januschka Schmidt is an interdisciplinary junior researcher focusing on the intersection of places, spirituality, and well-being. She has been working as an international scholar at universities in Europe and East Asia (particularly Japan). In her work, critical research methods take a central role as a tool to building sustainable research practices that have positive impacts on the communities she works with.

Karen Schucan Bird is based at the Social Research Institute of University College London. Her research and teaching spans the social sciences with specialist interests in gender and inclusivity, evidence use and policy, and domestic violence. As part of her teaching, Karen works with students and colleagues to develop evidence-informed initiatives that advance inclusive practices in higher education.

Federico Settler is Associate Professor in Sociology of Religion at the University of KwaZulu-Natal (South Africa). He has published widely on race, postcolonialism, migration, and their entanglements with religion. He is the author of a forthcoming book, *Frantz Fanon and Protest Cultures in South Africa*.

James Spickard is Emeritus Professor of Sociology at the University of Redlands, in the US. He has published widely on the sociology of religion, human rights, non-Western and Western social theories, and social science research design. His most recent book is *Alternative Sociologies of Religion: Through Non-Western Eyes* (New York University Press, 2017). His current project is a book on what is happening to religion in the contemporary world.

Martin Stringer was born in Tanzania, bought up in South Yorkshire, and took an undergraduate degree in Social Anthropology at Manchester University, specializing in religion. He taught in the Department of Theology and Religion at Birmingham University, becoming Head of College and Deputy Pro-Vice Chancellor with responsibility for Equality, Diversity, and Inclusion. He is currently Pro-Vice Chancellor for Education at Swansea University.

Seetha Tan is a graduate student in sociology at the University of Cambridge, where she specializes in political and economic sociology. Her thesis examines transnational political activism in the Lebanese diaspora in France. Her work aims to place critical citizenship studies, postcolonial diaspora studies, and decolonial theory into dialogue.

Dave S.P. Thomas (FHEA) is an occupational therapist (specialism in Occupational Science), a public health specialist, and doctoral researcher. He is a Senior Advisor at AdvanceHE with expertise in equality, diversity inclusion and leadership. He is the lead editor of *Doing Equity and Diversity for Success in Higher Education* (Palgrave Macmillan, 2021) and *Towards Decolonising the University: A Kaleidoscope for Empowered Action* (Counterpress, 2020).

Laura Wain is a graduate student in the Department of Sociology at the University of Cambridge. Her thesis focuses on the reproduction of coloniality through the production of indigenous tourism in Quebec, Canada. Her academic interests lie broadly in the field of decolonial thought and postcolonial theory, with a particular focus on global tourism.

Acknowledgements

It is with enormous excitement and humility that we editors are able now to thank all those people who made this volume possible – in the middle of a global pandemic and other worldwide issues and personal challenges. We are grateful to the many people who have been involved since its conception, beginning with members of the British Sociological Association and its study group for the Sociology of Religion who participated in two workshops where the first ideas for this volume were presented and discussed. Further discussions took place during workshops at two of our home institutions, Goldsmiths, University of London and the University of Kent (and in particular the University of Kent Centre for the Study of Higher Education).

It was Victoria Pittman, at Bristol University Press, who first shared our vision for a publication, and we are grateful for her early encouragement and direction. Shannon Kneis took over the project a little later on and expertly guided our proposal through reviews, revisions and eventually the final manuscript completion. We also want to thank the anonymous reviewers whose careful and constructive feedback provided important insights and opportunities for tightening the Introduction, the Epilogue and the volume as a whole and Gail Welsh for managing final proofs' quality.

The editors would like to thank many other individuals, including Afe Adogame, Jason Arday, Jocelyn Anita Barrow, Hilary Beckles, the late Gary Bouma, François Gauthier, Sari Hanafi, the late Otto Maduro, Eloísa Martín, Michael Okyerefo, Geoff Palmer, Kathleen M. Quinlan, and – of course – each other. As an editorial team we have spent the last three years in close consultation, sharing ideas, resolving problems and celebrating milestones and progress.

But none of this would have happened were it not for the authors of this volume's chapters. These are all hard-working academics with demands and constraints of full workloads and personal commitments (and did we mention a global pandemic?). They not only found the time to reflect, write and revise, but they also found the courage and the generosity to share their sometimes difficult, sometimes disappointing but ultimately encouraging attempts to put into practice what everyone else talks about in theory. Because of them we are able to offer this practical resource, this work in progress and, we hope, this small but important contribution to achieving our ultimate shared goal: justice and equality at all stages of our academic endeavours and careers.

One goal of this book is to empower individuals as well as institutions to make changes in their own practice when they want to, but the existence of this book is an acknowledgement of the greatest contribution of all: collaboration. We all get to where we are today because of our joint power in community to bring about real change, in ourselves and in the world around us.

Typographical Note

The editors capitalise the terms 'Black' and 'White' when used to denote racial groups. We do this for two reasons. First, 'races' are social constructs that change names and shapes from time to time and place to place. 'Black' and 'White' are not descriptive adjectives; they are the current names of (imagined) racial groups. Second, these groups are equal. Though some partisans capitalize their own group and lower-case others, we capitalize both to emphasize their equality. We also frequently use scare-quotes (for example, 'race') to indicate concepts that should not be read or used uncritically.

Some of our contributors have chosen to use different conventions. We have expressed our preferences to them but have let each of them make their own principled choices. (Out of similar respect, we have let contributors use their own national spelling conventions rather than convert them to British English.)

We thank Bristol University Press for letting us alter their house style on this matter. We also thank them for altering their standard reference style to include authors' full names rather than merely last names and initials. We want to avoid hiding our cited authors' diversity.

Introduction: Why Diversity, Inclusion, and Decolonization Matter

Abby Day, Lois Lee, Dave S.P. Thomas, and James Spickard

We live in an increasingly diverse society. In person and in our media spaces, we encounter people from different racial and ethnic groups, of different genders and sexual orientations, with different religions, education levels, incomes, occupations, languages, marital and family statuses, age, physical and mental abilities, and geographic origins. And we interact with them. Our democratic and humanistic ideals call us to respect them and to treat them as we all wish to be treated.

At the same time, our core institutions remain dominated by a small elite, crudely equated to 'White men of the Global North' (see Ahmed, 2017). This elite offers a much narrower set of perspectives and interests than are found in our diverse populations. For universities, this means that people from a small set of identity categories still dominate the production and dissemination of academic knowledge in teaching, writing, and research. The dominance of such elites poses challenges to all supposedly democratic institutions. In academic life, it distorts the knowledge that universities produce; it ill-serves students, most acutely those from non-dominant groups; and it threatens the humanistic values on which the modern university is founded.

Euro-American universities have long seen themselves as keepers of the Western tradition: that (imagined) constellation of Enlightenment values that proclaimed itself to be humanity's highest achievement and promised a '*mission civilisatrice*' that would improve life around the world. Those values included equality, individual freedom, and the importance of the pursuit of truth. These were seen both as good in themselves and as pathways to social flourishing. That is why university scholars were given the freedom to teach, to write, and to learn: only by doing so could they discover the truths that are supposed to set us all free.

Ironically, though, the scholarly pursuit of truth has revealed large gaps between these universities' values and their actual practices. Among other things:

• Universities do not treat people equally. Despite some progress, they continue to discriminate on the basis of gender, race, class, sexuality, religion, national origin, and a host of other attributes. They allow those with favoured status to join their student bodies and faculties; disfavoured groups are either admitted grudgingly or barred. This discrimination is often covert, but it is effective at keeping White male professional-class men – or people who act like them – at the top of the heap.

• They prioritize Euro-American knowledge and norms. University curricula continue to overemphasize the work of White males in literature, the arts, history, and social science. They structure scholarly practice along customary (and hierarchical) Euro-American lines. People who study these subjects and embrace these practices succeed; those whose interests or styles fall outside these boxes more often fail.

• They systematically hide the power relations that created Euro-American global hegemony or, at best, treat those power relations as part of a superseded past. British universities, for example, treat the British Empire as history rather than as a force that continues to structure socioeconomic and power relations around the world (Bhambra, 2014; Mehta, 2019). American universities offer courses on the history of slavery but not on the history of redlining – the 20th-century government-sponsored practice of denying African Americans the right to reside in all but the poorest parts of cities, which helped to create contemporary Black urban poverty (Coates, 2014; but see Wilson, 1987).

• Euro-American universities imagine that they are the pinnacle of excellence. In doing so, they conveniently forget the 'epistemicides' by which European powers (and their settler colonies) destroyed other civilizations' knowledge systems (Thomas, Chapter 7). They also forget the self-serving scholarly ranking systems that are structured to maintain the illusion of Euro-American intellectual superiority (Mann, Chapter 12).

In short, Euro-American universities are not the 'universal' institutions that they claim to be. They favour students and scholars who represent their traditional elites, and they systematically minimize intellectual contributions originating outside of them and outside the West. Their own values call them to account for these failings.

This volume investigates and presents practical responses to these profound issues; it contributes to work helpful for us understand elitisms in relation to the academy, but it focuses its lens on how individuals and institutions can best make change. In this, it builds on and learns from a wide and ever-growing critical engagement with different forms of elitism that shape and constrain the university. Over the 30 years since 1990, the gap between values and practice already described has led to various efforts to diversify academic personnel and fields of study, to include previously excluded or marginalized groups in university life, and to decolonize university curricula. Some of these efforts are driven by financial pressures, including the need to serve new student 'markets' and to expand their offerings into new academic fields. Social movements have shaped other efforts, particularly the women's movement and various racial and ethnic power movements (Black power, La Raza, AIM, Black Lives Matter). Decolonization movements have affected universities in Britain, France, and their former colonies. They are less common in the United States (US), as fewer Americans recognize US colonialism (hello, Puerto Rico!). Lawsuits play a role, too. These efforts gain momentum from their own limited success – when more of those outside of the elite progress through the universities, only to find their progress impeded still in significant ways. Together, such internal and external pressures are forcing universities to respond.

If recent years have seen a revitalization of the appetite for diversity and inclusivity that seeks to redress systemic inequalities, our understanding and ability to address them in everyday academic practice has not kept pace. This volume recognizes the scope for engaging and seeking to expand our understanding of inequalities that dog the university and limit its achievements in myriad ways. Yet it also recognizes the need to do much more to understand, share, and enhance the practical efforts that students, teachers, and scholars are making to overcome them. We seek to engage with what has been done and could be done to improve things, with initiatives that have and have not worked, and with the challenges that individuals and institutions face in implementing practical changes. Our 15 chapters cover issues that range from recasting course syllabi and redesigning pedagogy to developing more inclusive models of scholarship and resisting the neoliberal forces that dominate scholarly publication. Though they do not cover everything, they exemplify the ferment that seeks to bring equality and justice to higher education, and they support readers to develop their own understanding and use of, to use a phrase developed in this volume (Schmidt, Chapter 11), critical methods of teaching and research.

Diversity, inclusion, and decolonization

In this work, this volume engages the concepts 'diversity', 'inclusion', and 'decolonization'. These terms represent different ways of conceptualizing and critiquing forms of elitism. They address distinct power structures, but they overlap and intersect – and they converge in ways that make it possible to identify individuals and groups who are more or less advantaged within them.

One of the arguments we propose in this volume is precisely this: that elitism in the university is complex and intersectional in ways that no single set of initiatives – neither those pursuing diversity, those seeking inclusion, nor those wanting to decolonize – can capture alone. Meghji, Tan, and Wain (Chapter 2) show, for example, how diversity initiatives are often much more superficial than decolonization ones, while Ma's Chapter 3 reveals ways in which postcolonial critique may be more effective in highlighting forms of marginalization that arise from colonial history than it is at addressing other forms.

In creating this volume, we have found the concepts of the 'elite' and 'elitism' helpful precisely because they are more general and therefore more elastic: they can stretch to accommodate different forms of inequality. At the same time, they are less precise, and they lack the rich theoretical traditions of the sort that should shape our critical engagement with university research and teaching. We recognize that addressing and challenging elitisms and the hierarchies they rest upon involves the deep analysis that the theories and practices of diversity, inclusivity, and decolonization have produced. We offer no quick fix here. Instead, we offer an invitation to join us in engaging and challenging problematic hierarchies in the broadest sense – and to engage critically with critique itself, to always be asking if there is something we are missing.

We begin this volume with a sketch of these multiple lines of elitism – elitisms in the plural – as they manifest in the university, before setting out the practice-focused response that this volume offers.

Elitisms and the university today

We can start with teaching. Universities have long faced complaints about having elite-focused curricula and about serving the ruling classes rather than broader populations. Until the last quarter of the 19th century, for example, the best British and American universities centred their coursework on Latin and Greek literature and history, adding sciences and maths long before they added much attention to the modern world (LARA, 2019). This was designed to train their (male) students to rule and to give them a common set of intellectual references that excluded most of their countries' populations.

Interestingly, while Oxford and Cambridge students focused on the Roman Empire, 'schoolboys in India and Nigeria were learning the intricacies of Shakespeare's *Julius Caesar* and memorizing the lists of English kings through the wars of succession' (Elder, 1971, p 288). A Eurocentric curriculum was a way to make Indians and Nigerians think of themselves as British and thus not rebel.

The late 19th and early 20th centuries saw the founding of research universities on the German model, where scholars were encouraged to explore the natural world and push the boundaries of science. This could have altered curricula and expanded university access to the professional classes, but it did not; all but a few universities still served social, political, and religious elites. It was not until after the Second World War that governments recognized that national prosperity depended on having a workforce with technical skills. Their increased investments in higher education tilted curricula toward the sciences. Only then did university training become a common path to middle-class status (Bensman and Vidich, 1971), first in the US, followed by Britain, Germany, France, and other European countries.

Elitism still shaped who got to participate. Women were long excluded or marginalized, as were most ethnic and religious minorities. But shifting demographics, such as the end of the White post-war 'baby boom', forced the now larger number of universities to seek non-traditional students in order to maintain their revenues. Universities that had previously catered to the sons of the White professional classes found themselves teaching women, working-class, immigrant, and minority students in larger numbers than before. This presented new instructional problems and new issues of how to manage their inclusion.

Take economic issues. The editors of this volume have all taught students who lack access to their own computers, internet service, and sometimes even housing, or who work two or more jobs to support family members in need. Universities can do something to address the first two of these problems by providing computer labs, though this does not help students in the latter two situations. Nor does it mean that students' access to digital resources is equal: unrestricted access to a personal laptop at home is very different to limited access to a computer shared by several household users, let alone one in a public facility. How we meaningfully equalize access across social class lines remains an open question. Some faculty maintain textbook lending libraries; others record their lectures, which they provide to students whose work schedules prevent full-time schooling. Some set up student partnerships to ensure that everyone has resources. Some help students to navigate university aid bureaucracies, while a few have even paid an occasional student's fees. All this flies under school officials' radar; few university leaders ever think about the hurdles low-income students face.

There are other barriers to non-elite participation. At the faculty level, they include what Braveen Kumar (2020) calls 'homogeneity hiring', in which faculty and staff from White professional-class backgrounds fill posts with other people from White professional-class backgrounds because these hires fit the established model of what faculty and staff ought to be like. A similar process limits student diversity to 'promising' minority students who fit in with their White professional-class peers. Once admitted, they find themselves foregrounded as window-dressing on university brochures and websites – the university's way of virtue-signalling that it is more open to difference than is really the case. In the US, at least, rising student tuitions and fees are increasingly covered by predatory loans rather than grants. These make universities too expensive for most working-class students and leave those who do graduate so indebted that they need to take low-wage service jobs rather than pursue the further training that most professional-class jobs now require.

Cultural elitism is still alive and well. University core requirements are still dominated by European and American history, literature, art, and social sciences, plus introductory courses in natural science and maths. Many universities now gesture toward diversity by also requiring some sort of 'border crossing experience', by which is meant taking a course focused on 'minorities' or an activity providing exposure to a non-Western language, culture, history, or art. Yet this still puts the White, male, hetero-, cisgendered West at the centre of the curriculum. As one of our American editor's students put it, 'Coming from Compton [the heart of the Los Angeles Black ghetto], I cross a cultural border every time I step onto this campus!' White, professional-class Euro-America is still the cultural norm.

This elite domination thus affects the academy on many levels – ethical, epistemic, pedagogical, and economic, among others. It includes the dominance of perspectives from specific gender, ethnic, sexual, and class positions, as well as issues of Eurocentrism, androcentrism, Westernization, indigenization, and colonialism. These affect everything we do in the academy – teaching, writing, and research – and everyone who works there. That includes the elites whose views take centre stage.

Why diversity, inclusion, and decolonization matter

What do universities gain by diversifying their students and staff, helping people from all walks of life to feel included, and decolonizing their curricula and practices? Here are a few benefits.

First, admitting students from outside of traditional elites enriches university intellectual life. This is true in many respects, including for the quality of teaching that universities can provide. One of our editors teaches a course on homelessness, and scarcely a semester goes by without a student telling the class what it feels like to be homeless or marginally housed. Most students who take that course do so because they want to be social workers. They gain tremendously by having a peer give them their future clients' perspective on the problems they will be trying to solve.

The same benefit comes from having a racially, ethnically, religiously, linguistically, and sexually diverse student body. In-class discussions help students to see the world through other students' eyes. Students bring their unique knowledge and perspectives to the table, which can be a major source of learning for others. This kind of instrumental logic is not the only reason to challenge elitisms in the university, but it is a powerful illustration that a failure to do so profoundly limits the university's ability to produce real education.

The benefits of more diversity accrue only if all students feel that they are a welcome part of the university community. Diversity is not enough; they must feel included, as well. This is not just a matter of feeling safe; universities are supposed to help students grow, and that involves helping them to learn to thrive outside their comfort zones. But they need to feel that they have a place at the table and that their presence matters to others. They need to feel that their contribution is valued. Too often, universities' largely White faculty and Eurocentric curricula do not visibly recognize these students' worth.

This is, in fact, the message that various student movements have been giving to universities for what now seems like a very long time. From the women's movement's call for increased hiring of women faculty and better treatment of women on university campuses to Black, Asian, and Latino movements' call for better treatment and increased hiring of faculty of colour, to LGBTQ+ movements' call for an end to discrimination and for support of people's diverse sexualities, to differently abled students' insistence on educational access, the demand has been for universities to become the *universal* institutions they are supposed to be. Without this universality, effective teaching is impossible.

And more than teaching is at stake. Universities also generate and organize knowledge. Their professors and researchers discover new things and reveal new patterns that had heretofore been unseen. They integrate these discoveries and patterns into coherent ways of understanding the world. And they apply these discoveries and patterns to improve people's lives. These are three of the multiple scholarly tasks that the world asks of universities and their personnel (Boyer, 1990).

The problem here is this. If the knowledge that universities produce and organize is biased; if it is developed and proclaimed from only a particular socially dominant point of view; if it fails to represent the multiplicity of perspectives to be found in our globalized and multipolar world; if it fails to acknowledge the relations between the parts of that world and the historical forces that shaped those relations into the ones we experience today; then it fails in its epistemic mission. Its attempts to generate knowledge about the world hit their own 'glass ceiling'. With its enormous lacunae, its limited access to new knowledge and whole traditions of knowledge produced elsewhere, and its exclusion of the diverse perspectives needed to generate new critical readings and foster innovation, the still-colonial university is intellectually impoverished. For example, Euro-American ignorance of other societies' long traditions of recognizing and understanding the climate crisis is one powerful and tragic example discussed by Meghji, Tan, and Wain (Chapter 2).

This, in fact, is the charge levelled against universities today: that they promulgate a Eurocentric view of the world that ignores the contributions of non-Euro-American societies and supports the neocolonial power relations that continue to structure global society. Ending that intellectual colonialism is a key part of the current demand for university reform and part of the transnational demand for greater global equality – a demand for a 'decolonized university'.

The chapters in this volume by Meghji, Tan, and Wain (Chapter 2), by Thomas (Chapter 7), and by Settler (Chapter 15) go into detail about these decolonizing efforts, so we will be brief here. The decolonization movement has two main foci. The first is expanding the range of resources that scholars use for understanding the world beyond the 'great men' of the Euro-American tradition. This means reclaiming the knowledge and knowledge systems that colonial powers repressed, so that they can become an active part of the world's intellectual heritage. The second is dismantling the power relations that support Euro-American intellectual dominance. These are not just historic and financial; they are also built into such things as the structure of the publishing industry, journal and university ranking systems, and the status hierarchies that permeate academic life. Decolonizing these patterns calls for institutional as well as intellectual change.

The appetite for these changes seems to be growing among students and faculty in many parts of the world. The 2015–16 #RhodesMustFall and #FeesMustFall campaigns in South Africa (see Settler, 2019, and Chapter 15 this volume) and the near simultaneous 'Why Is My Curriculum White?' campaign at various British universities (Peters, 2018) addressed both forms of decolonizing, albeit in different measures. Students have continued to push (Swain, 2019), to such an extent that the Open University has listed decolonization as among the top ten trends in higher education in the coming decade (Ferguson et al, 2019, pp 15–17).

Meanwhile, decolonizing initiatives among faculty and intellectuals have multiplied (for example, Alatas, 2006; Bhambra, 2007; Connell, 2007, 2018; Grosfoguel, 2013; de Sousa Santos, 2014; Alatas and Sinha, 2017; Go, 2017). Many of these build on an earlier generation of postcolonial scholars, often of Middle Eastern or South Asian origin (for example, Said, 1978; Spivak, 1988; Bhabha, 1994), who criticized Western scholars' practice of speaking for colonized peoples rather than listening to them. Others, often from Latin America, focused on world-systems theory and on the realities of economic development and underdevelopment (for example, Lugones, 2007; Quijano, 2007; Mignolo, 2011). Bhambra (2014) explains that the presentation of modernity/coloniality as tightly bound concepts first articulated by Quijano shows that the Euro-American idealization of modernity and the fiction of rationally, individually created knowledge are consequences of colonialism, not the other way around.

These campaigns and intellectual movements have prepared the ground for our current situation. The public can no longer ignore systemic inequalities, which demand to be addressed. The COVID-19 pandemic has further highlighted racial and class disparities in many countries' health systems; the plight of low-paid service workers reminds us that not everyone has the option of working safely from home; the global Black Lives Matter protests demand the elimination of racially motivated over-policing; the pandemic-driven near collapse of international trade reminds people of their worldwide economic connections. All these events feed a revitalized appetite for diversity, inclusion, and decolonization as means of restoring justice to an unequal world. Many universities are trying to respond (Swain, 2019).

Why is change so hard?

Still, if everyone knows 'decolonizing the curriculum' and challenging elitisms across the university are good ideas, why then is the pace so slow? A 2020 *Guardian* investigation reported that only a fifth of British universities said that they were 'reforming their curriculum to confront the harmful legacy of colonialism' (Batty, 2020). The examples given suggest that these initiatives are limited in scope. For example, Queen Mary University of London reported that their decolonizing efforts occurred in one school only (English and Drama); Newman University also mentioned the English department, which apparently has but one course explicitly referencing decolonizing; the University of East London has run decolonizing workshops in its school of Art and Digital Industries, but not elsewhere. At the time of the *Guardian* report, only two universities (including Bristol, the publisher of this collection) had incorporated a commitment to decolonize in their strategic plan.

Yet the academics and students whom this study interviewed said they wanted universities to change the way that knowledge is created and presented. They wanted more than just a few non-White names added to the reading lists. Instead, they wanted universities to dedicate themselves to 'challenging and remaking the current pedagogy, which was rooted in imperial and colonial ideas about knowledge and learning, at an institutional level' (Batty, 2020).

Part of the reason for the minimal implementation of the decolonizing agenda is undoubtedly systemic. History is not littered with examples of privileged parties rushing to give up status and power. This, in fact, recalls the programme of colonialism itself: a matter of the colonizing countries using direct or indirect violence to gain power over the colonies' political and economic resources; it is no surprise that the process of relinquishing that power is likely to be complex and slow.

Adding to the problem, the two decades since 2000 have seen considerable neoliberal restructuring in British and, to a lesser extent, American and European universities; this has arguably narrowed their ability to ensure inclusivity (Holmwood, 2011). For example, the increased emphasis on quantitative measures of scholarship, teaching, and student outcomes leads universities (and other institutions) to focus on things they can count. That notably does not include curricular reform, especially when the measuring instruments are geared to the old curriculum rather than the new. Tuck and Yang (2012) point out that 'decolonisation is not a metaphor'; it is a messy and disruptive process. Universities and university personnel are not rewarded for taking on messy issues.

Such resistance to change makes some decolonization activists ask to what extent the colonial master's house can be truly dismantled. Who is responsible for decolonizing the academy and making reparations? What do reparations for past exclusion and disempowerment look like? Can we maintain the current global pressure to redress systemic inequalities? As Chinua Achebe (1994) and Ngũgĩ wa Thiong'o (1986) both remind us, the first step in the process of decolonization is to decolonize the mind. Simply put, promoting inclusivity requires collective action by a diverse range of persons, with the goal of abolishing inequality.

Ali Meghji and his co-authors (Chapter 2) share the view that decolonizing the university probably cannot be achieved via individual initiatives. Instead, decolonization requires a more paradigmatic change. Yet in developing this volume we have been struck also by the challenges that individuals face if they want to effect change in their own workplace. This is, of course, one outcome of the ongoing and tenacious hold of that colonial and elitist socio-epistemological paradigm that decolonization and other diversification initiatives seek to challenge. There are systemic, institutional barriers in place that work against individual initiative and intervention. Nevertheless, as we have worked on these issues over the years, we began to observe a gap between a positive will to change and the hindered ability to do so. We saw this firstly in our own practice, then in the practice of others around us, and finally as a trend in the way in which many of the anti-elitist movements we engage with in this volume approach their object.

That is why we chose to produce this collection: so we could present to ourselves and others as many concrete examples of deep, practical efforts toward diversity, inclusion, and decolonization as we could fit into a single volume.

This volume

Diversity, Inclusion, and Decolonization focuses on what we can all actually do, practically and theoretically, to bring about a more democratic and just academia. What have people tried? What has worked? What further visions do we need? How can we ordinary scholars contribute to the change that is needed? Our contributors detail the initiatives that both individuals and institutions have implemented to change academic practice in their everyday teaching, writing, and research practices. Our chapters locate these initiatives in wider theoretical contexts and reflect on these initiatives' achievements, their problems, and the work that they leave undone. The contributors explore what support institutions and colleagues can offer to others doing this work and how staff can manage the workload in their already busy, often over-stretched lives. We consider how students are involved in these processes and how they better could be. How are diversity, inclusivity, and decolonization negotiated in the classroom? What works? What does not? How can we democratize our scholarship? How can we open the academy to the complex, multipolar world in which we live?

We have organized these chapters into four sections, each dealing with one aspect of our topic. Part I: Changing Universities contains five chapters that provide an overview of the issues facing universities today.

- Prof. Martin Stringer reflects in Chapter 1 on his career in the UK as both an academic and a senior manager, currently as Pro-Vice Chancellor for Education at Swansea University. He shares his experiences of being passionate about diversity and the need to celebrate diversity within education. Despite identifying as gay, as Catholic, and to lesser extent as dyslexic, he did not engage directly in campaigning groups within the University, but effected change at policy and personal levels.
- In Chapter 2 Ali Meghji, Seetha Tan, and Laura Wain explore the differences between initiatives that focus on 'diversity' and 'inclusion', on the one hand, and 'decolonization', on the other. They argue that the former bring more people to the existing higher education table without fundamentally reconfiguring that table. They stress that decolonial thinking draws the connections between the wealth and power of the colonizing countries and the poverty and powerlessness of the global South, and they make some concrete proposals for righting this epistemic injustice.
- Lin Ma's Chapter 3 argues that postcolonial, decolonial, multiculturalist, and feminist scholars have typically neglected the presence and embodied knowledge of 'East Asians' – a significant case in its own right and an illustration of the blind spots that critical movements and initiatives may have. She shows how these scholars and their universities apply the racialized term 'East Asians' with insufficient reflection, and how they have failed to consider the unique challenges that many encompassed in this 'group' face within the context of Western universities – which too often see them only as a source of much-needed income. This chapter uses a case

study of Chinese international students in Britain and their relation to a locally dominant view of 'religion' to highlight how Eurocentric research frameworks reject certain knowledges as invalid and affirm an elitist agenda.

- Danny Braverman writes in Chapter 4 that disabled students experience disadvantage in higher education because institutions are informed and led by a medical framework instead of a social model of disability. Educators and managers follow equality legislation as they establish specialist teams to address issues of 'access', meaning that disabled students' needs are 'bolted on' rather than built in. Braverman looks instead to critical disability studies and describes how, as a teacher and dramaturg, he incorporates inclusive theatre practice where access is built in, allowing multiple points of entry and building a strong sense of community.

- Samantha Brennan, Gwen Chapman, Belinda Leach, and Alexandra Rodney report in Chapter 5 on a collaborative workshop specifically designed to share practitioners' everyday experiences of 'doing diversity'. The chapter illuminates the complex and messy relationships between policy and praxis and the extent to which institutional context can shape understandings of how policies are enacted, embodied, and experienced.

The four chapters in Part II: Diversifying Curricula examine teaching practices in search of better ways to reach normally excluded students and to include scholarship that is too often ignored.

- In Chapter 6 Karen Schucan Bird explores challenges involved in curricula reform in the UK, focusing on efforts to diversify reading lists. Bird provides tools and tips for educators seeking to review their syllabi, setting out ten practical steps for revising reading lists.

- In Chapter 7 Dave S.P. Thomas employs critical race theory as an analytical framework to understand academic debates that theorize race, gender, and intersectionality in relation to 'authentic knowledge'. He examines the role of Whiteness in maintaining myriad forms of epistemic inequality, focusing on post-secondary education curricula. Reflecting on a research project that aimed to disrupt heteronormative epistemologies and broaden perspectives, Thomas shows the impact of staff–student collaboration in reviewing reading lists to bring about curricula changes.

- In Chapter 8 Sara Ewing discusses the motivations, practices, and collaborations of the Decolonizing Research Methods project at Goldsmiths, University of London. The project consists of themed workshops that situate Western academic research in historical, political, and social contexts that are tied to colonial practices of difference and hierarchy. They work with a deliberately collaborative, flat teaching model that helps students to interrogate and contribute to issues of epistemology and methodology.

- Denise Buiten, Ellen Finlay, and Rosemary Hancock report in Chapter 9 on their experience of using intersectional feminist pedagogy to teach about gender-based violence in an Australian university. They describe how many students resist traditional ways of teaching about gender violence, either because they feel blamed or because the situations they know about are more complex than the ones they often encounter in teaching and research. This chapter shows how intersectional approaches offer new opportunities for teaching.

Part III: Diversifying Research and Scholarship contains three chapters that explore various ways of combating Eurocentrism in scholarly practice in the West and beyond.

- In Chapter 10 James Spickard advocates expanding the theoretical toolkit of one discipline, sociology, by taking seriously concepts arising in non-Euro-American civilizations. He illustrates this by using the Confucian concept of 'sacred relationships' and the 14th-century historian Ibn Khaldūn's concept of *al aṣabiyyah* to understand long-overlooked aspects of Western religious life.
- In Chapter 11 Januschka Schmidt presents a discussion of what she calls critical research methods. Schmidt identifies how power relations impact on and exclude forms of knowledge production, and considers critical research methods that can disrupt those power relations, with a focus on critical citation practices. The chapter also addresses how new, emerging, and other more vulnerable scholars can engage with critical research methods.
- In Chapter 12 Paige Mann describes the changes that have transformed the scholarly publishing industry. Now dominated by a few large, for-profit corporations that place increasing pressure on library budgets and shape scholars' career success, the publishing industry's control over journals and journal- and university-ranking systems determines where scholars need to publish, what they need to publish, and what scholarly conversations are possible – and preserves Euro-American hegemony over scholarship worldwide. This chapter suggests ways in which scholars can collectively challenge this system and regain control over access to their work.

The three chapters in Part IV: Overcoming Intellectual Colonialism describe aspects of intellectual colonialism outside the global North.

- In Chapter 13 Fabio Bolzonar explores the Westernization of social theory in contemporary China. He uses his experience as a teacher and lecturer at Fudan University (2015–17) to provide insights into the Eurocentrism of, in this case, Chinese sociology, and he suggests some classroom actions that can foster greater epistemic pluralism.

- In Chapter 14 Gretchen Abuso provides the Philippines as a case study of a postcolonial nation whose education system remains dominated by elitist and colonial perspectives. Focusing on the International Studies curricula in the country, this chapter provides practical methods and relevant materials that educators can use to emphasize local ethnic and cultural diversity in degree courses traditionally dominated by global North models.
- In Chapter 15 Federico Settler describes the production of a series of public performances and memorials at his South African university during the 2015–17 student-led effort to decolonize university curricula and lower university fees. These staff-led activities allowed students to reflect meaningfully on violence, resistance, and the racialized self while rethinking the purpose of the university and expanding students' and staff's conceptions of what counts as teaching and learning.

Finally, the editors of this volume offer an epilogue which reflects on these contributions and locates them within a broader picture of critique, resistance, and change.

An invitation

These chapters explore significant aspects of contemporary diversity, inclusion, and decolonization efforts. They do not cover them all; that is outside the scope of a single volume. Significantly, though, these chapters work together to show the potential of critical research and teaching practice. Instead of simply re-describing the problems, the chapters look towards to action. They do so by presenting experiences and insights from a number of national settings, since issues of elitism are framed in distinctive but related ways in those settings. For example, US universities tend to worry more about accommodating students from varied backgrounds and focus on programmes that promote 'diversity' and 'inclusion', while United Kingdom (UK) universities have engaged much more with the idea of 'decolonization' – yet these different conversations have much to offer one another. There is significant value, too, in the opportunity to reflect on what each approach might be missing in framing the issues as they do. Our contributors describe projects in the UK, the US, Canada, Germany, the Netherlands, Australia, China, the Philippines, and South Africa, plus a few that cross borders.

Each of the chapters describes a different effort to make universities more diverse and inclusive places, in terms both of whom they serve and of the knowledge they produce and convey. They are part of a large, as yet unattempted project – one that welcomes all people to engage in learning and teaching together. They come together to offer an invitation – to explore the possibility of what Achille Mbembe calls the 'pluriversity', reforming and replacing the 'university'. The pluriversity would embrace a process of knowledge production that is open to epistemic diversity. It ... does not necessarily abandon the notion of universal knowledge for humanity, but ... embraces it via a horizontal strategy of openness to dialogue among different epistemic traditions. To decolonize the university is therefore to reform it with the aim of creating a less provincial and more open critical cosmopolitan pluriversalism – a task that involves the radical refounding of our ways of thinking and a transcendence of our disciplinary divisions. (Mbembe, 2016, pp 36–37)

Mbembe recognizes the barriers to such a transformation, some of which we will revisit in the Epilogue. Neither he, we, nor our contributors are ready to describe a path taking us that far. But we are ready to take more than just small steps – and this volume offers 15 practical pathways to improving university teaching, research, and scholarship.

This volume is the result of our own enquiries into how we can do more as academics to challenge the colonial and other elitisms of the institutions in which we work; elitisms in which we are necessarily complicit. We, as editors, came to this volume with more questions than answers. Yet we do have some expertise to offer.

Abby Day is Professor of Race, Faith, and Culture in the Department of Sociology, Goldsmiths, University of London, and her research explores gender, generations, and ethnicity in relation to the cross-cultural meaning of 'belief'. Her recently published sociology of religion textbook (Day, 2020) is the first of its kind to begin the process of decolonizing that curriculum.

Lois Lee is also a sociologist and Senior Lecturer at the University of Kent, UK, where her work explores world-views and existential cultures in 'modern' and 'late modern' societies, focusing on the atheisms and humanisms that are so bound up with Euro-American intellectual elitism and their concept of the university.

Dave Thomas is an occupational therapist, a public health specialist and the Student Success and Engagement Manager at the University of Kent. His research uses critical race theory and adopts a 'race-focused' approach in exploring the relationship between university students' perceptions of the cultural sensitivity of the curriculum and their engagement, as measured by their interaction with teachers and their interest in their programme of study. This research, and indeed his scholarly outlook, grows from a deep engagement with contemporary structural inequalities – what Professor Ibram X. Kendi (2019) calls 'racist policies' – and the need for social justice. He is the lead editor on two books which explore issues of elitism and exclusion in the university: *Doing Equity and Diversity for Success in Higher Education* (Thomas and Arday, 2021) and *Towards Decolonising the University* (Thomas and Jivraj, 2020).

James Spickard is Emeritus Professor of Sociology and Anthropology at the University of Redlands (US), best known for his work on non-Western social theories, and most recently *Alternative Sociologies of Religion: Through Non-Western Eyes* (2017). His fieldwork and teaching have focused on people on society's margins: immigrants, minority religions, those living in extreme poverty, social activists. His work is particularly concerned with helping students and scholars to understand what their ordinary ways of observing the world prevent them from seeing.

All of us take critical approaches in our research, and all of us seek to uncover hierarchies. It is also true that we all of us have experienced some of the imbalances of power that this volume addresses at the sharp end, though in other regards we all have identities that locate us within the elite demographics that the Western university has favoured and favours still. We have different histories and are part of different identity categories, and this variety has been of value to us as students of the critical academic practices that this volume explores – an illustration to us of what 'mere' diversity can achieve.

But most importantly, we come to this volume as willing students of diversity, inclusion, and decolonization in the university. We are all teachers as well as researchers. We all spend time working closely with undergraduate and graduate students, and we have all had a chance to see their intellectual and personal gifts. Two of us have been at it long enough to see major demographic changes in our classrooms, and all of us have seen the barriers that minority and non-traditional students face – and we all have experimented with ways to overcome them. The work that has resulted in this volume sought to expand our own practical toolkits, as well as those of others. And it is as working teachers and researchers that we came to the practical focus of this volume. Theory is crucial, but it pays its dues by helping people to change their everyday lives. The intellectual and political movements documented earlier have made great strides in helping us to understand what is wrong with higher education; our own and our students' experiences tell the same story. What this volume asks is, what can people do to change it? How can we reform our universities so that they are truly universal? We invite readers to join us in asking these questions, in establishing critical research and teaching methods as the norm, as well as in exploring and sharing our different responses to them.

References

Achebe, Chinua (1994) ' "The Art of Fiction 139", Interview by Jerome Brooks', *The Paris Review*, 36(133): 142–165.

Ahmed, Sara (2017) *Living a Feminist Life*. Durham, NC: Duke University Press.

Alatas, Syed Farid (2006) *Alternative Discourses in Asian Social Science: Responses to Eurocentrism*. New Delhi: Sage.

Alatas, Syed Farid, and Sinha, Vineeta (2017) *Sociological Theory beyond the Canon*. London: Palgrave Macmillan.

Batty, David (2020) 'Only a fifth of UK universities say they are "decolonizing" curriculum', *The Guardian*, 11 June. [online] Available from: https://bit.ly3sC0KgR [accessed 29 March 2021].

Bensman, Joseph, and Vidich, Arthur (1971) *The New American Society: The Revolution of the Middle Class*. Chicago: Quadrangle Books.

Bhabha, Homi K. (1994) *The Location of Culture*. London: Routledge.

Bhambra, Gurminder K. (2007) *Rethinking Modernity: Postcolonialism and the Sociological Imagination*. Basingstoke, UK: Palgrave Macmillan.

Bhambra, Gurminder K. (2014) 'Postcolonial and decolonial dialogues', *Postcolonial Studies*, 17(2): 115–121

Boyer, Ernest L. (1990) *Scholarship Reconsidered: The Priorities of the Professoriate*. Princeton, NJ: Carnegie Foundation for the Advancement of Teaching.

Coates, Te-Nehisi (2014) 'The case for reparations', *The Atlantic*, June. [online] Available from: https://bit.ly/30g6PmL [accessed 6 March 2021].

Connell, Raewyn (2007) *Southern Theory: The Global Dynamics of Knowledge in Social Science*. Cambridge: Polity Press.

Connell, Raewyn (2018) 'Decolonizing sociology', *Contemporary Sociology*, 47(4): 399–407

Day, Abby (2020) *Sociology of Religion: Overview and Analysis of Contemporary Religion*. London: Routledge.

De Sousa Santos, Boaventura (2014) *Epistemologies of the South: Justice against Epistemicide*. New York: Routledge.

Elder, Joseph W. (1971) 'The decolonization of educational culture: The case of India', *Comparative Education Review*, 15(3): 288–295

Ferguson, Rebecca, Coughlan, Tim, Egelandsdal, Kjetil, Gaved, Mark, Herodotou, Christothea, Hillaire, Garon, Jones, Derek, Jowers, Iestyn, Kukulska-Hulme, Agnes, McAndrew, Patrick, Misiejuk, Kamila, Ness, Ingunn Johanna, Rienties, Bart, Scanlon, Eileen, Sharples, Mike, Wasson, Barbara, Weller, Martin, and Whitelock, Denise (2019) 'Innovating pedagogy: Open University Innovation Report 7'. [online] Available from: https://bit.ly/3a7RSZa [accessed 14 April 2021].

Go, Julian (2017) 'Decolonizing sociology: Epistemic inequality and sociological thought', *Social Problems*, 64(2): 194–199.

Grosfoguel, Ramón (2013) 'The structure of knowledge in westernized universities: Epistemic racism/sexism and the four genocides/epistemicides of the long 16th century', *Human Architecture: Journal of the Sociology of Self-Knowledge*, 11(1): 73–90.

Holmwood, John (ed) (2011) *A Manifesto for the Public University*. London: Bloomsbury.

Kendi, Ibram (2019) *How to Be an Antiracist*. New York: Penguin.

Kumar, Braveen (2020) *Twitter Post*, 4 December, 8:07am. [online] Available from: http://bit.ly/3mTwDP3 [accessed 29 March 2021].

Lara (2019) *History of a Liberal Arts Education* [Online]. Liberal Arts School Review. [online] Available from: https://bit.ly/3tjydNE [accessed 13 April 2021].

Lugones, Maria (2007) 'Heterosexualism and the colonial/modern gender system', *Hypatia*, 22(1): 186–209

Mbembe, Achille Joseph (2016) 'Decolonizing the university: New directions', *Arts and Humanities in Higher Education*, 15(1): 29–45

Mehta, Suketu (2019) *This Land Is Our Land: An Immigrant's Manifesto*. New York: Farrar, Straus, and Giroux.

Mignolo, Walter D. (2011) *The Darker Side of Western Modernity: Global Futures, Decolonial Options*. Durham, NC: Duke University Press.

Ngũgĩ wa Thiong'o (1986) *Decolonising the Mind: The Politics of Language in African Literature*. Melton, Woodbridge: James Currey.

Peters, Michael Adrian (2018) 'Why is my curriculum White? A brief genealogy of resistance', in Jason Arday and Heidi Safia Mirza (eds) *Dismantling Race in Higher Education: Racism, Whiteness and Decolonising the Academy*. Cham: Springer International Publishing, pp 253–270.

Quijano, Aníbal (2007) 'Coloniality and modernity/rationality', *Cultural Studies*, 21(2): 168–178

Said, Edward W. (1978) *Orientalism: Western Conceptions of the Occident*. New York: Pantheon.

Settler, Federico (2019) 'Curating violence: Reflecting on race and religion in campaigns for decolonizing the university in South Africa', *Religions*, 10(5): 310

Spickard, James V. (2017) *Alternative Sociologies of Religion: Through Non-Western Eyes*. New York: NYU Press.

Spivak, Gayatri Chakravorty (1988) 'Can the subaltern speak?', in Cary Nelson and Lawrence Grossberg (eds) *Marxism and the Interpretation of Culture*. Champaign: University of Illinois Press, pp 271–316.

Swain, Harriet (2019) 'Students want their curriculums decolonised. Are universities listening?', *The Guardian*, 30 January. [online] Available from: https://bit.ly/2Qptf38 [accessed 14 April 2021].

Thomas, Dave S.P., and Arday, Jason (eds) (2021) *Doing Equity and Diversity for Success in Higher Education: Redressing Structural Inequalities in the Academy*. London: Palgrave.

Thomas, Dave S.P., and Jivraj, Suhraiya (eds) (2020) *Towards Decolonising the University: A Kaleidoscope for Empowered Action*. Oxford: Counterpress.

Tuck, Eve, and Yansg, K. Wayne (2012) 'Decolonization is not a metaphor', *Decolonization: Indigeneity, Education, & Society*, 1(1): 1–40.

Wilson, William Julius (1987) *The Truly Disadvantaged: The Inner City, the Underclass, and Public Policy*. Chicago: University of Chicago Press.

PART I

Changing Universities

1

Negotiating Diversity, a Personal Reflection

Martin Stringer

Introduction

One of my first jobs in higher education was as a part-time tutor in the Department of Anthropology at the University of Manchester in 1987. Just over 30 years later I am now Pro-Vice Chancellor for Education at Swansea University. Much of the time in between, 23 years, was spent at the University of Birmingham. When Theresa Ogbekhiulu, the full-time Officer for Education at our Students' Union asked me, just a few days ago, what was the thing I was most proud of in my time working in higher education, I replied, very quickly, that it was to see so many students, and so many colleagues, grow, develop and achieve more than they thought possible. Theresa, herself, is a clear example of that, from arriving in her role two years ago, a shy international student from Nigeria, who had begun her career at Swansea on our access programme, to becoming a confident activist who is drawing on all her own experiences to transform the responses, not just of Swansea University but also of the higher education sector across Wales, to race and racial discrimination.

In this chapter I want to use some of my own experience, and the attempts I have made over the years to support others, to give a very personal perspective on the development of equality, diversity and inclusion in British higher education from the 1980s to the current day. I would not describe myself as an 'activist', far from it, but I have always been passionate about diversity and the need to celebrate diversity within education. I want to ponder on a number of examples from my own experience to try to understand the range of possible approaches to what might be called 'activism' around equality, diversity and inclusion within higher education, whether that relates to sexuality, gender, faith, race or disability.

1980s radicalism

As an undergraduate I was closely involved with the chaplaincy at Manchester University, but this was never the limit of my engagement, either with faith-based groups or in terms of my own 'activism'. I attended the Christian Union on occasion and supported a couple of colleagues who took a radical subsection of the Christian Union and used it to challenge the traditional political parties for control of the Students' Union, winning elections and developing a new and radical agenda. These activists went on to be among the founders of Church Action on Poverty and continue to run this from their Salford office to the present day. I also attended the occasional meeting of the Student Christian movement (SCM) and it was with SCM that I first really encountered gay Christian theologies and the preferential option to the poor, but could never really get my head around their particular approach to liberal theology.

This was Thatcher's Britain. Born in Tanzania, to white parents, I was brought up on the South Yorkshire coal field. I went to university in 1980 and the miners' strike took place while I was studying in Manchester. I could see the devastating effect it had on the communities where I was bought up, something that turned me away from both major political parties. Radical ideas were swirling around, and, like all good students, I was searching for an identity and a position (a faith position, a political position, even a position in relation to my own sexuality) within all these many currents. I remember one wonderful event organised by the Christian Anarchists in an empty warehouse/squat in London. There was something very thrilling about the activities, with some really amazing talks. Of course, it was all a little mad – 'throw love, not bombs' – but it was also stimulating and has stayed with me over the years. AIDS was also emerging as the 'gay' issue, and being gay came with a radical, oppositional edge, a rejection of mainstream heterosexual society and all that that stood for. We had to fight for the right to be different.

I have no memory of the University as an institution ever engaging with issues of gender, race or sexuality. A very inspiring lecturer spent the time to help me to recognise and work around my dyslexia. There was no official University support that I was aware of, and the lecturer had no training, just an innate response to what I needed at that moment. My only engagement with issues of race came through the church and the work of a somewhat crazy priest who had been at the heart of the Moss Side riots in 1981 and continued to work within the community, encouraging them to assert their rights, challenge their oppression and discover their dignity as human persons.

From undergraduate study, I went to Tanzania, the country of my birth, to work in a hospital for nine months, and then came back to Manchester to study for my PhD. Through conversations with Jim Cotter, one of the more creative and radical voices within the gay Christian community, I set up my own journal, *Creating Futures*, drawing inspiration from Brechtian montage and the work of the Marxist anthropologist, Michael Taussig. It only ever ran to five issues, but generated a range of very interesting responses from friends and colleagues alike. I also visited Chicago for three months and buried myself in the community organising traditions of the city through the tutelage of an amazing Columbian Jesuit. Thanksgiving that year, shared with the Latino community, was something utterly unique. I also attended the local Gay Christian group which met in the university's Friends Meeting House. However, through all my time in Chicago I was very conscious of Hyde Park, the neighbourhood in which the university is situated, as an enclave of 'respectability' within the wider desolation of the South Side. My hosts, an academic couple who were expelled from South Africa for their opposition to apartheid, told me never to cross the park into the black neighbourhoods because they were so dangerous. I ignored them and found in those neighbourhoods a passion for life within the midst of deprivation that I was already used to from Dar es Salaam in Tanzania and from Moss Side in Manchester.

1990s challenges

On completion of my PhD, I moved into church-based community work, funded by the Church Urban Fund and I worked with 13 Anglican churches on the East side of Manchester, helping them to reach out to young families in the area. What struck me most forcefully from this very hands-on work, was that there was so little of any lasting value that I could do for these people. My role ended up being one of giving the congregations confidence to be visible and supporting the clergy. It was after five years of this work that I made the decision that if I really wanted to make a difference to the lives of the people of inner-urban Manchester, I was not going to do it on the ground, through community work or pastoral care. We could win some small battles, but the bigger war was being fought elsewhere. I knew that I had to establish myself with a reputation and a voice that would be listened to by those in power if I really wanted to change the lives of these people. I therefore set out into an academic career, to put myself in a position where I vainly hoped that I could truly 'make a difference'.

In September 1993 I moved to Birmingham to take up a role as lecturer in the sociology and anthropology of religion in what was, at that time, a small, struggling Theology Department in the midst of a very self-consciously 'secular' university. It was a very interesting move and, in many ways, has completely changed the way I thought about activism. I continued to work with the people of the city, particularly with a struggling Baptist church with a largely Afro-Caribbean congregation, with a Yemeni Muslim educational charity and with the Sikh community in Handsworth, just north of the city. I also integrated all this into my teaching, setting up with colleagues a very popular course in black, gay and feminist theologies. I was 'out', if anybody cared to ask, as both a Catholic and gay. In all the time I worked in the Department of Theology (and Religion as it was to become), however, I had no contact with either the university LGBTQ (lesbian, gay, bisexual, trans and queer) network or the chaplaincy. I did not want to be involved in 'activism', or campaigns within the University itself.

The 1990s were a significant decade for the development of a number of diversity issues. The LGBTQ community struggled against Section 28, and Stonewall established itself as the leading campaigning group on this issue. The Disability Discrimination Act was finally passed in 1995, some 30 years after similar acts on gender and racial discrimination. The decade ended with the Lawrence Report and the definition of institutional racism. There was also significant movement within higher education, but this was primarily at the group level, impacting upon a small number of individuals, rather than across institutions as a whole. Almost all the work of the decade was undertaken primarily by those who shared the characteristics under discussion and there was little cross-fertilisation between the different campaigns. It was not surprising that the relevant sections of our black, gay and feminist theology course were taught by a black colleague, a gay man and a female colleague, respectively.

Despite identifying as gay, as Catholic and to lesser extent as dyslexic, I did not engage directly in the campaigning groups within the University. Part of this I put down to the excuse that I am just not clubbable. If I am honest, however, I did not expect to like the kind of people who I thought would go to such groups, although without ever attending I had no idea who attended and therefore no way of knowing whether I would get on with them or not. I had continued to have some links with the Gay Christian Movement nationally (and it was still the 'gay' Christian movement in the early 1990s), but I did not find either their brand of Christianity or their projection of what it meant to be gay to my liking, and I guess I really expected to find much the same, essentially 'well-meaning liberals' in the chaplaincy and the LGBTQ network. I told myself that it wasn't for me. However, I am still not convinced that this is the real reason I avoided both groups. If I am honest, I did not want to be sucked into the endless activities that both groups generate, and, perhaps more important, I did not want to be 'labelled' as an activist or as a troublemaker. This was, looking back, clearly something of a mistake on my part.

Where my activism was apparent, however, if not in the joining of groups or campaigning for the cause, was in supporting colleagues and, above all, students. I was the go-to person on the staff for students who wished to take a principled approach to their dissertations. Obviously, I had several gay or lesbian students approach me, seeking support and advice, either academically or personally. However, I also had conservative Evangelicals who felt uncertain about how to approach theological issues within a notably liberal department. Likewise, Muslim women who wanted to express their Islamic identity within their dissertation, either alongside or working against a more explicitly feminist approach. Finally, black women, wanting to explore womanist approaches to theology and religion more generally, also came to seek advice and support in their work. Some of these students realised that by studying and writing within the sociology of religion they could express a position that was more difficult to sustain within a strictly theological context. Many, however, were looking for affirmation of their own position, and the opportunity to express something of their own identity and something of their own 'radical' political or theological thinking. It was in supporting and encouraging such marginalised students that much of my 'activism' within the University expressed itself, an important role in and of itself.

2000s managerialism

My approach to students in the 1990s, and the activism that was associated with supporting students to be themselves and to express themselves, became particularly appropriate as I moved from a primarily teaching and research role to one of management and leadership in the early years of the new millennium. I always said at the time that much of this managerial role consisted of transferring the supporting role that I was used to playing in relation to students, to my colleagues and other members of staff. I always understood the leadership role, in part, as one of supporting, encouraging and providing a voice for members of staff. Many colleagues, especially the women, often felt marginalised, as if the 'University' failed to listen to them, or as victims trapped within institutional structures that did not provide them space to develop. From simply providing a space in which I offered to listen, and knowing the real importance of being listened to, even when nothing further can happen, to defending the case of many female and black, Asian and minority ethnic (BAME) colleagues in a room of other white men in the promotions committees, I saw my role as one of supporting and enabling colleagues to flourish.

On more than one occasion I have talked through with colleagues how they should not be afraid of conducting research in radical areas such as queer studies, black theologies or whatever the equivalent might be in other disciplines. They were convinced that processes such as the Research Excellence Framework (REF) or internal review and promotion were stacked against them. They probably were, but that, I argued, was no reason to stop doing what was vitally important to them and to their sense of identity as researchers. Likewise, on teaching, giving confidence, allowing colleagues to express themselves, to have a view on the proposals of others in meetings, to advocate on behalf of the more marginal students, this was all part of what I chose to do. This was what being an activist meant to me in middle management, often a delicate balance between protecting and advocating, deflecting the worst of the institution's stupidity, while allowing all voices to be heard in proposing alternative solutions.

It was also in the first decade of the 21st century that equality, diversity and inclusion became more significantly embedded in the structures and institutional lives of the universities. The development of the Athena SWAN charter in 2005, growing out of the work of female academics in science, technology, engineering and medicine (STEM) subjects and backed by the Medical Research Council as a prerequisite for funding, made a number of institutions sit up and take the place of women in science, medicine and engineering seriously. The establishment of the Equalities Challenge Unit in 2006 provided, for the first time, a sector-wide body that prepared reports on the experience of minority groups within higher education. The Stonewall Workplace Equality Index was launched in 2005 as the Corporate Equality Index and changing to its current name in 2006. The Runnymede trust, among others, promoted work on the BAME attainment gaps and some of the earliest work on inclusive curricula was developed in this decade. The passing of the Equalities Act in 2010 identified a series of protected characteristics and established a Public Sector Equality Duty that all higher education institutions had to respond to. Once again, however, as in the 1990s, much of this work was developed along parallel lines, with little cross-reference between the different characteristics or their campaigns. In many institutions this is still the overriding position, with Athena SWAN and BAME attainment, for example, being the responsibility of very different parts of the institution.

2010s intersectionality

As I moved further up the chain of command, I found myself with more opportunity not only to guide colleagues through the systems but also to change the systems themselves. I also found myself in an interesting and somewhat embarrassing position. Having studiously avoided the chaplaincy and LGBTQ network for much of the previous 15 years, I was now being approached by both to act as a spokesperson, and as an advocate within the senior management team. I did not have to do anything, or at least nothing more than provide my name to publicity material or all-staff e-mails. It is very clear that there is direct correlation between the presence an openly gay or lesbian senior manager at an institution and their Stonewall Workplace Equality rating, or to turn that around, it is much easier to rise in the rating if the openly gay or lesbian leader is prepared to offer their support to activities that they have probably had very little role in organising or driving. That is not, of course, to undermine or minimise the very important work that so many members of our LGBTQ networks group do day in and day out. The leader has nothing to support without the work of many different members of the institution. It just felt rather strange, and not a little embarrassing, from the position of a newly promoted senior manager.

But this was not all that 'activism' meant within the context of senior management. I was particularly lucky in one way, that having spent nine months as an interim Head of College, looking after the College of Arts and Law, I was appointed as Deputy Pro-Vice Chancellor (DPVC), and deputy to the Provost at Birmingham University in January 2011, and was essentially left to define my own job. I had no formal power. As a DPVC I sat on none of the senior committees of the University, and I had a role that had no authority in any of the five Colleges. I had a different kind of position, the ability to persuade and encourage, if not to command and order. I chose to take on a number of projects from across the University. I transformed the employability strategy, putting Birmingham at the forefront of work in that area. I introduced a new process for professional development review and introduced training for all academic line managers. I also took up three of my great passions: I revitalised the University's Africa strategy; I led the University's community engagement strategy, focusing once again on the people of the city; and I took on the challenge of equality, diversity and inclusion.

Birmingham did not have an outstanding record on equality and diversity at the time, although, as in most institutions, there were clear pockets of outstanding work, especially in the Medical School. I set out, very deliberately, to work across all the protected characteristics as set out in the Equality Act. I worked to bring people together, to encourage those working on Athena SWAN to learn from those involved in disability rights and to encourage BAME activists to engage with those from the LGBTQ community. I also worked at all times across both staff and student agendas, seeing BAME attainment as an issue for the whole institution, not a problem for interested part-time officers within the Students' Union. As a team we worked on processes, on data collection, on the student and staff journeys, looking at all points where unconscious bias could be seen to function. We instigated training programmes, and I insisted that the senior managers, the Vice-Chancellor (VC) and Heads of College, attended alongside Students' Union Full Time Officers, academic and professional services staff and students reps. Above all, we celebrated. I instigated a cycle of events through Black History Month, Disability Awareness Week, Interfaith Week, LGBTQ History Month and Women's International Day. We ran blogs, we invited speakers, we gathered to share food and we filled the Bramhall auditorium for celebrations, films, and seminars. One of the highlights was in encouraging the VC to speak during Disability Awareness Week on the consequences of an accident many years ago that meant walking remained extremely painful. It opened many eyes across the institution to a very different side of their boss.

Throughout all this work, I was very keen not to neglect religion. It was the one characteristic that many people at the University found particularly difficult. Birmingham had a 'secular charter', and many colleagues took this, especially when I first arrived in the 1990s, as a stance that banned religion, religious debate and even the teaching of religion from the institution. We had strong Jewish, Muslim, Sikh and Hindu societies within the Students' Union and we had held annual interfaith events organised by the chaplaincy, but religion was never really understood in the same light as sexuality, race or gender as a question of diversity and inclusivity. It was still felt that being dismissive towards those who were religious, especially when it was felt that such people were opposed to our positive messages around sexuality and gender, was permissible and acceptable. I gave a talk during Interfaith Week on the secular charter, and talked about the way, in a nonconformist foundation with a strong Quaker heritage, the secular charter was originally seen as a means of enabling a range of religions to express themselves freely, without the domination of either Anglicans or Catholics. This was the tradition that I suggested that Birmingham should be celebrating, particularly in such a religiously diverse city at the start of the 21st century.

My work at Birmingham came together in a university-wide equalities conference, opened by the VC and attended by over 400 staff from across the institution. When I left, my work was recognised to the extent that I was replaced by two DPVCs, one of whom had equality, diversity and inclusion as their specific brief. The University has continued to develop, through the appointment of several significant leaders in the area of gender equality and critical race theory, as well as leading the national work on the LGBTQ-inclusive curriculum.

Ironically, my current role and work in Swansea University gives me much less opportunity to undertake this kind of activism. I have to worry about National Student Survey scores, curriculum development, student engagement, REF preparations, space and timetabling, new apprenticeships, the arts and culture strategy and so on and so forth. I continue to support the work of the LGBTQ Network and we are very proud of our Stonewall Workplace Equality Placement achievements, including a commendation for the Network, which I can claim no credit for at all. I also support the work of Athena SWAN and the work of wonderful colleagues, including fellow PVC Hilary Lappin-Scott, whose work on gender equality in STEM has been nationally recognised. We have an academy devoted to inclusivity and learner success that supports a wide range of work across the University around BAME attainment, as well as retention and attainment among students from the full range of under-represented groups. I work with colleagues around protected characteristics, and we have a strong story to tell about the diversity of students we take in and the very high levels of employability that all students achieve across the institution. I also work very closely with my immediate colleagues to constantly renew and refresh our staff recruitment, promotions and Professional Development Review policies, putting particular emphasis on transparency and equality of opportunity. There are still many issues and problems across the institution in terms of equality, diversity and inclusion. That is inevitable, but there is a strong commitment to making things better, and, what is more, this is embedded in the day-to-day life of the institution, our sense of 'Swanseaness', and not an added extra. That is something that attracted me to Swansea in the first place.

Looking to the 2020s

Am I still an activist? It is a very difficult question to answer. I still hold strongly to my commitment to support individuals, to encourage them to grow and to excel and, above all, to be themselves. I want to encourage all our students, and our staff, to be activist and fight for those things that they are really passionate about. I find myself somewhat in awe of colleagues who are committed to improving the lives of asylum seekers, who put in time as members of governing bodies in struggling schools, or as members of the city council, who work with residents to improve the lives of the more deprived neighbourhoods in the city, who give of their time to act as translators in the courts or for social services, or to teach in the prison. In some moments I envy such people, their commitment, the drive that makes this work so essential for them, the time they make in the midst of already busy lives to devote to such activities, but I also know that that is simply an excuse. To do, or not to do, to get involved, or not to get involved, is a question of priorities, and I find most of my priorities are devoted to the University, and perhaps my wish to finish the latest book.

So, what became of my decision, on leaving community organising in Manchester, to become important and influential enough to have a real impact on the decisions that affect the lives of the people of the city? Part of me, I have to say, is no longer quite as clear about what those policies and actions actually are. My political position has become so much more complex, as I guess has the whole economic and globalised world that we now live in. Politics more generally has become distracted from such issues, obsessed with Brexit, and more recently with COVID. A voice on any other subject simply would not be heard in today's media- and social media- obsessed world. The drive is still there. Solutions, however, appear so much more difficult to achieve. I still have the dream, perhaps a task for my retirement …

Ultimately, however, for me, activism has always been about making time and space for others, to enable individuals to explore their own passions and identity, and to support them as they set out, whether through research, creativity, political engagement or sheer bloody-mindedness, to make a difference on the world around them. We need to give everybody that opportunity and support, irrespective of their background, the particular range of characteristics that make up their own identity, and irrespective, within some reason, of the choices they make in life. While that is, for me personally, what activism has always been, often leading me to be seen as a 'radical' in terms of my views and out of step with many in the institutions I have worked in, this is also, I believe, what universities are also about. They are places where people can explore, experiment, grow, gain in confidence, make mistakes and develop the passions that are going to help them to change the world.

2

Demystifying the 'Decolonizing' and 'Diversity' Slippage: Reflections from Sociology

Ali Meghji, Seetha Tan, and Laura Wain

Introduction: critiquing the decolonizing-diversity slippage

Colonialism and education have always been linked. Indeed, one significant way that European empires naturalized the 'superiority' of Western knowledge was by setting up educational institutions, including universities, in the colonies. These would teach in imperial languages and focus on a Western canon, which would buttress the view that 'knowledge' comes from the West while 'the rest' merely has tradition, superstition, and pre-modern beliefs. Even after the collapse of many colonial administrations in the 20th century, universities in newly 'independent' nations continued to function as they had done before. They continued to reproduce ideas of Western superiority and non-Western backwardness (Uys, 2010). It is fair to say, therefore, that calls to 'decolonize' the university are certainly not recent and, indeed, that struggles against universities and structures of knowledge more generally have been part of anti-colonial insurgency for several centuries.

The decade since 2010 has seen increasing calls from British university student movements to 'decolonize the university' and 'decolonize the curriculum'. In a typical neoliberal response, British universities quickly co-opted the terminology of 'decolonizing' as a marketing tool to signal themes such as 'equality', 'diversity', and 'openness' (Ahmed, 2015). This meant that, for instance, City University of London's Decolonizing the Curriculum campaign was itself endorsed by a member of the royal family.

In this chapter, we wish to address this conceptual 'fuzziness' surrounding debates over decolonizing curricula, paying special attention to how the project of decolonizing is quite different from the discourse of 'diversity'.

Part of the reason why decolonizing the curriculum is so different to merely 'diversifying' is because decolonizing knowledge involves a radical critique of epistemology. If one were to construct a reading list for social theory – for instance – where more than 50 per cent of the taught authors were people of colour, this would not necessarily mean that one had a 'decolonized curriculum'. This is because decolonizing involves a fundamental engagement with how colonialism and coloniality shape the practices of knowledge production, the classification of knowledge, and the hierarchies and schemes by which knowledge is valued. It is of course a meaningful enterprise to engage in diversity initiatives that will – to use the same example – increase the number of people of colour on reading lists. However, to conflate such diversity initiatives with decolonizing would be imprudent, not least because the former focuses on *representation*, whereas the latter focuses on the reconstitution of knowledge practices and values.

Unfortunately, even critical academics have made this conflation. Thus, we regularly see claims that decolonial thought is needed in British universities because it 'draws our attention to the whiteness of the university staff body' (Doharty et al, 2020, p 2), because minority scholars 'work […] themselves into the ground by sitting on and contributing to, a disproportionate number of […] Race Equality Staff networks, and Race Equality launches' (Doharty et al, 2020, p 9), and because 'the knowledge producers within (United Kingdom) academic institutions are still disproportionately white' (Johnson, 2020, p 91). Thus, we see calls for the increased representation of people of colour at all staff levels, accounts of the experiences of faculty of colour in British universities, and the use of scholars of colour to act as the face for Race Equality Staff networks. Though these are valuable in themselves, they do not decolonize the university's core ways of thinking.

In short, what we see in Britain is a constant slippage from a vocabulary of 'decolonizing' and 'decoloniality' to one that uses terms such as whiteness and anti-racism. The result is an empirical focus that is centred more on the experiences of minoritized students and staff than on structures of knowledge production and coloniality more broadly.

It is in the context of such conceptual fuzziness that we use this chapter to clear up some of the debates as to what 'decolonizing' actually implies for curriculum reform and knowledge production. In doing so, we show how such discussions of decoloniality go far beyond the remit of equality, diversity, and inclusion. In particular, we argue that decolonizing knowledge production involves a dismantling of the Eurocentrism that dominates the current global political economy of knowledge production. This Eurocentrism is characterized by bifurcation: the supposition that one can study 'the West' without regard for its global interlinkages. And it is characterized by Orientalism: the idea that the non-West is a pre-modern 'Other' to the West. In dismantling this Eurocentrism, decolonizing knowledge involves opening up different schemes of thinking and knowing – pushing us towards forming relational analyses across time and space and valuing varying methodologies that have been devalued by Western hierarchies. This chapter, therefore, intends to be a resource we can use as we push forward the decolonial option in British universities.

Three principles in decolonizing the curriculum

From this brief introduction, it is apparent that decolonizing has 'two sides'. On the one hand, it is partly defined in terms of what it is *against*. In this case, what decolonizing is *against* is quite clearly the dominance of Eurocentrism and its component parts of Orientalism and bifurcation. However, decolonizing knowledge ought to be defined not just by what it opposes, but also by what it stands for. Here, it is clear that decolonizing knowledge stands for relational analyses that link phenomena across time and space. And it stands for justice against European epistemicide (which is the devaluation and even erasure of non-Western knowledges carried out as part of the colonial process).[1] For this reason, we have decided to structure this chapter through a discussion of each of these component parts, starting with the critique of Eurocentrism.

Decolonizing knowledge and the attack on Eurocentrism

When people hear charges of Eurocentrism in sociology, they typically think of the well-founded criticism that the sociological canon tends to be dominated by European or Western thinkers. Indeed, it is true that the canon has developed this way across the world, as Syed Farid Alatas (2010, p 29) highlights: 'Typically, a history of social thought or a course on social thought and theory would cover theorists such as Montesquieu, Vico, Comte, Spencer, Marx, Weber, Durkheim, Simmel, Toennies, Sombart, Mannheim, Pareto, Sumner, Ward, Small and others. Generally, non-Western thinkers are excluded.'

However, the critique of Eurocentrism is not necessarily a critique of European thinkers. Rather, it is a critique of a standpoint, where sociology adopts 'a particular position, a perspective, a way of seeing *and* not-seeing that is rooted in a number of problematic claims and assumptions' (Alatas and Sinha, 2001, p 319). Following Go (2016), it is useful to see Eurocentric thought as being characterized by two problems: Orientalism and bifurcation.

As Saïd (1978, p 2) comments, Orientalism 'is a style of thought' emerging in the colonial era 'based upon an ontological and epistemological distinction made between "the Orient" and (most of the time) "the Occident"'. Central to the work of those theorizing Orientalism is the idea that the binaries and 'ontological and epistemological' distinctions between the West and the East (Saïd, 1978), the Occident and Orient (Ahmed, 2006), or simply what Hall (1992) labels the West and the rest, *are produced by the West*. Moreover, these binaries produced by the West are not value neutral; they inherently convey a supposition of 'Eastern' or 'Oriental' difference and inferiority. Orientalist discourses thus rely on hierarchical binaries between the West and the rest, such that the sanctity of Western Christianity can be compared to the savage tribal customs of indigenous Americans and Africans, the cleanliness of Western cities can be contrasted to the squalor of the Middle East and South Asia, Western sexual respectability can be contrasted to the promiscuity and amorality of African women, and the civility of everyday life in the bourgeois West can be contrasted with the rudeness of the East (Hall, 1992).

Decolonizing the curriculum involves directly exposing and challenging how such Orientalist discourses are integral to much of the knowledge systems that we canonize. Take for instance sociology, and the way that both Max Weber and Karl Marx are unanimously canonized figures in 'Introduction to Sociology' courses *across the world*. Both Marx and Weber were attempting to explain the Western transition to industrial capitalism, or what we can also label broadly as 'modernity'. However, in order to explain this Western transition into capitalism, both Marx and Weber placed an orientalist bias at the core of their theories. For instance, Marx (1973, 2004) argued that Western societies transitioned from feudalism into capitalism as we get a shift in the means of production (which were becoming increasingly industrial), and an unequal ownership over these means of production that created the driving force of class antagonism between the workers and bourgeoisie. To Marx, this tension between the two classes was then the spirit of capitalism, as the workers earned just enough for subsistence, while the bourgeoisie extracted the surplus capital from the workers' labour. Marx contrasted this class struggle as a driving force for development in the West against what (in the *Grundrisse*) he labelled the 'Asiatic mode of production' that he said typified the so-called East ('Asiatic societies'). This mode of production, Marx argued, produced a stagnant society, due to the absence of a dynamic class struggle and a state-centralized economy with no private ownership of land. Similarly, Weber (1959, 2000, 2002) argued that central to the Western development of capitalism was a 'Protestant ethic', characterized by an asceticism which rejected the search for everyday pleasures and instead fostered a stringent dedication to work. This ascetic will to work, Weber argued, combined with the growth of European cities and the increased specialization of the workforce, led to the industrialization of the West as we know it. Weber compared this situation in the West with what he saw as stagnant societies in the East – the Chinese, Indian, and Muslim 'worlds' – who were seen to have religions of 'sensuality' that did not have the discipline required for industrial work.

Both Marx and Weber, then, produced 'arguments in terms of broad, simple, contrasting oppositions which mirror quite closely the West–Rest, civilized–rude, developed–backward oppositions of "the West and the Rest" discourse' (Hall, 1992, p 223). Through crystallizing this West/rest binary, Weber and Marx consequently offered internalist accounts of capitalism and modernity that made it appear as though capitalism developed in the West because of particular conditions *within* the West (the class structure, the Protestant ethic), while it did not develop in the rest of the world because of factors internal to those parts of the world (Hinduism, Islam, Confucianism, the 'Asiatic mode of production'). Such internalist accounts of capitalism and modernity occlude any analysis of the connections between the West and the rest in the development of capitalism. They hide the fact that, as Frantz Fanon (1963, p 102) put it, the West is 'literally the creation of the Third World', as the 'third world' – in the form of colonies or imperial territories – provided the labour, land, and natural resources for the overdevelopment of Western economies. Weber may have labelled China as a stagnant society, but he did not note how the Spain's colonization of the Americas enabled it to steal enough silver and gold to bring the Chinese economy to the brink of collapse (Dussel, 2002); Marx may have labelled India as stagnant and in need of an economic revolution, but he failed to note that over nine billion British pounds' worth of capital was channelled from India into the British economy between 1765 and 1938 (Patnaik, 2017). Can we really say, therefore, that either Marx or Weber offered complete accounts of modernity when neither of them fully explicated the centrality of colonialism to Western industrialization?[2] By ignoring the connections between the West and the rest, Marx and Weber's Orientalism led them to commit the second principle of Eurocentrism: bifurcation.

Bifurcation is characterized by the belief that one can separate the West from the rest of the world and can analyse the West outside of its global links (Bhambra, 2007). This strategy presents canonical theories as universal in a way that denies any sense of agency, reality, or existence to those in the global South.

Foucault, for instance, is treated as a canonical social theorist as well as a key figure in the arts, humanities, and social sciences more broadly. However, his theory of disciplinary power (2019) is guilty of precisely the epistemic bifurcation that we have been discussing. He argued that in Western Europe, around the time of the 18th century, there was a shift in the exercise of power, where criminals ceased to be punished through the 'spectacle of scaffold' (that is, public execution and/or torture) and instead were hidden away in prisons. Foucault's argued that this model of power in the prison can be generalized to understanding disciplinary power in society, where citizens are regulated through surveillance and a normalizing gaze. The issue with Foucault's account of disciplinary power is not *just* that it focuses only on Western Europe; had Foucault linked the 'covert' surveillance-style power in the metropoles with the overtly violent exercise of power in the colonies, then this would indeed be a critical argument. The issue with Foucault's viewpoint is that he offers no justification for why he focuses *only* on Western Europe for modelling this theory of power. It is here that we see the assumed universality of the West that is buried into the disciplinary unconscious. Further, this disciplinary unconscious leads us to a Eurocentrism which offers, at best, a thoroughly obfuscated vision of social realities. As Connell (2006, p 261) puts to Foucault:

> One hundred years after the execution of Damiens the regicide, when Foucault's 'reticence' was supposedly in full flow, the British executed a large number of men they captured while suppressing the 'Indian Mutiny' in 1857–58. They did it in public, with exemplary brutality, including mass hangings and floggings, caste degradation of leaders, and blowing rebels from the cannon's mouth. Public, spectacular, collective punishments remained a favored technique of British and French colonialism far into the twentieth century. Notable examples are the punitive massacres at Setif and Kerrata in 1945, to intimidate the populations of northern Africa, just after France itself had been liberated from the Nazis.

The bifurcation in Foucault's account of disciplinary power, therefore, fails to provide a convincing account of social reality, given that 'his theory arbitrarily cuts "Europe" off from its colonies – as if imperial and colonial history were not also Europe's history' (Go, 2016, p 89).

From these critiques of Orientalism and Eurocentrism, therefore, we can see how decolonizing the curriculum is calling for something radically different to 'diversifying' the curriculum. We are not talking about merely adding Southern authors around a Eurocentric core. We are, rather, seeking to expose and critique that very Eurocentric core itself *in the realm of epistemology*. To this extent, it is useful to think of 'diversity' as maintaining an epistemic equilibrium, while decoloniality destroys this epistemological tradition in the hope to build anew. This is a subtle but central point. Decolonizing the curriculum is *not* just about tearing down what we have (that is, it is not defined simply in terms of what it is opposed to); it is also about opening up new ways of thinking and knowing. In this chapter, we want to focus on two particular avenues of knowledge and social thought that decolonizing the curriculum opens up: relational analysis across space and time, and justice against epistemicide.

Decolonizing is a relational process

It is quite ironic that decolonizing the curriculum is often seen in media outlets as being akin to burning all the books written by European authors. In fact, this attack could not be further off the mark. Decolonizing the curriculum is foundationally about opening up *relational* modes of thoughts which fundamentally seek to link together social processes. When we are thinking about decolonizing our curriculum, therefore, it is useful to ask ourselves not 'What do we need to get rid of?' but, rather, 'What decolonial links can we build here?' Such decolonial links can be both spatial and temporal.

Spatially, building decolonial links involves showing how events or social processes in the West are fundamentally intertwined with social processes in the global South. This could involve, for instance, showing how the increase of vegan diets and purchasing of electric cars in the West to tackle the climate crisis is linked to the exploitation of women and child labour in the global South (Meghji, 2020). Temporally, building decolonial links involves showing how the logics, processes, and practices put in place during colonialism continue to shape the present and future world. Sticking with the topic of the climate, this may involve, for instance, linking the current climate crisis with the desire for unlimited capital accumulation and extractivist capitalism set in motion by European colonialism (Dussel, 1999).

When we are trying to decolonize our curricula, therefore, we are really asking ourselves, 'What is the bigger picture?' Focusing on the bigger picture allows us to escape the lure of Eurocentric bifurcation and Orientalism and turns us towards the global interconnectedness of social relations. Let us illustrate this with a couple of examples.

Take, for instance, the case of the militarization of the police in the United States (US); there is no doubt that this is a contemporary issue when we think of police violence towards Black and indigenous Americans. However, analysing such policing has to engage in decolonial thought's transnational and temporal linking. As Go (2020) points out, the militarization of the US police, beginning in the early 20th century, involved importing techniques, tactics, and organizational frameworks from the US's colonial military interventions – particularly from its war in the Philippines. To this extent, Go shows how there is a historical link between contemporary policing and the US colonial missions *and* a spatial link between US 'racism at home' and its 'imperialism abroad'. Including these connections gives us the 'bigger picture'.

To use another example of such linking, we can consider the phenomena of nationalism and national identity. Decolonial thought views such social phenomena through a transnational and temporal lens. In Britain, for instance, one of the symbols of national identity is tea; indeed, as Stuart Hall (1991) put it, 'what does anybody in the world know about an English person except that they can't get through the day without a cup of tea?' However, as Hall (1991) continues: 'Not a single tea plantation exists within the United Kingdom. This is the symbolization of English identity [...] Where does it come from? Ceylon – Sri Lanka, India. That is the outside history that is inside the history of the English. There is no English history without that other history.' Hall's analysis of English identity, therefore, stretches far beyond the temporal limits of the present day and far beyond the geographical confines of the nation-state. He shows that Britain's historical colonial expropriation, as well as the labour of those colonized by the British Empire, have fundamentally shaped what it means to be 'English'. This is why Hall refers to himself as 'sugar at the bottom of the English cup of tea'.[3]

In this respect, Hall shows how claims that Britain or England are 'white countries' involve a severe distortion of history; the fundamental entanglement between Britain and its colonial territories means that colonized people were in fact essential to the making of British identity – the very same identity which nationalists try to protect and define as 'white' in the present day.

When we are talking about decolonizing our curricula, therefore, we are really talking about stretching our imagination in order to '(re)structure global narratives' of the present to include 'the empirical connections forged through histories of colonialism, enslavement, dispossession and appropriation' (Bhambra, 2014, p 149). This is, again, essentially different to what it would mean to diversify a curriculum. Diversifying a curriculum may involve incorporating different points of view, or indeed voices from different social locations, but it does not necessarily entail the decolonial mission of binding together connected histories and their resulting presents. To use the same examples as previously illustrated: one could teach a course on policing in the US and incorporate the various pertinent critiques of policing and racism from authors of colour, such as Michelle Alexander (2012) or Keon Gilbert and Rashawn Ray (2016). However, if such a course does not draw the connections between American policing 'at home' and American imperialism 'abroad', then it is not strictly decolonial. Similarly, one could teach a course on British identity with a diverse set of authors, but if the course does not look at how British identity is fundamentally linked to British Empire, then it would not be decolonial either.

Justice against epistemicide

Just as a 'diverse' curriculum does not necessarily engage in decolonial linking, it also does not guarantee that it offers any justice against *epistemicide*. Before we define epistemicide in detail, let us clarify the problem through an example.

Take Geoffrey Cronjé, who is often portrayed as a pioneer of social science in South Africa in the 1930s (see Meghji, 2020). If Cronjé were on a reading list, one could say 'look, this reading list is diverse because we have a South African author!' However, what was the actual content of Cronjé's work? Well, he argued that the white Afrikanervolk in South Africa were the pure race, and that the racial groups of South Africa ought to be segregated in order to protect the purity of this white race; this is what earned him the title the 'mind of apartheid' (Meghji, 2020). In this case, Cronjé may satisfy many people's criterion for making a reading list 'diverse', because he is writing from outside of the West; but, given, that he reproduced Western ideas of racial inferiority, there is no way that we could classify inclusion of his work as part of the decolonizing mission. The issue here, therefore, is one of justice against epistemicide.

Epistemicide refers to how European colonialism involved a devaluation of 'other' ways and forms of knowing and knowledge that differ from those of the supposedly superior West (de Sousa Santos, 2014). Through this Western epistemicide, the religious, political, and cultural beliefs and practices of those in the global South — including Southern theories of what it means to be human, of sexuality and gender, of political rights and institutions, religions, and so on — are recast as merely superstition, 'magic', tradition, or pre-modern. Colonialism devalues Southern ways of thinking by refusing to treat them as legitimate knowledge systems. Epistemicide, therefore, is part and parcel of Western universalism — the idea that the Western knowledge system is *the only* knowledge system that applies to the whole world.

Decolonizing the curriculum does not just involve incorporating authors from the global South for the sake of it. Rather, decolonizing the curriculum looks to the forms of knowledge that have been erased through epistemicides, it values these knowledges, and it explores what questions and realities these knowledge systems can open up that are obfuscated in the Eurocentric tradition.

Take, for instance, proverbs. In the Western knowledge system, proverbs are construed as traditional folklore sayings. But what if we changed our perspective, and instead saw proverbs as meaningful expressions of knowledge about particular social processes? Indeed, this is exactly what Olutayo (2014) does, arguing that 'proverbs present deep meanings that contextualize and structure embedded social relations, social structure, culture, and accompanying development within the contextualized meaning of the immediate local/culture group'. We can see how Olutayo's point works in the context of agency. Agency is a key concept in Western social science, but it is often approached as representing individual will and freedom and is juxtaposed to structural or group constraints. However, as Olutayo shows by looking at West African proverbs, many social groups have much different conceptions of agency. Thus, Olutayo (2014, p 235) cites the Yoruban proverb that 'A tree does not make a forest' and the Akan proverb that 'A person is not a palm-tree that he should be self-complete [or self-sufficient]'. Olutayo (2014, p 235) connects these proverbs to the common African saying that 'One hand cannot lift a load up to the head. The left hand washes the right hand and the right hand washes the left for the hands to be clean. It is when all hands come together that confidence (independence) exudes.' Each of these proverbs, Olutayo (2014) argues, demonstrates the point that various social groups construe agency as being something achieved *within* instead of *in spite of* group membership; in other words:

> The individual is situated within a community where he exists and is also socially constructed into a social being. There exists therefore a symbiotic relationship between the individual and his community [...] the sanctity of the physical individual is rather meaningless without the community, as the essence of an individual lies within the community within which he exists. The physical and individual being must thus be transformed to a social being in order to be relevant in [their] society. (Omobowale and Akanle, 2017, p 45)

In this case, we see that decolonizing the curriculum requires us to substantially rethink what counts as knowledge, which forms of knowledge we value, and which knowledge-producing methods (for example, proverbs) need to be incorporated back into our curricula in order to avoid continuing the project of Western epistemicide. Of course, a consequence of this mission for 'justice against epistemicide' is that we end up discovering that there are many areas of inquiry that Western traditions of social thought have neglected through their devaluation of Southern knowledge systems. Perhaps a clear example of this is the climate crisis, and how Western sociology has largely neglected this topic until recent years.

Despite the centrality of the climate crisis to our collective lives on Earth, it is a relatively understudied area in Western sociology (Wainwright, 2011). However, the realities of climate change and climate crises have been central in Southern perspectives. As Meyer (2008, p 219) clarifies, 'Indigenous people are all about place. Land/*aina*, defined as "that which feeds," is the everything to our sense of love, joy, and nourishment. Land is our mother. *This is not a metaphor.*' Given that 'land' is construed in this way by many indigenous people across the world, such people have been theorizing about climate crises ever since the beginnings of colonialism in the 15th century. In fact, colonialism began the (still-continuing) destruction of such indigenous environments (Whyte, 2017; Darrah-Okike, 2020). Indeed, it is through spotting this link between colonialism, the birth of capitalism, and environmental destruction that so many Southern, decolonial intellectuals have put the climate crisis at the centre of their paradigms. And they did so long before Western theory caught onto the problem.

For instance, almost a century ago, Du Bois (1954, p 3) commented on how the driving logic of neocolonial capitalism was 'private profit from low wages of colored workers and low prices for *priceless raw materials* over the earth' [emphasis added]. As Du Bois pointed out, colonial capitalism – fostered through the actions of empires that wanted to horde, capitalize, and profit from the world's resources – was always committed to the destruction of the environment in the name of economic growth. Dussel (1999, p 17), too, summarizes this logic of environmental destruction when he comments that: 'Capitalism, mediation of exploitation and accumulation (effect of the world-system), is later on transformed into an independent system that from out of its own self-referential and autopoietic logic can destroy Europe and its periphery, *even the entire planet*' [emphasis added]. To decolonial thinkers, the climate crisis has therefore been emblematic of the problem of coloniality. As Wynter (2003, pp 260–261) clarifies, the climate crisis is a manifestation of the struggle between 'man' (the West) and 'humans' (the sub-persons across the global South):

all our present [...] struggles over the environment, global warming, severe climate change, the sharply unequal distribution of the earth resources (20 percent of the world's peoples own 80 percent of its resources, consume two-thirds of its food, and are responsible for 75 percent of its ongoing pollution, with this leading to two billion of earth's peoples living relatively affluent lives while four billion still live on the edge of hunger and immiseration, to the dynamic of overconsumption on the part of the rich techno-industrial North paralleled by that of overpopulation on the part of the dispossessed poor, still partly agrarian worlds of the South) – these are all differing facets of the central ethnoclass Man vs. Human struggle.

We have gone into such detail on this topic for a deliberate reason. Adding 'different' perspectives to Western knowledge is not only important because it brings 'diversity' and different points of view to the table. Rather, one of the central missions of decolonizing the curriculum is to look to forms of knowledge that have been erased in the name of Western universalism, to value these knowledges, and to bear witness to the vast amounts of critical analyses that are opened up when such knowledges are valued. The climate crisis is a great example of this because it shows how looking to 'other' knowledges is not simply a nice, tolerant thing to do. It is, instead, an essential epistemic mission if we are to save the world. We are talking about a situation in which it is realistic that soon there will be no world to decolonize simply because the world does not exist. Yet it is not as if this is simply a 'new topic'; there are traditions of thought that have been theorizing such climate disasters since the 1400s. Indeed, it is within these centuries-old traditions that we may locate both the epistemologies and the practices that can help us to avoid such climate catastrophes; thus the centrality of decolonial perspectives to the future existence of our world.

Concluding thoughts and practical reflections: a world beyond diversity, inclusion, and equality

Thinking about the climate encourages us to concentrate on how the questions of 'what is decolonizing the curriculum?' and 'why decolonize the curriculum?' are interrelated. This is simultaneously a project of epistemology and a project of justice. Indeed, scholars such as de Sousa Santos (2014) have used the notion of cognitive justice to refer to how decolonization can provide social and material justice to those in the global South only if it also promotes epistemic justice – by valuing of all those knowledge systems that have been erased and/or devalued through Western epistemicide. It is for this reason that we think it prudent to avoid conflating decolonization of the curriculum with debates over diversity, inclusion, and equality.

Shirley Chisolm famously talked about bringing your own seat to the table if you aren't given one. However, this is a different kind of rhetoric and practice to that promoted in decolonizing curricula initiatives. Let's again talk about sociology. Do we want to give Du Bois a seat at the 'Introduction to Sociology' table, even if that table itself does not fundamentally challenge the Eurocentric Orientalism and bifurcation at the heart of sociology's emergence and continuing logic? Do we want to have intellectuals from the global South sitting at the table simply so we can say that our dinner party is not all white? Or do we instead want to value these voices as authoritative, knowledgeable agents? Do we want to invite people from the global South to the table only if they can contribute towards discussions happening in the West? Or are we ready to accept that the table itself needs to be substantially changed?

Of course, this is not a critique that diversity initiatives are bad per se; it is, rather, a question of the different scopes of decolonizing and diversity: the latter wants representation, while the former wants to reconfigure knowledge practices themselves.

These are but a few rhetorical questions to get us thinking about how serious a challenge decolonizing a curriculum can be. Given that it is such a challenge, we do not pretend that we can offer any 100 per cent effective blueprint for 'decolonizing your curriculum'. But we do have a series of suggestions and thinking points for teachers (and students) to consider:

- *De-universalize any canon*: It is counter to the decolonial mission to present any theory as being a 'theory of everything'. At the heart of the decolonizing project is a desire to show that all knowledge comes from particular standpoints; all knowledge, to some extent, is provincial. This does not mean that no knowledge or theory is useful; it simply means that no particular knowledge can claim omniscience. However, as Alatas and Sinha (2001) remark, rejecting the idea that a canon is universal does not imply that the authors within this canon are not useful to think with. Take, for instance, sociology's holy trinity of Marx, Weber, and Durkheim. These three thinkers are often presented as offering universal theories of modernity or capitalism, all of which decolonial critics have pointed out to be Eurocentric (see Bhambra, 2007). However, such thinkers can still be useful in non-universalizing ways. Instead of teaching a class on 'The Sociology of Marx', for instance, you could teach a class on social class and the industrial revolution, which avoids bifurcated accounts of capitalism and incorporates the work of Du Bois (2014) or Williams (1944) on the importance of enslavement and colonialism to industrialization. Similarly, a course on Weber could be recast as a course on religious ethics and the development of capitalism, which would allow for incorporating Shari'ati's (1980) work on Islam and economic revolution. Likewise, rather than teaching 'The Sociology of Durkheim', one could teach a course on social theory and ethnography, contrasting Durkheim's presentation of indigenous people with the work of those using similar methods from more critical perspectives – such as Kenyatta's (1979) work that portrays the Gikuyu people *not* as 'pre-modern' but as having a highly structured, complex social life that was devastated by colonial rule.

• *Look for links even if you were not taught them yourself:* Through this de-universalizing of the canon, we come to see that there are lots of epistemic links that can be teased out in our teaching and learning. By focusing our teaching on these links, we can again present students with more connected understandings of the world. Take, for instance, Bourdieu and Foucault in sociology. Both thinkers are often presented as being involved in metropolitan debates over metropolitan societies, such as the struggle between French Marxists, structuralists, and existentialists (see Saïd, 1989; Connell, 2006). Neither of these figures needs to be presented this way. It was in his involvement with Algerian anti-colonialism (where he engaged with the works of Frantz Fanon) that Bourdieu developed his canonical concepts of habitus, field, and capital (Puwar, 2009). Similarly, it was through his involvement in anti-imperialism in Tunisia and Iran (where he came across the works of Ali Shari'ati) that Foucault came to theorize 'power' as a network of relations. Further, just as Bourdieu encountered Fanon, and Foucault encountered Shari'ati, so too did these two anti-colonial intellectuals Fanon and Shari'ati correspond with each other in Paris; we do not just need to link Northern thinkers to Southern thinkers, but we need to link thinkers more generally (including South–South links).

- *Value Southern thought regardless of its Northern applicability*: Given that all three of this chapter's authors work in Britain, and that this book is published in Britain for a largely British audience, we need to emphasize the point that we ought not to value just Southern theory(ies) if it helps us to understand something about the West. As Connell (2010) argues, if we value Southern theory only in terms of the question 'What can the West gain from this?', then we simply reproduce the epistemic structure that decolonizing knowledge seeks to displace. At a practical level, this point can therefore be taken in different ways. On the one hand, it means that when we are teaching Southern theories, we ought not to teach them solely in terms of their contributions to Northern theories. For instance, it would be disingenuous to only teach a thinker like Ali Shari'ati through his contributions to Western Marxism. While Shari'ati (1980) was indeed interested in struggles against capitalism and drew upon Marx's work to think about revolution in Iran and beyond, he also generated his own sociological theory which was rooted in the teachings of Shi'a Islam. It would thus be disingenuous to only focus on the 'Western' aspect of his oeuvre.
- *Decolonizing knowledge does not have a finishing point*: Decolonizing knowledge must be understood as an ongoing process rather than something that has a finite end. For sociology, for instance, this means that there is no specific end goal for decolonizing the discipline; there is no point at which we can collectively agree that the decolonial mission has been achieved. By thinking of decolonizing knowledge as a process – or, indeed, as an approach – we not only rid ourselves of any complacency but we also remind ourselves that the decolonial links we can draw and form in our social thought are endless, so long as we retain open minds.

From these four points alone, it is quite clear that decolonizing knowledge is a challenge. We are basically saying that it involves a complete reworking of our global epistemic, material, and ontological hierarchies. And this is where we leave the chapter: if decolonizing curricula is about challenging global epistemic hierarchies, then to what extent is it really useful to think of this project as something that can be achieved by a single institution, let alone a single course organizer? This is again why decolonizing curricula goes well beyond debates over diversity; in order to decolonize curricula, we need to decolonize a total world system.

Notes

[1] See Chapter 7 of this volume for further discussion of this topic.
[2] We use 'complete' here to signal that we do not necessarily think that either of these theories is 'bad'. They simply ought not to be taken as universal accounts of modernity.

[3] We have been told that a tea plantation does now exist in Britain; however, we believe Hall's point stands.

References

Ahmed, Sara (2006) *Queer Phenomenology: Orientations, Objects, Others.* Durham, NC: Duke University Press.

Ahmed, Sara (2015) 'Doing diversity work in higher education', in Clair Alexander and Jason Arday (eds) *Aiming Higher: Race, Inequality and Diversity in the Academy.* London: Runnymede Trust, pp 6–7.

Alatas, Syed Farid (2010) 'Religion and reform: Two exemplars for autonomous sociology in the non-Western context', in Sujata Patel (ed) *The ISA Handbook of Diverse Sociological Traditions.* Los Angeles, CA: Sage, pp 29–39.

Alatas, Syed Farid and Sinha, Vineeta (2001) 'Teaching classical sociological theory in Singapore: The context of Eurocentrism', *Teaching Sociology*, 29(3): 316–331.

Alexander, Michelle (2012) *The New Jim Crow.* New York: The New Press.

Bhambra, Gurminder (2007) *Rethinking Modernity: Postcolonialism and the Sociological Imagination.* London: Palgrave Macmillan.

Bhambra, Gurminder (2014) *Connected Sociologies.* London: Bloomsbury.

Connell, Raewyn (2006) 'Northern theory: The political geography of general social theory', *Theory and Society* 35(2): 237–264.

Connell, Raewyn (2010) 'Learning from each other: Sociology on a world scale', in Sujata Patel (ed) *The ISA Handbook of Diverse Sociological Traditions.* Los Angeles, CA: Sage, pp 40–51.

Darrah-Okike, Jennifer (2020) 'Theorizing race in Hawai'i: Centering place, indigeneity, and settler colonialism', *Sociology Compass*, 14(7): e12791.

de Sousa Santos, Boaventura (2014) *Epistemologies of the South: Justice against Epistemicide.* New York, NY: Routledge.

Doharty, Nadena, Madriaga, Manuel, and Joseph-Salisbury, Remi (2020) 'The university went to "decolonize" and all they brought back was lousy diversity double-speak! Critical race counter-stories from faculty of colour in "decolonial" times', *Educational Philosophy and Theory*, 53(3): 233–244.

Du Bois, W.E.B. (1954) 'The status of colonialism', Special Collections and University Archives, University of Massachusetts Amherst Libraries. [online] Available from: https://bit.ly/3mcNHAe [accessed 11 July 2019].

Du Bois, W.E.B. (2014) *Black Reconstruction in America: An Essay Toward a History of the Part Which Black Folk Played in the Attempt to Reconstruct Democracy in America, 1860–1880.* Oxford, New York: Oxford University Press.

Dussel, Enrique (1999) 'Beyond Eurocentrism: The world-system and the limits of modernity', in Fredric Jameson and Masao Miyoshi (eds) *The Cultures of Globalization.* Durham, NC: Duke University Press, pp 3–31.

Dussel, Enrique (2002) 'World-system and "trans"-modernity', *Nepantla: Views from South*, 3(2): 221–244.

Fanon, Frantz (1963) *The Wretched of the Earth*. New York, NY: Grove Weidenfield.

Foucault, Michel (2019) *Discipline and Punish: The Birth of the Prison*. London: Penguin.

Gilbert, Keon, and Ray, Rashawn (2016) 'Why police kill black males with impunity: Applying public health critical race praxis (PHCRP) to address the determinants of policing behaviors and "justifiable" homicides in the U.S.A.', *Journal of Urban Health*, 93(Suppl 1): 122–140.

Go, Julian (2016) *Postcolonial Thought and Social Theory*. New York, NY: Oxford University Press.

Go, Julian (2020) 'The imperial origins of American policing: Militarization and imperial feedback in the early 20th century', *American Journal of Sociology*, 125(5): 1193–1254.

Hall, Stuart (1991) 'Old and new identities, old and new ethnicites', in Anthony King (ed) *Culture, Globalization and the World System: Contemporary Conditions for the Representation of Identity*. Minneapolis, MN: University of Minnesota Press, pp 41–68.

Hall, Stuart (1992) 'The West and the rest', in Bram Gieben and Stuart Hall (eds) *Formations of Modernity*. Cambridge: Polity, pp 275–332.

Johnson, Azeezat (2020) 'Throwing our bodies against the white background of academia', *Area*, 52(1): 89–96.

Kenyatta, Jomo (1979) *Facing Mount Kenya*. London: Heinemann.

Marx, Karl (1973) *Grundrisse: Foundations of the Critique of Political Economy*. London: Penguin.

Marx, Karl (2004) *Capital: A Critique of Political Economy*. London: Penguin.

Meghji, Ali (2020) *Decolonizing Sociology: An Introduction*. Cambridge: Polity.

Meyer, Manulani Aluli (2008) 'Indigenous and authentic: Hawaiian epistemology and the triangulation of meaning', in Norman Denzin, Yvonne Lincoln, and Linda Tuhiwai Smith (eds) *Handbook of Critical and Indigenous Methodologies*. Thousand Oaks, CA: Sage, pp 217–232.

Olutayo, Akinpelu Olanrewaju (2014) '"Verstehen", everyday sociology and development: Incorporating African indigenous knowledge', *Critical Sociology*, 40(2): 229–238.

Omobowale, Ayokunle Olumuyiwa, and Akanle, Olayinka (2017) 'Asuwada epistemology and globalised sociology: Challenges of the South', *Sociology*, 51(1): 43–59.

Patnaik, Utsa (2017) 'Revisiting the "drain", or transfer from India to Britain in the Context of Global Diffusion of Capitalism', in Shubhra Chakrabarti and Utsa Patnaik (eds) *Agrarian and Other Histories: Essays for Binay Bhushan Chaudhuri*. New Delhi: Tulika Books, pp 278–317.

Puwar, Nirmal (2009) 'Sensing a post-colonial Bourdieu: An introduction', *The Sociological Review*, 57(3): 371–384.

Saïd, Edward (1989) *Orientalism*. London: Penguin.

Shari'ati, Ali (1980) *Marxism and Other Western Fallacies: An Islamic Critique*. Markfield: Islamic Foundation Press.

Uys, Tina (2010) 'Dealing with domination, division and diversity: The forging of a national sociological tradition in South Africa', in Sujata Patel (ed) *The ISA Handbook of Diverse Sociological Traditions*. Los Angeles, CA: Sage, pp 235–245.

Wainwright, Steven (2011) 'Review essay: Is sociology warming to climate change?' *Sociology*, 45(1): 173–177.

Weber, Max (1959) *The Religion of China*. The Free Press: Glencoe, IL.

Weber, Max (2000) *The Religion of India*. The Free Press: Glencoe, IL.

Weber, Max (2002) *The Protestant Ethic and the Spirit of Capitalism: And Other Writings*. London: Penguin.

Whyte, Kyle (2017) 'Indigenous climate change studies: Indigenizing futures, decolonizing the Anthropocene', *English Language Notes*, 55(1): 153–162.

Williams, Eric (1944) *Capitalism and Slavery*. Chapel Hill, NC: University of North Carolina Press.

Wynter, Sylvia (2003) 'Unsettling the coloniality of being/power/truth/ freedom: Towards the human, after man, its overrepresentation – an argument', *CR: The New Centennial Review*, 3(3): 257–337.

3

Doing Diversity Inclusively: 'East Asians' in Western Universities

Lin Ma

Introduction

This chapter responds to a growing demand for recognition of plural forms of knowledge production in higher education. It focuses on Chinese and other students from so-called 'East Asia', a racialized term. An often-forgotten group, they remain peripheral, despite the joint contribution of anti-imperialist, postcolonial, multiculturalist, feminist, indigenous, and diversity scholars. This marginalization calls for reflection. For example, in current inclusion approaches, progressive gender quotas in referencing may apply only to gendered, western names, and decolonial initiatives appeal only to those invested in understanding colonialism. While other examples abound, this chapter discusses how 'East Asians' are racialized and subject to western racism and coloniality. Ignorance and misrecognition of this group prohibit diversity agendas from including them on equal, participatory terms. To illustrate this, I contrast two inclusion approaches. In British universities, ethnic Chinese international students are included by enrolment; however, as non-white, non-western foreigners, they struggle with knowledge production that alienates theirs and with campus structures insufficiently supporting them. Meanwhile, universalist Christians may recognize these students' global orientations but include them by misinterpreting their 'religious' inclinations for potential evangelical conversion. Significantly, these two approaches co-produce and reproduce the Eurocentric secular-versus-religious divide by ethnically sorting students into differentiated channels of integration.

As Nye (2019, p 3) argues, campus diversity that 'keeps intact the shell' of knowledge structures reduces itself to an institutional showcase. To facilitate participation of long-standing others requires diversity work that decolonizes a knowledge system that excludes, misrecognizes, and mispresents marginal perspectives. This chapter starts by locating 'East Asian' international students in Britain. Identifying their marginality, I acknowledge Christian attempts for universalist inclusion. Through a United Kingdom (UK)-based study, I illuminate how academic categories impact upon student experience on campus.

Racialized 'East Asian' students in postcolonial Britain

Historians trace the arrival of foreign students in Britain back to its colonial era. Handpicked sons of noble families in African colonies became cultural-savvy facilitators for colonial trade expansions (Perraton, 2014; Walker, 2014; Pietsch, 2015). In 1875, the Indian colonial government recruited British professors to produce loyal 'Anglicised Indian elites' (Walker, 2014, p 329). In North American colonies, British settlers established the first universities, seeking 'to perpetuate in colonial communities the privilege of the Established Church enjoyed in England' (Pietsch, 2015, p 17). These colonial legacies remain visible today: eight of the 'top ten' countries sending most international students to UK universities are former colonies (Perraton, 2014).

Where to locate China in the world transition to the postcolonial era? Increased by 21 per cent since 2013–14, Chinese students accounted for 23 per cent of UK international students[1] in 2017–18 (UKCISA, 2019). However, 88 per cent of all China's overseas students were self-funded (MoE, 2018), suggesting the absence of postcolonial intergovernmental connections. Rather, the increase of Chinese entrants to British universities reflects Chinese middle-class families' desire for cultural access to anglophone centres (Matthews and Sidhu, 2005).

Apart from Hong Kong, mainland China together with other countries[2] in 'East Asia' experienced a co-ethnic colonial imperialism from Japan. Albeit ephemerally, this experience encourages culturalist, rather than racial, attributions in interpreting colonialism. Indeed, contemporary Chinese appear less sensitized to postcolonial racial dynamics. Compared with black African students opting for British universities known to recruit and support black students (Andrews, 2018), Chinese students are known to 'choose a university with less Chinese students' (Spencer-Oatey and Xiong, 2006, p 49).

But are Chinese exempted from European racism? In *Becoming Yellow*, Michael Keevak (2011) traced a change in European racial depiction. Before the mid-18th century, the Chinese and Japanese were 'white' to European travellers and missionaries. However, this changed in the late 18th to 19th centuries, when European colonialism dominated the world and China lost its equal standing as a civilization. A 'scientific' racial taxonomy emerged, and reclassified the Chinese, among others in 'East Asia', as Mongolians. Expanding the established 'black' and 'white' racial system, European race scientists created this colour-based taxonomy and assigned 'yellow' to the Chinese, Japanese, and Koreans, who could no longer be 'white'. They belonged to an existing category of 'other', namely, the Mongols, whose ancestor had induced much horror in Europe (Keevak, 2011, pp 64–71). Nonetheless, contemporary Chinese dismissed the pseudo-science on Mongoloids and mythologized yellow by relating it to the Yellow River and the Yellow Empire. Without rejecting the phenotypical racialization, they claimed a fractional cultural ownership of it.

Quintessentially, the notion of 'East Asians' remains racialized. Examining British media coverage, Brooks (2017) identified neocolonial and neoliberal narratives of 'East Asian' students. She included ethnic Chinese students from mainland China, Hong Kong, and Taiwan, and those from South Korea, Japan, and Mongolia. Despite an exemplar British lecturer challenging the view of Chinese learners as 'culturally brainwashed' (by Confucianism or Maoism), most articles portrayed Chinese education in negative terms: rote-learning, pushy, or exemplary results (of the 2012 PISA [Program for International Student Assessment] tests) as unrepresentative of China and 'East Asia' (Brooks, 2017, p 2369). This culturalist lens also applies to racialized British 'East Asians'; articles were concerned with their 'un-British' pushiness and their outnumbering white British pupils (Brooks, 2017, p 2371).

Besides these neocolonial narratives, Brooks found that the articles discuss ethnic Chinese students in universities not as learners, but as financial contributors to a profitable UK export (Brooks, 2017, p 2372). Under such neoliberal narratives, racialized Chinese and other non-white, non-western international students are particularly vulnerable. They are collectively and individually referred to by misrecognition, that is, as 'cash cows', 'backdoor immigrants', or 'neoliberal subjects' to be 'knowledgised' by the globally branded western teaching (Robertson, 2011; Madge et al, 2015; Andrews, 2018). Examining racial abuse on campus, the UK's National Union of Students (NUS, 2012, p 5) found that ethnic Chinese students are the most[3] common victims, with 30 per cent reporting a racial-hate incident between October 2010 and February 2011. During the COVID-19 pandemic, YouGov (2020, p 23) recorded in June 2020 that 76 per cent of Chinese had a racial slur directed at them, compared with 64 per cent for all the Black, Asian and Minority Ethnics (BAME).

That Chinese are non-white renders them to the British category of BAME, but this belonging is not a straightforward one. As a Hong Kong Chinese student, Tan (2018) reflected on 'East Asian' ambivalence and her learning to self-identify as 'a foreign woman of colour' in the anglophone west. Students from 'East Asia' fall into a crack. They face racism and ethnic alienation, both on and off campuses, but they do not immediately possess the fluency in a political language that British BAMEs have.

Newsome and Cooper (2016) found that UK international students are subject to 'neo-racism'. Theorized by Lee and Rice (2007), neo-racism builds on biological racism and justifies group superiority via cultural difference and national origin according to nation-states' geopolitical and developmental statuses. Thus globally constituted, neo-racism is also identified outside the west. Indeed, Jon (2013) researched an internationalized Korean campus and found that local Korean students favoured international students from the United States (US) and the UK, despite their ethnic affinities with other Asian students. In other words, international students are not marginalized only by their minority statuses in white-majority universities. As Stein and Andreotti (2016, p 236) argued, it is a racist imaginary[4] of western supremacy that 'positions western nation-states as over and above Other nation-states' and 'produces Others *within* and *at* the border of the nation-state' [original emphasis]. Vocabulary change may help, but scholars and practitioners need to develop studies that 'scramble the persistent and ubiquitous grammar of the dominant global imaginary' (Andreotti, 2016, p 236).

So far, British universities recruit students from 'East Asia', but this inclusion does little to protect them from neoliberal racism or the globally constituted western supremacy. Linguistically and culturally disengaged, many Chinese students retreat into ethnic space, but some resort to religion. Compared with British and European students, they were 'slightly more likely' to use chaplaincy services (UKCOSA, 2004, p 43). Yu (2017, p 130) found that over a third of her non-Christian Chinese students had a local church experience in the past six months. Asking whether Christian inclusivity exemplifies an alternative approach to diversity on western campuses begs two questions: how Christianity has positioned race, and whether it could escape its culturalist undertones.

The culturalist origin of European racism

With these questions, this section revisits the earliest European thinking on race. Ostensibly religious, it retrieves a culturalist power that underpins racial grouping before the secular-versus-religious divide. Unlike racial phenotypes, cultural identities are convertible and cultivable. Through an example of overseas 'East Asian' interaction with western-centric ideas about religion, this section highlights how a religious approach to racialized culture contributes to the inclusion and exclusion of knowledge and people from 'East Asia'.

Philosopher Adam Hochman (2020) traced the etymon of race, 'raza', to 15th-century Spanish classifications of Jews and Moors as of non-Christian blood lineage. Despite conversion, they were not trusted, which triggered 'the first medieval example of true anti-Semitism', followed by the Spanish *Limpieza de Sangre* (Purity of Blood) statutes, starting in 1449 (Hochman, 2020, p 652). This history illustrates how power reinforced and corrupted medieval Christianity, an exclusionary version that appears counterintuitive. Today, secular governance triumphs once Christendom, and Christians, especially evangelicals, welcome converts and take pride in their racial diversity.

Nevertheless, rarely do these changes – the Christian turn to inclusivity and the European path to secularization – acknowledge the effects of encountering 'others', that is, non-Christian and non-Europeans. This omission creates difficulties in understanding why these people's knowledge becomes subjugated, despite secular and religious inclusions. After Columbus arrived in America in 1492, the Spaniards had their Christian cosmology shaken upon encountering Amerindians external to the biblical knowledge. They reacted in two ways: to convert, and to secularize the divine law to the natural law, both justifying their colonial rule (Jahn, 2000, pp 35–37). Centuries to follow witnessed the transatlantic colonialist expansion, the declined power of Christian reasoning, and the unleashed power of science that aims to encapsulate the entire human realm. A racial taxonomical offshoot emerged, classifying all peoples by self-serving white European criteria.

Although racial scholars disagree upon whether a continuity exists between the religious-based raza and the better-known racial taxonomy established over three centuries later, the signified white European dominance remains. Despite ethnic diversifications in both secular and religious domains, imperial unconsciousness creeps into existing social theories and concepts (Go, 2016). Take the notion of 'East Asians', for example. When Brooks (2017) identified implicit racism in British media narratives, she included Mongolians without recalling the racist construct of 'East Asians'. When US-based Chinese Professor Fenggang Yang (2018, p 1) founded the 'East Asian Society for the Scientific Study of Religion' to address current 'improper understanding and misunderstanding', he included the Chinese, Japanese, South Koreans, Singaporeans, and Vietnamese. The curious grouping, however, represents the majority of racialized Chinese in the US Chinese Exclusion Act. In the 1960s, they formed Asian American alliances against racism and imperialism. But Yang regarded 'East Asia' as 'neither Euro-centric nor North-Atlantic-centric' (Yang, 2018, p 1). In support, sociologist José Casanova (2018, p 2) explained that 'East Asia' constituted 'a pre-existing geographic and cultural civilisational region' with shared integration of 'Confucianism, Buddhism and Taoism'. In this knowledge claim, what characterizes China represents 'East Asia', and regional cultural affinity is defined by religion.

With culture racialized, this religious characterization is also problematic for recognizing secularity only to pre-modern China. In 1584 the earliest Jesuit to China, Matteo Ricci (Casanova, 2018, p 7), remarked on its absence of 'religion' (as Judeo-Christianity) and, despite noticing the 'Moors', he did not consider them as part of Chinese society. At the time neither Europeans nor Chinese had foreseen China's upcoming decline to European ascendancy. Upon hearing about pro-secular Confucianism, together with Buddhism and Taoism, some European thinkers even considered it as 'what was needed in Europe' (Casanova, 2018, p 8).

Since Communist China, however, this secularity has become both politicized in China's ideological pursuit of modernity and diminished in the western-centric religious approach to culture. Under these lenses, contemporary non-religious Chinese were either Confucian elites or militant atheists. Sociologist Peter Kivisto (2014, p 26) even generalized Chinese international students as 'the products of a doctrinaire education system in China [that] roundly condemned not only religious institutions, but religious belief'. Politically charged, this perception presumes that institutional atheism manufactures atheist individuals, and so, where ruling ideology practices atheism, individuals detest religion and beliefs accordingly. The next section explains why this is false.

Under the religious approach to culture, religious Chinese appear approachable, albeit marginalized. On the one hand, religion in English, argued Nongbri (cited in Nye, 2019, p 15), embraces an ostensible universality in the history of white Protestant expansion, further enabled by European colonialism across the globe. In this process, some Christians secularized their divine law for sustained rule (Jahn, 2000). Some others sought to integrate different cosmologies. World religions thus appeared 'seemingly without a history' but as a shadow category 'already taken shape underground' (Masuzawa, 2005, p 11) and defined by their resemblance to the dominant Protestant theology (Asad, 1993). Outside academia, such categorization had everyday significance; accessing right and power that European Christians once had, one has to become one or belong to a compatible religious structure. Long into the postcolonial era, critical scholars of Chinese religion continue to follow western theories placing God-belief at the centre, and the pre-modern-thus-religious assumption (Puett, 2013).

On the other hand, the definition of religion has been contested and expanded, through both academic interests in non-Christian, non-western societies and through social change within the west. Once we recognize rejections to propositional beliefs, as mainstream British religious scholars do, we need new categories for secular identities (Lee, 2017), including religiously affiliated non-believers (Day, 2012)[5] and the non-religious with or without spiritual beliefs (Woodhead, 2016). In this complex landscape, locating the non-religious Chinese in Britain appears ever more challenging. We know little about their reasons for embracing or rejecting religious identities when available. Grace Davie (2018) suggested that moving away from Eurocentric frameworks is a necessary first step, but caution is needed as next steps are taken. First, novel manifestations in the 'postsecular' do not emerge from a vacuum and may have been there all along. Significantly, this continuity applies to religious belief as well as non-belief. Second, religious diversity goes hand in hand with movement of people. They update our discussion of secularity, secularization, and secularism. Yet perspectives from these people do not often penetrate various boundaries inside which consequential discussions happen.

Altogether, studies of non-European societies often approach culture via racialization followed by religion, whose definition was modelled after Judeo-Christianity with later reflective expansions. The coupling of race and religion transforms racism into culturalism, not dissimilar to neo-racism theorized in secular domains (Lee and Rice, 2007; Newsome and Cooper, 2016). Secularity in the west is largely associated with the waning power of Christianity, but this lens applies awkwardly elsewhere. Consequently, Chinese are arbitrarily presumed to be non-religious as either Marxist-indoctrinated or Confucian elitist, and religious out of pre-modern legacy. These conceptualizations contribute to inclusion and exclusion in universities, and Chinese students remain marginalized, as their perspectives are disregarded.

Chinese beliefs and Christian inclusivity: UK-based study

Illustrated in what follows are results from a mixed-methods study of UK-based Chinese international students and their involvement at local British evangelical Christian sites. The qualitative data are from ethnography and life-story interviews with Chinese international students encountering or converting to Christianity in Britain. Similar to Day's (2012) method, I followed an open-ended, exploratory approach to allow my participants to lead in sharing stories and thoughts. The quantitative data came from a 2017 survey (n=270, response rate 0.22) with newly arrived[6] Chinese students on degree-oriented programmes at a university-affiliated language centre.

Table 3.1 shows that more than 72 per cent of newly arrived international students from China identified as non-religious, 12 per cent identified with Buddhism, 8 per cent with Chinese Folk Religion, followed by 1 per cent identifying with Daoism, and Protestantism.

Westerners may question this combined 1.6 per cent Catholic–Protestant identifications as low, although this small sample of young, educated Chinese students is not representative of Chinese society. This issue is polemical. White (2017, p 104) observes a 'Western fascination' with Chinese Christians and a 'Western hope' for the growth of Christianity in China. To be accurate, this 'western' hope reflects a Christian-centric west. Conversely, Chinese elites tended to downplay Chinese Christian percentages and hoped for an 'unreligious' and 'rationalistic' portrayal of China (C.K. Yang 1965 in White, 2017, p 103).

Table 3.1: Religious identity upon arrival

What is your current religious identity?	Percentage (n=254)
None	72.4
Buddhism	12.2
Chinese Folk Religion (敬祖/拜仙/施道/信神灵)	8.3
Daoism	1.2
Protestantism	1.2
Islam	0.8
Catholicism	0.4
Other (including, 'myself', 'nature', 'technology', 'truth philosophy', 'Buddhism-and-Chinese Folk Religion', 'communism', 'Jehovah's Witness')	3.5

Language also keeps a cultural record. Whereas early Jesuits introduced Catholicism to China as *tianzhu jiao*, 'a religion of the Heavenly Master',[7] Protestants translated Protestantism as *jidu jiao*, 'a religion of Christ', and actively claimed the Christian identity. Respondent-centred, this survey deliberately employs religious categories used in China; yet the 'other' category demonstrates further linguistic and cultural ambiguities. Several wrote down 'Buddhism *and* Chinese Folk Religion', as this combined option was unlisted, a few 'Jehovah's Witnesses' provided the extra note 'not Christian'.

The comparatively low religious identifications may match Kivisto's perception of Chinese students, but further empirical data disprove it.

Table 3.2 shows one multiple-choice question[8] from the survey, and Figure 3.1 shows its results. The results illustrate a little-known Chinese belief system.

On average, respondents have five transcendental beliefs simultaneously. Despite 18 per cent of respondents not believing in anything, 42 per cent had one to four beliefs from the list. The most common beliefs are: (1) *yuanfen*, an indigenous Chinese concept, explained later, (2) animism, in Chinese that is, 'everything has a spirit', and (3) moral reciprocity. Together, these results show that Chinese students hold beliefs but do not identify themselves religiously. For example, 26.1 per cent of respondents believe in Dao (see Figure 3.1), the core concept of Daoism, yet only 1.2 per cent identify as Daoist (see Table 3.1).

These well-believed Chinese concepts, however, are little known to pastoral care providers and are thus denied as spiritual resources on campus.

Table 3.2: Snapshot of a survey question

	Yes, I believe it exists	No, I don't believe it exists	Not sure	Never heard of it
Destiny, fate (宿命)				
Soul (灵魂)				
Dao (道)				
Predestined relationship (缘分)				
God the Creator (造物主上帝)				
Jesus Christ (救赎主耶稣)				
Muhammad (先知默罕默德)				
Buddha (佛)				
Immortal gods (神仙)				
Ghosts (鬼)				
Demons (恶魔)				
Heaven (天堂)				
Hell (地狱)				
Reincarnation (转世)				
Karma (轮回)				
Retribution (moral reciprocity, 报应)				
Eternal life (永生)				

As the qualitative part of this study includes 15 eventual Chinese student converts to Christianity (compared with 16 who had explored Christianity but did not embrace a Christian identity), all converts had moments of subjective crisis – relating to or accentuated by overseas studies – during which local evangelical Christians provided care and support. Five vignettes are discussed later.

Yuanfen was most believed (68.2 per cent) by my UK-based respondents. So was it also in CRCS's (2016) US-based Chinese student sample (61.1 per cent): their respondents selected 缘分 (*yuanfen*) in Chinese or 'predestined relationship' as its translation. *Yuanfen* is a prevalent Chinese understanding of interpersonal relationships, including that between a person and an object, an animal, a location, a job opportunity, and so on. It describes fated relations, for example between parents and children, or couples; they ask each other, given *yuanfen* in the next life, if they would opt to enter the same relationship again. *Yuanfen* also encourages detachment and honours transient encounters.

Figure 3.1: Chinese beliefs upon arrival (n=255–260)

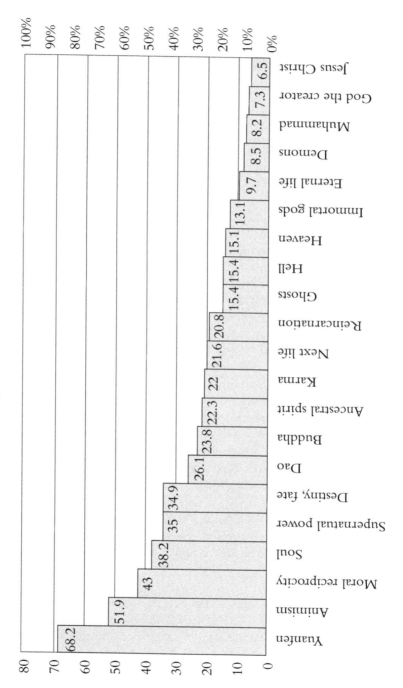

In response to an unsuccessful job application or unrequited love, the Chinese phrase *you* (having) *yuan*, *wu* (not having) *fen* suggests that a serendipitous encounter does not guarantee sustained relationships, and that is fine. Its English translation of 'predestined relationship', however, forges a plausible connection to predestination and salvation. As a lay minister encourages the Chinese students to reason: it must be God-the-Christ who pre-decides. The following vignette is from a Chinese student who became Christian since coming to the UK.

'I don't believe in karma. That's Buddhist stuff. It's not allowed, you know. We say Jesus is the only way, and we can't worship any other thing … *yuanfen* is fine, because it's not from a religion.'

Scholarly definitions of religion affect individual attitudes to belief. To the Chinese, *yuanfen* can be traced back to Chinese Folk Religion and Buddhism as an extended belief in karma – deeds in this life may affect next or later lives. Karma from a recognizable 'religion', Buddhism, has to be discarded by biblical Christians. But '*yuanfen* is fine', because it is not a 'religious' belief and is therefore non-threatening to the 'true' status of her adopted Christian identity and framework.

Western teaching of Asian religions mainly involves historical texts, with colonial legacies little challenged. This observation leads to Nye's (2019, p 13) proposal to 'teach from the present backwards' so that the postcolonial present is understood with past forces that have created it. Thus, the problem is not just about recognizing non-Christian cultural and transcendental systems as 'religion', a privileged status that Christianity has had. But such framing should not further privilege Christianity as the standard.

For modern converts to Christianity in adulthood, subjective sense-making is of paramount importance. Typically, they do not abandon pre-existing knowledge but strive to reconcile the past with the present knowledge structure.

'I compared Jesus with Confucius. I think Confucius is good, but he never claimed himself to be God. He's completely confined by his time, but Jesus is for the entire humankind. Confucius didn't ask the most important question.'

After encountering Christianity in Britain, this student had a revelation of Christ at a moment of crisis. She struggled and reasoned, and decided that the question that has shaped the religious history of Europe and European understanding of humanity is, after all, "the most important question". Convinced, she was baptized on the first Easter that she spent in Britain. Although Confucianism is not a recognized religion in China, Chinese international students came to re-examine it in their updated context.

Alienated on their overseas student journey, Chinese students search for empowerment. This context prompts them into specific belief accounts. The following is another Chinese student convert who come to evaluate and reposition spiritual beings.

> 'The religious world is huge. … We Asians have other spiritualities, like our ancestral spirits. The problem is you don't know the position of your ancestor in the whole spiritual world. Theoretically, the spiritual world shouldn't interact with the human world but we Christians understand they can influence us, and after we accept God, we are children of God.'

Animism, 万物有灵, believed in by many Chinese students, is less of an -ism but respects that everything in nature, including rocks, trees, rivers, and so on has a spirit beyond its material contour. Once considered primitive, such thinking is 'just about paying attention'; as Harvey (2014, p 220) argues, 'You don't have to believe anything'. In ancient China, ancestral–spirit rituals served the human domain by creating 'as if' scenarios through which ideal relationships are cultivated (Puett, 2013, pp 98–99). Yet, dismissing this explicitly stated purpose, many ritual scholars follow a default reading of humans in traditional societies as more 'religious-oriented' and thus outside a recognized modern humanity. Such reading reifies the modern versus pre-modern societal hierarchy and retains the taken-for-granted notion of 'religion' after its universalized prototype of Protestantism, applied to comprehending its others (Puett, 2013, p 100). The sense of disempowerment these Chinese students experienced has prompted them to reason as to why Christianity is better, more important and more reasonable in their immediate context. Ultimately, the marginalized location they migrated into requires self-empower and when they lack such resources, spiritual empowerment becomes inviting and to many, a necessity (Ma, 2021).

As a holistic site, the Christian setting that includes Chinese students is permeated with physical, psychological, and social dynamics, and further embedded in the liberal, secular universities that have enrolled these students. Besides student converts finding joy and solace in Christian faith, those who explored but did not convert to Christianity provided different belief accounts.

> 'Gradually, I went less as I should return to my real life … I believe in something outside human power. But even I believe that, I don't necessarily believe in your God … God can only be one, but there are many other religions. They have their God, and some religions have many gods, there're many possibilities. … Many things gods don't manage, and I should just do what *fanren* do.'

Often governed by moral reciprocity, the third most-believed concept in my survey, Chinese students feel guilt after entering Christian circles only to realize their inability to fulfil the conversion expectation. They took the demand so seriously that they could not deny their disbelief and had to withdraw. For this student, belief in plurality prohibits her from becoming Christian. To be *fanren*, earthly beings, resolved the conversion tension for her, but a struggle in fitting in on campus continued. As another Chinese student who also remained non-religious reflected: "If Chinese students could fit in easily, they wouldn't all try the church. ... We wouldn't narrow our socializing circles only to the Christians."

Overall, this study reached two findings by contrasting Chinese belief patterns from the survey with narratives of Christian faith-explorers and converts. First, Chinese non-religious identity is not equivalent to the absence of transcendental beliefs. It can mean the coexistence of several beliefs. Second, this non-religious, pluralist outlook generates varied effects. While it hardly facilitated their secular integration on campus, its openness renders them engaged in evangelical Christian sites, whereby student converts reposition pre-existing beliefs, and those who cannot do so withdraw gradually.

Conclusion

'East Asians' are indispensable in western universities and worth rethinking. As this chapter shows, racialization underpins the notion of 'East Asians' in powerful ways, both externally imposed for categorization and internalized for cultural ownership. Without explicitly calling out its racist construct, we risk reinforcing racism and transforming it into culturalism. Subject to western supremacy in knowledge production, ethnic Chinese are misplaced by initiatives challenging this epistemological dominance. On liberal campuses, these progressive movements rely on a political language and contextual understanding that is foreign to international students, especially those from outside the anglophone west. Although biblical Christian language and culture is equally alien, ethnic Chinese international students are supported to acquire them. Predominantly non-religious to begin with, they hold transcendental beliefs that are unrecognized and marginalized on secular campuses.

Christian inclusivity on campus may have been exemplary in including linguistically and culturally marginalized international students. Indeed, Chinese students report evangelical Christians as one of the few, if not the only, local groups proactively including them. Yet, what religion is and does is defined and internalized via a Eurocentric secular-versus-religious divide. While student converts find a home in globalized Christianity through their willingness to reposition their beliefs, those who cannot do so remain non-Christian or non-religious but disengaged in British universities that have enrolled them in the first place.

How could campus diversity include them on equal, participatory terms? It goes without saying that we should be anti-racist. But our understanding of modern racism matters. What it means to different racial groups (that is, the black, the Asian, the Chinese, and so on) and in various academic fields (that is, studies of race, culture, religion, history, gender, and so on) cannot be examined in isolation. Nor can we rely on vocabularies and categories that are knowingly racist, or unrepresentative of actual lives on campus. Chinese and other marginalized students cannot be excluded or reduced to a diversity showcase. Their perspectives must be heard, understood, and engaged with for a truly plural knowledge structure. To facilitate participation, we must not stop at decolonizing the 'white' curriculum but include widely, address critiques, and reflect diligently.

Notes

[1] Indian students, the second-largest group, accounted for 4 per cent of UK international students in 2017–18.

[2] China, Japan, Korea, and Vietnam share memories of Japanese imperialism. Britain had, however, established an 'informal' empire based on trade and economic power, rendering China semi-colonised in 19th century.

[3] Followed by ethnic Asian students at 19 per cent.

[4] Unlike imagination, social imaginary refers to values that we act upon.

[5] Anglicans of an anthropocentric type do not place God-belief as the core but something humanist, spiritual, and secular.

[6] The survey included international students who had been in the UK for three months or less. This was so as to capture attitudes and perceptions before significant socialization.

[7] Chinese Muslims call their God, 'Allah, the True Master', as localized through both ancient Chinese and regional languages.

[8] This question is modelled after CRCS's (2016) large-sampled survey (response rate 0.23) with US-based Chinese international students whose lengths of stay were uncontrolled (from less than a year to over nine years).

References

Andrews, Kehinde (2018) 'The challenge for Black studies in the neoliberal university', in Gurminder K. Bhambra, Dalia Gebrial and Kerem Nişancıoğlu (eds) *Decolonising the University*. London: Pluto Press, 129–144.

Asad, Talal (1993) *Genealogies of Religion: Discipline and Reasons of Power in Christianity and Islam*. Baltimore: Johns Hopkins University Press.

Brooks, Rachel (2017) 'Representations of East Asian students in the UK media', *Journal of Ethnic and Migration Studies*, 43(14): 2363–2377.

Casanova, José (2018) 'Locating religion and secularity in East Asia through global processes: Early modern Jesuit religious encounters', *Religions*, 9: 349.

CRCS, Centre on Religion and Chinese Society (2016) *Purdue Survey of Chinese Students in the United States: A General Report*. [online] Available from: https://bit.ly/3tXZm99 [accessed 27 April 2021].

Davie, Grace (2018) 'Thinking theoretically about religiosity, secularity and pluralism in the Global East', *Religions*, 9: 337.

Day, Abby (2012) 'Post-secular identities: Non-religious Christians'. *Scripta Donneriani Aboensis*. Turku: Åbo University.

Go, Julian (2016) *Postcolonial Thought and Social Theory*. Oxford: Oxford University Press.

Harvey, Graham (2014) *The Handbook of Contemporary Animism*. London: Routledge.

Hochman, Adam (2020) 'Is "race" modern: Disambiguating the question', *Du Bois Review: Social Science Research on Race*, 16(2): 647–665.

Jahn, Beate (2000) *The Cultural Construction of International Relations: The Invention of the State of Nature*. London: Palgrave Macmillan.

Jon, Jae-Eun (2013) 'Realising internationalisation at home in Korean higher education', *Journal of Studies in International Education*, 17(4): 455–470.

Keevak, Michael (2011) *Becoming Yellow: A Short History of Racial Thinking*. Princeton: Princeton University Press.

Kivisto, Peter (2014) *Religion and Immigration: Migrant Faiths in North America and Western Europe*. Cambridge: Polity.

Lee, Jenny, and Rice, Charles (2007) 'Welcome to America? International student perception of discrimination', *Higher Education*, 53(3): 381–409.

Lee, Lois (2017) *Recognising the Nonreligious: Reimagining the Secular*. New York: Oxford University Press.

Ma, Lin (2021) 'Religious pursuit? Chinese international students encountering Christianity in Britain', *Journal of Contemporary Religion*, 36(3): 401–420.

Madge, Clare, Raghuram, Parvati, and Noxolo, Pat (2015) 'Conceptualising international education: from international student to international study', *Progress in Human Geography*, 39(6): 681–701.

Masuzawa, Tomoko (2005) *The Invention of World Religions: Or, How European Universalism was Preserved in the Language of Pluralism*. Chicago: University of Chicago Press.

Matthews, Julie, and Sidhu, Ravinder (2005) 'Desperately seeking the global subject: International education, citizenship and cosmopolitanism', *Globalisation, Societies and Education*, 3(1): 49–66.

MoE, Ministry of Education (April 2018) 2017 'Increase in numbers of going abroad and returning after studies'. [online] Available from: https://bit.ly/3nrtvuM [accessed 27 April 2021].

Newsome, Linda, and Cooler, Paul (2016) 'International students' cultural and social experiences in a British university: "Such a hard life [it] is here"', *Journal of International Students*, 6(1): 195–215.

NUS, National Union of Students (2012) *No Place for Hate: Hate Crimes and Incidents in Further and Higher Education: Race and Ethnicity*. [online] Available from: https://bit.ly/3expvVP [accessed 27 April 2021].

Nye, Malory (2019) 'Decolonising the Study of Religion'. *Open Library of Humanities*, 5(1): 43: 1–45.

Perraton, Hilary (2014) *A History of Foreign Students in Britain.* London: Palgrave Macmillan UK.

Pietsch, Tamson (2015) *Empire of Scholars: Universities, Networks and the British Academic World, 1850–1939.* Manchester: Manchester University Press.

Puett, Michael (2013) 'Critical approaches to religion in China', *Critical Research on Religion*, I(I): 95–101.

Robertson, Shanthi (2011) 'Cash cows, backdoor migrants, or activist citizens? International students, citizenship, and rights in Australia', *Ethnic and Racial Studies*, 34(12): 2192–2211.

Spencer-Oatey, Helen, and Xiong, Zhaoning (2006) 'Chinese students' psychological and sociocultural adjustments to Britain: an empirical study', *Language, Culture and Curriculum*, 19(1): 37–53.

Stein, Sharon, and Andreotti, Vanessa (2016) 'Cash, competition, or charity: International students and the global imaginary', *Higher Education*, 72(2): 225–239.

Tan, Ning-Sang (March 2018) 'For East Asian students, claims to BME identity are complicated', *Varsity*. [online] Available from: https://bit.ly/2QrEMj1 [accessed 27 April 2021].

UKCISA, UK Council for International Student Affairs (2019) International Student Statistics: UK Higher Education. [online] Available from: https://bit.ly/32Sw0wY [accessed 27 April 2021].

UKCOSA, UK Council for Overseas Student Affairs (2004) *Broadening Our Horizons: International Students in UK Universities and Colleges.* London: UKCOSA.

Walker, Patricia (2014) 'International student policies in UK higher education from colonialism to the coalition', *Journal of Studies in International Education*, 18(4): 325–344.

White, Chris (2017) 'Counting Christians in China: A critical reading of A Star in the East: The rise of Christianity in China', *Cultural Diversity in China*, 2(1): 101–109.

Woodhead, Linda (2016) 'The rise of "no religion" in Britain: The emergence of a new cultural majority', *Journal of the British Academy*, 4: 245–261.

Yang, Fenggang (2018) 'Religion in the Global East: Challenges and opportunities for the social scientific study of religion', *Religions*, 9: 305.

YouGov (2020) Racism_BAME_June2020. [online] Available from: https://bit.ly/3gEfxEI [accessed 27 April 2021].

Yu, Yun (2017) 'Church participation as intercultural encounter in the experiences of Chinese international students in the UK'. PhD thesis, University of Glasgow.

4

This Island's Mine: University Teaching as Inclusive Dramaturgy

Danny Braverman

Prologue: setting the scene

Before the action of the class starts, I prepare the space. I'm lucky; I'm in a studio. There is no fixed seating and I have 30 minutes to prepare. Typically, when teaching in a United Kingdom (UK) university, the space is preconfigured in 'sage on the stage' mode (King, 1993), where banks of students face the font of wisdom. You'd be fortunate to have a five-minute turnaround. This, however, is a 'black box' studio with some audio–visual equipment. The lack of natural light is compensated by the ability to control lighting. I can project images and I can play music. There are walls which I can reimagine, including moveable theatrical drapes. I have enough chairs for participants and a trestle table. I get to work. I have prepared a sign – deciding it will be handwritten. Cued by Harrison Owen (2008) and his advice about setting up Open Space Technology I appreciate that handwritten signs are friendlier, more welcoming and less corporate than something printed. The sign outlines the central question of the workshop: 'How does understanding global issues affect our work on play texts?', written purposely in plain English. I could have written: 'An exploration of postcolonialism in The Tempest', but it was important not to present a barrier of assumed knowledge. I have, after all, responded to students expressing their alienation from theory courses, who have told me that terminology and lack of familiarity with the canon present barriers for them. I have prepared something typed, but it is projected: the lyrics to Bob Marley's 'Redemption Song'. I scatter the chairs around the space randomly. I place other materials for work later in the session on the trestle table – pens, paper, masking tape, exercise books (for students that want to jot something down). I arrange the materials like a buffet, as if I'm setting up a party. I want the space to be convivial, to spark curiosity and to encourage conversation and creativity. Just before my guests are due to arrive, I play 'Redemption Song' on repeat and realise that no matter how much you prepare, the value of the event will always be an act of co-creation with others. This triggers the good kind of performance anxiety I've experienced many times before a show. Teaching is performance; students are audience–participants who alternate between moments of reception and creation. Teaching space curation is often unexamined in universities, but as a dramaturg I can't help but consider how time, colour, light, sound, image and text combine to set the scene. In a perfect world, I'd take smell and taste into account too, like a nervous house vendor baking bread and brewing coffee before prospective buyers arrive. However, College rules state that no food or drink (except water) are permitted in this studio, and I didn't have the wit then to create a more welcoming smell with, say, essential oils.

In a way, this is a meta-chapter. Dramaturgy is both its core theme and informs its form. The preceding paragraph is analogous to the lead-up to the performance itself. The meaning of any event is circumscribed by the journey to it. Just as a show's impact depends on the crowd's buzz in the foyer, so a class depends on the institution's atmosphere and the set-up of the teaching space. Correspondingly, this chapter has an opening that intends to welcome you, the reader; it aims to intrigue so that you'll read on. What immediately follows in this section acts as a prologue; providing you with a map for your journey, a sense of the themes and narrative to follow.

Dramaturgy is a notoriously slippery term, with broad applications. This is partly complicated by the dramaturg's role: in many theatre contexts it is discreet, with functions ranging from critical friend to researcher, to in-house philosopher (Turner and Behrndt, 2008). In practice, acts of dramaturgy are performed by many creatives, and are chiefly concerned with composition, arranging the different elements of performance. There are many principles that can govern dramaturgy. This chapter's structure and my own theatre-making practice are concerned mostly with what Fiona Graham (2017) terms the 'concatenate pole' of dramaturgy, supporting the Aristotelian view that narrative structure is the drama's most important element.

I use the assorted elements to compose a journey for my audience/students. I want that journey to have a shape; a beginning, middle and end. I realise also that assumptions about audience may fit awkwardly with the notion of the active learner. However, audiences are never passive. Indeed, my own theatre-making has been informed by the work of theatre/drama practitioners such as Augusto Boal (1979) and Dorothy Heathcote (2015), who place interactivity at their practice's heart.

My dramaturgical approach to teaching is also influenced by Disability Studies. Drawing particularly from Swain and French's (2000) formulation of the affirmative model of disability, I see benefits in disability consciousness for creating profound learning experiences. This means that inclusive practices are built into teaching's design, rather than bolted on following individual adjustments. There is an obvious parallel here with the 'aesthetics of access' as articulated by Jenny Sealey of Graeae Theatre Company (Sealey and Lynch, 2007), and now widely practised by artists such as Jess Thom and Rachel Bagshaw and companies such as Cardiff's Hijinx. Here, elements such as audio description, sign language, captioning and a relaxed environment suitable for neurodiverse people are woven into performance. In setting the scene for my class, the creation of a 'soft opening' was informed particularly by the movement for relaxed performance in theatre. This challenges many of university teaching's orthodoxies: the start time is relatively fluid; students can come and go as they please; they can interrupt; and they can participate at a level where they feel comfortable – including just observing rather than actively participating if that's their choice. Of course, for the class to maximise learning, I want the students to engage actively. So, it is my responsibility as the teacher-dramaturg to create a compelling and engaging journey for them.

This chapter's dramaturgy follows a classic three-act structure. Act One parallels the script writer's notion of the 'inciting incident', the impetus being to find better ways to teach students with hidden disabilities. Therefore, Act One harnesses the 'social model' of disability (Barnes, 2012) to analyse the barriers that those students face, particularly regarding conventional approaches to teaching theory. Act Two, characteristically the longest act of a traditional play, explores possibilities. I posit a different approach to designing teaching by digging more deeply into underpinning disability theory. This was the foundation for the practical experiment of *The Tempest* workshop itself, which I'll describe and analyse as it unfolded. Act Three will, as Dorothy Heathcote (2015) describes it, drop 'from the particular to the universal', seeking to name general principles underpinning an inclusive dramaturgy approach to university teaching.

Having set the scene and introduced our journey through a prologue, let us open the curtain on Act One.

Act One: What is the managerialist-adjustment model?

Caliban's famous speech in *The Tempest* starts with the bold declaration: 'This Island's mine, by Sycorax my mother, / which thou takest from me' (Shakespeare, 1999). This resonates not just with colonialism but with other thefts of rights. If we consider education as a colonised island, a case can be made that disabling barriers constrain and limit the non-normative student. Caliban goes on to declare that Prospero originally showed him kindness and even taught him 'how / to name the bigger light, and how the less, / that burn by day and night'. However, Prospero's teaching came at a cost to Caliban, imprisoned in 'this hard rock, while you do keep from me / the rest of the island'. In the neoliberal university, disabled students are attracted, recruited and offered support from disability-specific schemes, but still have lower levels of achievement and participation (Office for Students, 2019). There may not be segregated 'special needs' provision in universities, but integration is on non-disabled terms, and should not be confused with inclusion (Leite, 2012).

The social model of disability was a breakthrough in Disability Studies, particularly in the UK, as it identified the dominant medical model that emphasises normalising and curing disability, and proposes instead a human rights focus on the physical and attitudinal barriers that society creates, preventing disabled people from full participation (Barnes, 2012). The social model has been critiqued and expanded, but analysing disabling barriers remains a useful tool in addressing educational disadvantage. Ironically, the language of 'access' and 'adjustment' driven by equalities legislation reflects a generally agreed shift to social-model thinking by the academy, but the universities' measures are experienced as barriers by many disabled students, mainly because they need to wrestle with bureaucracy. As Magnus and Tøssebro state: 'when applying for supports the individual will always run the risk of being met with suspiciousness and rejection, to be considered not deserving' (Magnus and Tøssebro, 2014, p 320). While mechanisms such as reasonable adjustment agreements are well meaning, they tend to address physical barriers rather than the more complex area of disabling attitudes and psychological barriers arising through how disabled people experience ableism. While disabled students still struggle for concrete adjustments, there are discernible access improvements: a wheelchair user may have improved physical access to teaching spaces; a deaf student to signing and captioning; a blind student to text-to-speech software; and a dyslexic student to their readings printed on coloured paper. Even without these measures, and despite financial arguments excusing lack of access, there is usually agreement that disabled students should have these concrete adjustments put in place ... when time and resources permit. Typically, however, few core studies incorporate as role models the work generated by disabled people. Furthermore, in, say, literature or theatre studies, rarely are representations such as Dickens' Tiny Tim or Shakespeare's Richard III systematically critiqued from a disability perspective. Disabled students' peers and teachers may also unwittingly display unconscious bias: a chronically ill student may be perceived as lazy; a student with attention deficit hyperactivity disorder (ADHD) is criticised for talking too much; a deaf student must navigate an 'eyes-closed visualisation' exercise.

When I was considering how to improve disabled students' experience at Goldsmiths, it was quickly clear that the vast majority of disabled students had what are frequently termed 'invisible disabilities'. Indeed, all the Reasonable Adjustment Student Agreements produced for undergraduates in my department, Theatre and Performance, for 2020–21 indicated that all our disabled students declared 'invisible disabilities'. These were mostly concerned with neurodiversity (46 per cent) – a term which I use to include dyslexia, dyspraxia, ADHD, autism – or mental health (50 per cent). The Office for Students (2019) recommends that universities and colleges respond to the needs of disabled students by adopting the social model of disability. While its terminology broadly aligns with that model, closer examination reveals characteristics aligning more with medical-model thinking. Diagnosis and medical evidence are mandatory for obtaining 'reasonable adjustments'. Documents are framed by outlining a 'condition' or 'disorder' to be verified by people in what Vic Finkelstein terms as 'professions allied to medicine' (Finkelstein, 2001, p 7). The adjustments can be read therefore as a 'cure' to a 'problem'; a way to normalise impairment. Indeed, there is now a standard menu of adjustments purporting to adequately address needs such as considering assignment deadlines, recording lectures, allowing for lateness/absence and alerting lecturers not to put a student 'on the spot'. This is what Sheila Riddell and Elisabet Weedon refer to as 'managerialist methods' to tackle disability inequality (Riddell and Weedon, 2014, p 39). I argue that most university disability-access processes reflect a 'managerialist-adjustment' model.

However, are disabilities as 'invisible' as is claimed? Certainly, neurodiversity often presents as behaviour deemed aberrant in traditional academic settings and is often coterminous with episodes of mental distress. Clearly, for example, Jeff Gawthorpe's description of his ADHD symptoms while a student shows that his 'invisible disability' would have been apparent: 'I've been to GPs [general practitioners] dozens of times both exhibiting and describing the core symptoms of ADHD: racing mind, inability to relax, fidgeting, feeling overwhelmed, terrible sleep quality, anxiety, and treatment resistant depression' (Beckett, 2017).

Despite adjustments, a student with these experiences is often unable to suppress their manifestations. Moreover, the act of trying to supress behaviours so as to appear 'normal' is likely to worsen poor mental health. Correspondingly, a student with a fluctuating chronic health condition such as inflammatory bowel disease or diabetes will have their stamina and cognition impaired at different times. The structures of university life, governed by timetables, deadlines, preparatory reading, scholarly writing conventions and often complex navigation of rooming arrangements, present barriers to full participation. There is a presumption that the prototypical student will easily navigate these default organisational arrangements and that what is needed is adjustments to the status quo. The managerialist-adjustment model is therefore a 'bolted on' approach, requiring the non-normative, disabled student to conform to institutional norms, often in ways that are not possible for them.

Unsurprisingly, students with 'invisible disabilities' will feel pressured to appear 'normal'. There are stigmas (Goffman, 1990) clearly associated with these disabilities, which UK studies confirm leads to the added barrier of fear of disclosure (Riddell and Weedon, 2005; Stanley et al, 2011), with most students, according to Jennifer Marie Martin (2010, p 259), not disclosing their mental health issues to university staff. This shows that the roughly one in eight of Goldsmiths' Theatre and Performance students who officially declare a mental health condition to gain reasonable adjustments is likely to be significantly underestimated.

Dramaturgical performance analysis can further examine disabling barriers in typical university learning experiences. Whitmore's (1994, p 16) semiotic approach shows that an audience constructs or decodes a performance's meaning depending on, for example, their education, cultural heritage, social experience, mood, physical impairment and concentration ability. Audience members and learners approach events with their own individual 'horizon of expectations' (Jauss and Benzinger, 1970, p 8). For many educators, this means designing classes so that learning is appropriately differentiated. By contrast, the dramaturg will take a less individualised approach, aiming to build a sense of community based in shared identity, friendship and celebration – key elements for students' university experience. Consideration of these elements is missing in the managerialist-adjustment model of disability as disabled students navigate the added barriers of stigma, disclosure and the emotional labour of burdensome bureaucracy.

Analysing the scenography of typical lecture theatres (that almost always, ironically, constrain theatricality) reveals a specific learner–teacher relationship: the teacher-performer presenting to receiving students; the plethora of electricity points for laptops; the neutral-coloured walls with little stimulus; fixed seating; the ubiquity of PowerPoint. The space beyond the lecture theatre is often unwelcoming too, particularly for neurodiverse students: the signage can be confusing; the noise and bustle unnerving; and the 'cost-effective' turnaround times between lectures tight.

Many lecturers know how to provide narrative shape to the given time for a learning experience, typically just short of an hour. This is often hampered by the notion of 'delivering learning outcomes' – terminology that is rarely problematised. The 'delivery' aspect assumes that the lecturer's primary role is akin to the postal service: deliver the 'learning outcome' package to the doorstep. The reception of the 'outcome' is the primary, highly problematic, metric by which successful teaching is often measured. If the 'learning package' is not received, it is arguably not always the fault of either lecturer or student, but a systemic problem baked into an inadequate pedagogy.

By contrast, concatenate dramaturgy is contingent on an emotional journey where a diverse audience reaches plot points together. When teaching theory, intellectual insights can be treated as analogous to plot points, each building on the last. If significant numbers of students do not grasp key insights, their experience will be frustrating and might even activate anger. This frustration can be compounded by the need to bring prior knowledge to the learning experience, most often in the form of preparatory reading. Here, many students experience the barrier of unfamiliar terminology, which is particularly problematic for, say, dyslexic students and those whose focus and concentration is affected by their impairment. If the drive to 'deliver learning outcomes' means that a lecturer feels compelled to embed challenging preparatory reading, a parallel can be seen with an audience member's first bad experience of Shakespeare where it was assumed they were already familiar with the text.

The question then arises: if the managerialist-adjustment model does not adequately enshrine students' disability rights, is there a more inclusive approach?

Act Two: What if theory were taught using the principles of inclusive dramaturgy?

As Clarissa Hope Lynch states in her interview with Jenny Sealey (Sealey and Lynch, 2007, p 62): 'Access is embedded in every production to enable accessible performing and spectating' through a multisensory narrative of spoken/signed languages and visual/aural technology. In relaxed performances, audience members can arrive and leave, and involuntary sounds are incorporated spontaneously. These examples show how artists go beyond the social model of disability, with its emphasis on addressing an ableist deficit, and are more aligned to the principles of universal design (Center for Universal Design, 1997) and Swain and French's 'affirmative model' of disability.

Swain and French (2000, p 569) describe the affirmative model as depicting non-tragic, positive social identities which address 'the limitations of the social model through the realisation of positive identity encompassing impairment, as well as disability'. Their affirmative model shows that being disabled brings benefits to the learning experience. This is clearly the case for neurodiverse students, often adept at the kind of divergent thinking that can deepen conceptual learning. Again, artists can signal new ways of thinking. Benedict Phillips' (2005) work centres on his experience of dyslexia and includes his 'lexic to dyslexic dictionary'. His performance piece *The Agenda of the Aggressive Dyslexic* (Phillips, 2020) has taken his practice to higher education. In witnessing Phillips' residency at the Royal Conservatoire of Scotland, fellow neurodiverse artist, dyspraxic dancer/choreographer Aby Watson (Watson and Phillips, 2019) described how Phillips reversed the medical and deficit discourse of dyslexia by conceiving of memory as a coil of cassette tape and emphasising the strengths of three-dimensional and visual thinking.

People experiencing poor mental health can also frame their experiences more affirmatively in learning environments. Perhaps more so than in other areas, students experiencing poor mental health are locked into the medical model of disability; it is challenging for them to accept fluctuating conditions when they want to return to earlier times without mental distress. They are often caught in dualistic thinking about their identity, between hoping for a permanent state of being 'well' and fearful that their mental health status is their defining characteristic. Again, arts practice can illuminate more inclusive ways of working. Rather than looking to erase students' experience, or exposing them to the pressures of disclosure, the teacher can encourage a more nuanced sense of identity as part of the group. In theatre studies and other arts practice, a collective identity as artists can be useful. Hui et al (2019, p 297) praised the benefits of the non-medical and non-stigmatising environment of a community arts and mental health project, where 'people may perceive themselves more positively, and develop a sense of belonging through their artistic activities'. Artists can bring elements of autobiography to their work, while maintaining agency over their level of disclosure. Teachers must therefore create a safe environment, with clear confidentiality boundaries, opening invitations that validate personal stories as a key part of learning and without pressure for students to disclose.

For teachers, the next step is to design university learning experiences informed by the innovations of disabled and community artists (often we are both) where, as Glass, Meyer and Rose (Glass et al, 2013, p 107) assert, 'The arts push us to recognize and consider the multiple, flexible ways in which people learn and interact with the world.'

The concept of 'universal design' complements the affirmative model by moving on from the social model. The concept was first developed by designers, architects and engineers as 'the design of products and environments to be usable by all people, to the greatest extent possible, without the need for adaptation or specialized design' (Center for Universal Design, 1997). Universal design therefore negates the necessity for disabled people 'to "declare" a disability for a socially just, respectful and adaptable workplace, leisure facility or educational institution to emerge' (Brabazon, 2015, p 26).

Returning to the studio

Over ten minutes, six students come into the studio in ones and twos. I have invited all students, but especially encouraged those that self-define as disabled. Of the six, five identify as being neurodiverse and/or experiencing poor mental health; one is non-disabled, but interested in experiencing a more inclusive approach to teaching. There are students here who identify as dyslexic, dyspraxic and ADHD, with mental health diagnoses that include post-traumatic stress, eating disorders, anxiety and depression. As host, I greet them, prompt talk about 'Redemption Song' and point out the lyrics projected on the wall. They either sit or stand, moving chairs around to configure relaxed conversations. I ask them if they know the song; they all do, and know it's about slavery. We talk about the line: 'emancipate yourself from mental slavery'. Christine says that for her the line is about "recognising your family, your background, will have some very … difficult history. Terrible things have been inflicted on you, back generations. But also good things. Don't let the shadows rule your mind." There's a murmur of recognition.

When we've settled, I point to the handmade sign on the wall: 'How does understanding global issues affect our work on play texts?' and ask if they will agree to discussing this question for the next couple of hours. I remind them of the ground rules we've agreed in previous sessions: that this is a relaxed space, people can come and go; that there are no right answers; that we're primarily looking at a practical way to explore theory … but not to worry about that for now. I always start in a circle, so we gather our chairs. Although I'm leading, I want to establish a sense of parity. As the session progresses, I know that I will also take part. Personal stories will play their part in our exploration of the topic. Pedagogically, I take a cue from bell hooks (1994, p 186) and her analysis of teachers sharing their experiences: 'Sharing experiences and confessional narratives in the classroom helps establish communal commitment to learning.' I frame this simply by saying "I won't ask you to do anything I'm not prepared to do myself." It is important for me to be open about my own positionality – after all, we are talking explicitly in this session about race, and our mutual interest is disability. I am a cis, white, straight, middle-class man – so, already, there are potential tensions in terms of building trust and rapport with a group where none of the participants shares all these characteristics. However, I am a disabled Jew. This is an intersectional identity which I can partly conceal. I am open from the beginning of the workshops about my disabled identity as someone experiencing chronic illness. Although for some this would have become clear when I was undergoing radiotherapy and needed to walk with a cane, the barriers I experience are often hidden. My disclosures about chronic illness are important: I may experience periods of exhaustion; my diabetes can manifest in cognitive fog; and my stoma may mean a bag leakage where I must leave the room suddenly. Disclosure is not just to create mutual recognition, but also to model the benefits of 'coming out' as disabled and the affirmative aspects of impairment. My Jewishness is also known to students, largely as they study my solo show *Wot? No Fish!!* (Braverman, 2013), and I don't suppress the mannerisms and Yiddish-inflected vernacular that are part of my personality.

A core aim of the session is to build what the theatre anthropologist Victor Turner (1982) would term *communitas*, a sense of temporary community. So,

I ask an open and friendly question to the students in a circle: "How are things this week?" Barbara, whose communication style is fun and garrulous, launches into a monologue about their workload: "I'm sooo stressed," they say, "I've got two essays I'm totally lost with; I'm loving my practical project." There are nods of agreement. Others pitch in about their workload too, with the core narrative that practical assignments are the 'reward', the essays are like 'eating your greens'. This provides me with a natural segue into the main session. "I hope," I say, "that by working practically this afternoon, we'll blur the distinction with theory, but as you know, this is an experiment to see if these techniques work – so please let me know if there's any terminology we use you don't understand." Just as an overture in a musical or opera, or the call-and-response rituals of stand-up comedy, traditional storytelling or rock gigs establish a community of attention, I judge that the group are now 'in the room'. The disparate energies that inevitably form the beginning of any class have now been converted to a greater sense of common purpose. The welcoming environment and circle check-in have done their jobs, and we are ready to launch into the content. It may have taken half an hour for this to be established, but it is not time wasted.

I change the projection to a Peters' projection map of the world, showing the true proportions of land masses. "Do you notice anything different about this map?" I ask. Initially, students comment that it 'looks weird', until someone says: "Britain looks small"; and so a conversation ensues about maps and how they affect how we think about nations, continents and cultures. Dominic adds that he has seen a map shown "upside down, which makes you think about how the North is assumed to be dominant". We talk about the map that showed the British Empire in pink and how surprisingly large Kazakhstan is. I then invite students to recreate the continents on the floor of the studio with signs and masking tape. I say: "Let's start by going to where we are now." As a group we tightly cluster on the tiny patch that is the UK. Without making it explicit through words, we are experiencing being on the margins of a much bigger world. Because the exercise requires us to be tightly huddled, this exercise has a sense of intimacy. As drama students, the group is comfortable with touch – I make a mental note that not all groups would find this easy and that this first physical exercise could, in other circumstances, jeopardise group cohesion. Then I say: "Now move to where one of your parents was born." The group scans the floor-map and I can see them considering which parent to choose. Christine, Dominic and Barbara stay in the 'UK', trying in a tight space to distinguish different regions. I join Christine in what we decide is London. Dominic places himself a fraction 'north' of us in Sheffield; Barbara stakes a claim for a slightly westward Devon. Meanwhile, Eva has found 'Poland', Zac has gone to 'Hong Kong' and Sofia to 'Thessaloniki, Greece'. Already fragments of family stories are emerging. Barbara, so often the initiator, says her mum is still in rural Devon and can't understand why Barbara will "never go back there"; she's a confirmed Londoner now. I chip in that my identity is pure East London, but my mum, although born in Hackney, migrated across the North Circular Road to a leafy suburb when she was a child (I use the term migration ironically, but deliberately). Zac says his mum came from Hong Kong, but his dad is Indian. It was a difficult choice where to place himself for the exercise, but his mum talks more about her "homeland", dad is reticent about his life in India. Eva, new to London, in contrast to Barbara, finds herself feeling "like a foreigner", despite London's diverse communities. And so, the stories of family tumble out; there are nods of recognition and gentle prompts for people to amplify. We then expand the exercise across past generations. We go to where our grandparents came from, and great-grandparents. We find out that part of Christine's family were the Windrush generation, another branch came from India too – she has this in common with Zac, to their mutual surprise. Christine, it transpires, is encyclopaedic about the patterns of her family migration. She tells us how part of her family wasn't "originally from Jamaica", that they'd been taken as slaves from West Africa. "Old pirates, yeah, they rob I!" sings Dominic. We laugh, recognising a connection made. I tell the group how my great grandparents came from different parts of the Pale of Settlement, including Poland. However, as I move to Poland, I can see Eva is deep in thought. "No," she says, "my great grandfather wasn't in Poland a lot of the time. During the war, as a child, he was sent to Siberia." She goes on to tell the family story of displacement, that her grandmother made a dramatic return to Poland, but that she was told that her great-grandfather had a terrible childhood, torn away from his home. "Until now," she says, "I thought I was the only member of my family ever to move from Poland – but, no, you see, I'd forgotten about my great-grandfather!"

We then shift the focus of the game from the past to the future. We visit places where we wouldn't like to end up and discuss why, say, Afghanistan or Columbia are considered dangerous. We visit places we'd like to live and discuss why the United States is so often perceived as a 'promised land'. At each phase of the exercise, I give the stories and opinions space to breathe. The group is exploring communalities and difference, unwittingly discussing their sense of place and, underpinning it all, within each story we start to understand that geopolitics has had a huge effect on our sense of self.

We shift back into a circle formed across 'the Equator', dropping from the particular to the universal (Heathcote, 2015). This is a playwriting reflex, as well as fundamental to Heathcote's process drama. Good plays have strong controlling ideas, which thoughtful dramaturgy brings subtly to the surface, so the flow of characters' emotional journeys isn't unsettled by an 'author's message'. As an example, the moment in Arthur Miller's (2013, p 46) *Death of a Salesman* when the protagonist Willy Loman stoops to pick up his new, younger boss's lighter, in one movement sums up the worker's loss of dignity under capitalism. Kolb (1984), in another parallel between dramaturgy and teaching, alerts us with his cycle of experiential learning to the way conceptual tools surface following concrete experience. It is worth noting here that traditional university teaching methods often start with concepts – which can so often be alienating – rather than having them derive from experience. I frame the discussion to look at the reasons why people move around the globe; which are choices, which are desperate needs, which are forced? It is only then that we define colonialism, referring to the room around us as our map of the world. We see where European powers took control of other parts of the world, and how that intersects with our own stories.

Now is the time to introduce our play. I say we will look at *The Tempest*, but don't assume that students know the play. We move our chairs to face the screen and, in role as cinema-goers, watch a short, animated version of *The Tempest* story. We split into pairs and I invite the group to work now as actors, preparing to perform the short section of the second scene of the play where we first meet Caliban, starting with the famous 'This island's mine …' speech. Despite being drama students, I am aware that some members of the group could feel unsettled by the text and the job of reading aloud. Each pair has their own separated space, and they are invited to find any position they find comfortable to read the passage. I chunk the exercise into stages. First, "just have a read together", I say. I float between the groups. If they are tripping up over unfamiliar language, I lightly coach them. Then I call them to attention to think about the power relationship between Caliban and Prospero; they are to mark up their scripts with status numbers between 1 and 10 to explore the power dynamics. One pair says this is a difficult task; isn't Prospero always a 10 and Caliban always a 1? It's then that we discuss the role of interpretation; that they can experiment with different power differentials. We acknowledge that, hugely problematic as it is, Prospero is threatened by Caliban's alleged attempt to 'violate the honour of' his daughter, Miranda. We discuss parallels, that those in power feel threatened by, as one student puts it, "dilution of their precious gene pool". Having marked up scripts in this way, we shift into performance mode. The scene is projected, so there is no need for script in hand. As pairs try out the scene, the others become audience–directors. The key question is: what meaning can we generate from this text? Zac says he's fascinated by Caliban's last line in the section: 'the red plague rid you for learning me your language'. "I resonate with that," he says, "I feel that I've been denied my real language." He expands. "Well, in drama we have to do this – read Shakespeare – learn all that. My form is hip-hop, but it's not seen as proper drama." A thought then occurs to me. I ask the group if they mind if we look at something else, something not in my lesson plan. So, we return to our cinema-goer formation and I show Jonzi D's (2015) TED talk. In his talk, Jonzi starts with the provoking question: "Why is hip-hop not part of the national curriculum for performing arts?" He goes on to discuss his own journey through hip-hop performance; his encounters with dominant Western dance forms through his training; the fraught decision to turn down an MBE because of its imperialist connotations. At one point, he says: "I ended up leaving the London Contemporary Dance School with this body, this hip-hop body, colonised," punctuating the end of this sentence with his arms posed in a ballet third position. The students erupt into laughter.

Our final practical exercise is to try out rehearsed readings of the scene. Each group scours the internet for images of colonialism, which they project as creative juxtapositions. The images include a white volunteer teaching children in India, a Union Jack flag and a Bible. We talk about how these images could inform a production of *The Tempest* that brings out its postcolonialist themes. "What if Prospero's book was a Bible," says Maria. As she speaks, I can see her contemplating the role of the missionary in colonisation.

Finally, presented almost as an afterthought, I project a couple of quotations from theory texts: 'Every empire, however, tells itself and the world that it is unlike all other empires, that its mission is not to plunder and control but to educate and liberate' (Said, 2003).

> Every colonized people – in other words, every people in whose soul an inferiority complex has been created by the death and burial of its local cultural originality – finds itself face to face with the language of the civilizing nation; that is, with the culture of the mother country. The colonized is elevated above his jungle status in proportion to his adoption of the mother country's cultural standards. (Fanon, 2008, p 9)

I ask: "If you now had to write an essay about postcolonialism and *The Tempest*, would you be able to link this theory to the meaning of the play in production?" The students all say that they have a grasp now and that an essay would be easier. However, having to read the whole text is still a barrier, it still feels like 'eating your greens'. This tells me that the centrality of the scholarly text in university teaching will continue to be a barrier for these students. Nevertheless, the ideas have excited the group when unpacked practically and accessibly. We have made a start, but there's more work to do.

Act Three: What next? Being realistic in changing university teaching

As Tara Brabazon (2015) suggests, a university can choose between a concept of universal design, assuming a plurality of users at the outset, or a policy of retrofitting when disabling features of a policy, idea or architecture are removed. Although Brabazon is primarily concerned with 'architectures, ideas and policies', by extension we can apply this thinking to teaching methodologies. Universal design would entail a change in thinking, where the prototypical student is no longer non-disabled. This would challenge several shibboleths, particularly that theory is substantially 'delivered' through preparatory and follow-up reading. Alternative methodologies, where reading complements a much more multilayered approach, would need to be employed by teachers who have, almost by definition, succeeded in navigating ableist systems. Applying universal design principles would entail substantial added labour for teachers with already heavy workloads, underpinned by a shift in their consciousness that questions fundamental pedagogic assumptions. Furthermore, the managerialist-adjustment model determines administrative structures too; access agreements have been enshrined as the primary practice to address disability equality. Retrofitting is therefore a more achievable first step to providing a gateway into embedding universal design principles in the future.

Inclusive dramaturgy offers useful tools for retrofitting existing courses. It can guide teachers through ways that theatre-makers design events to simultaneously resonate with individual audience experiences and create *communitas*. Teachers can give greater consideration to creating a shared group identity by greeting students as 'guests', as we might an audience. The teaching space can be reconfigured with music played, senses of touch and smell judiciously used and convivial chat encouraged. Recognising that a class, like a play, takes the student on an emotional journey, teachers can find ways to validate personal testimony, shared safely and confidentially, with teachers prepared to share their own stories too. We can focus intellectual content towards deepening understanding of ourselves within the wider world, aiming for shared insights and pleasurable 'light bulb' moments, where the class reaches the same point in the 'plot' together. Teachers can embrace more embodied learning experiences too, with exploration and articulation through image, poetry, sound and symbol, lifting ideas from the page and so motivating students to engage with their readings. In this way, we begin to address the psychological barriers to learning that so often result in anxiety, feelings of inferiority, shame, fear of disclosure and the anger that arises from exclusion.

The craft of dramaturgy is a complex consideration of how every element of performance combines to compose an experience, with the audience as co-creators. The best performance and teaching both generate a delicate balance of invitations for individuals to generate their own meaning and a celebration of community. The best performances and classes are also memorable; they come back to us for the rest of our lives, not as regurgitated facts, but as multidimensional lenses to better understand the world. As teachers, we often struggle to design experiences where students don't just grasp something fleetingly with the instrumental and temporary purpose of gaining the best possible grades, but that have the kind of lasting impact of the best performance. If we start to perceive disabled students affirmatively as co-creators who bring powerful divergent contributions, our teaching can inspire everyone in the room.

References

Barnes, Colin (2012) 'Understanding the social model of disability', in Nick Watson, Alan Roulstone, and Carol Thomas (eds) *Routledge Handbook of Disability Studies*. New York: Routledge, pp 12–29.

Beckett, Michelle (2017) 'Jeff's story – adult ADHD'. [online] Available from: https://bit.ly/3gHrBoJ [accessed 18 February 2021].

Boal, Augusto (1979) *Theatre of the Oppressed*. London: Pluto Press.

Brabazon, Tara (2015) *Enabling University: Impairment, (Dis)ability and Social Justice in Higher Education*. New York: Springer International Publishing.

Braverman, Danny (2013) *Wot? No Fish!!* London: Bread and Circuses Arts.

Center for Universal Design (1997) 'The principles of universal design'. [online] Available from: https://bit.ly/2SbOztZ [accessed 19 February 2021].

Fanon, Frantz (2008) *Black Skin, White Masks* (10th edn). London: Pluto Press.

Finkelstein, Vic (2001) 'A personal journey into disability politics'. [online] Available from: https://bit.ly/3aNO1kj [accessed 18 February 2021].

Glass, Don, Meyer, Anne, and Rose, David H. (2013) 'Universal design in the arts', *Harvard Educational Review*, 83(1): 98–119.

Goffman, Erving (1990) *Stigma: Notes on the Management of Spoiled Identity* (5th edn). London: Penguin.

Graham, Fiona (2017) *Performing Dramaturgy*. Wellington: Playmarket.

Heathcote, Dorothy (2015) *Dorothy Heathcote on Education and Drama*. London and New York: Routledge.

hooks, bell (1994) *Teaching to Transgress: Education as the Practice of Freedom*, New York: Routledge.

Hui, Ada, Stickley, Theodore, Stubley, Michelle, and Baker, Francesca (2019) 'Project eARTh: Participatory arts and mental health recovery, a qualitative study', *Perspectives in Public Health*, 139(6): 296–302.

Jauss, Hans Robert, and Benzinger, Elizabeth (1970) 'Literary history as a challenge to literary theory', *New Literary History*, 2(1): 7–37.

Jonzi, D. (2015) 'Hip-Hop Theatre: recognition without permission', *TEDx Warwick*. [online] Available from: https://bit.ly/3vpbFeT [accessed 9 March 2021].

King, Alison (1993) 'From sage on the stage to guide on the side', *College Teaching*, 41(1): 30–35.

Kolb, David (1984) *Experiential Learning: Experience as the Source of Learning and Development* (5th edn). London: Prentice-Hall.

Leite, Sonia (2012) 'From exclusion to inclusion going through segregation and integration: The role of the school and of the sociopedagogical mediator', *Procedia – Social and Behavioral Sciences*, 69: 47–53.

Magnus, Eva, and Tossebro, Jan (2014) 'Negotiating individual accommodation in higher education', *Scandinavian Journal of Disability Research*, 16(4): 316–332.

Martin, Jennifer Marie (2010) 'Stigma and student mental health in higher education', *Higher Education Research and Development*, 29(3): 259–274.

Miller, Arthur (2013) *Death of a Salesman* (e.edition). London: Penguin Random House.

Office for Students (2019) 'Beyond the bare minimum', *sight* 4. [online] Available from: https://bit.ly/3aOipLA [accessed 7 March 2021].

Owen, Harrison (2008) *Open Space Technology: A User's Guide*. San Francisco: Berrett-Koehler Publishers.

Phillips, Benedict (2005) *A Benedictionary*. [online] Available from: https://bit.ly/3aNkebv [accessed 8 March 2021].

Phillips, Benedict (2020) 'The Agenda of the Aggresive Dyslexic'. [online] Available from: https://bit.ly/3eENouu [accessed 8 March 2021].

Riddell, Sheila, and Weedon, Elisabet (2005) *Disabled Students in Higher Education: Perspectives on Widening Access and Changing Policy*. London: Routledge.

Riddell, Sheila, and Weedon, Elisabet (2014) 'Disabled students in higher education: Discourses of disability and the negotiation of identity', *International Journal of Educational Research*, 63: 38–46.

Said, Edward (2003) 'Blind imperial arrogance', *LA Times*. [online] Available from: https://lat.ms/3xp1Zmm [accessed 28 April 2021]

Sealey, Jenny, and Lynch, Clarissa Hope (2007) 'Graeae: An aesthetics of access – (de)-cluttering the clutter', in Susan Broadhurst and Josephine Machon (eds) *Identity, Performance and Technology; Practices of Empowerment, Embodiment and Technicity*. London: Palgrave Macmillan, pp 60–73.

Shakespeare, William (1999) *The Tempest*. London: Bloomsbury Publishing.

Stanley, Nicky, Ridley, Julie, Harris, Jessica, and Manthorpe, Jill (2011) 'Disclosing disability in the context of professional regulation: A qualitative UK study', *Disability and Society*, 26(1): 19–32.

Swain, John, and French, Sally (2000) 'Towards an affirmation model of disability', *Disability and Society*, 15(4): 568–582.

Turner, Cathy, and Behrndt, Synne K. (2008) *Dramaturgy and Performance*. Basingstoke: Palgrave Macmillan.

Turner, Victor (1982) *From Ritual to Theatre: the Human Seriousness of Play* (18th edn). New York: Performing Arts Journal Publications.

Watson, Aby, and Phillips, Benedict (2019) 'How to be a dyslexic artist'. [online] Available from: https://bit.ly/3aLUdcw [accessed 19 February 2021].

Whitmore, Jon (1994) *Directing Postmodern Theater: Shaping Signification in Performance*. Ann Arbor: University of Michigan Press.

5

Emergent Tensions in Diversity and Inclusion Work in Universities: Reflections on Policy and Practice

Samantha Brennan, Gwen Chapman, Belinda Leach,
and Alexandra Rodney

Introduction

Amid growing population diversity, universities face the challenge of including historically under-represented students, staff, and faculty (Kobayashi, 2009; Tienda, 2013; Karakasoglu, 2014; Henry et al, 2017). While diversity can be mandated and is a precursor for inclusion, inclusion is a normative target stemming from voluntary action and requiring complex reorganization, which presents challenges for universities (Tienda, 2013). As Winters puts it, inclusion work involves 'creating an environment that acknowledges, welcomes and accepts different approaches, styles, perspectives and experiences, so all can reach their potential and result in enhanced organizational success' (Winters, 2014, p 206). This work demands answers to pressing questions: how do universities create an inclusive environment? How do we transform our institutions?

This chapter examines a collaborative workshop designed to mobilize knowledge about 'doing diversity and inclusion' that was organized jointly by the University of Guelph, Canada, and Bremen University, Germany, two institutions with a long-standing strategic partnership. The workshop brought together 50 students, staff, administrators, and faculty to share practical actions for better serving under-represented community members. The universities share societal positioning, size, and many research interests, as well as a commitment to changing university structures to foster inclusion. Over the course of the workshop, interesting insights emerged, including differences in priorities and histories, structure, and strategy, producing an opportunity for constructive and creative thinking about how to address shared and divergent aspects of inclusion.

The presentations and conversations that filled our two days together vividly described the lived experience of doing diversity and inclusion work. The workshop was designed to include people doing the work from different perspectives, holding different positions in relation to diversity and inclusion policies and practices. Participants ranged from those who are the objects of policies to those who set policy, enact it, advocate for it, work against policy, struggle with it, and work outside it. While the workshop was intended to generate a framework for creating sustainable inclusion strategies, and to identify and develop recommendations for policies and practices, it raised substantially more questions than answers and revealed tensions that emerge when doing diversity and inclusion work on university campuses. These tensions serve as the context in which students, staff, faculty, and administrators must work to advance inclusivity agendas. To be clear, the tensions we focus on here are analytical and not interpersonal strains between participants. We do identify one moment of friction in the workshop discussed later, in the section on who is doing the work – the only overt instance we are aware of. Tensions provide a valuable focus for analysis because they are indicative of institutional forces that contribute to both enabling and impeding change. Identifying tensions confirms the limitations placed on all actors by the structures that shape individual and institutional behaviour, but tensions also have the capacity to be productive and creative. They can reveal roadblocks to change and suggest where energy toward change is best directed. Tensions then are useful for critically analysing both resistance to and movement toward change within the university context.

The chapter aims, first, to critically reflect on the knowledge and experience exchanged at the workshop by identifying and analysing the emergent tensions observed in participants' contributions. Second, we aim to provide insights into the complexity and transformative potential of post-secondary institutional processes. The chapter's major contribution is use of an analytical lens that is grounded in the day-to-day experiences of staff, students, faculty and administrators working from different positionalities in varying ways, seeking to transform governance, curricula, spaces and places. The literature on diversity and inclusion in higher education reviewed briefly in this chapter is critical of ineffective, top-down, policy initiatives. Our analytical framework pairs that critique with feminist and postcolonial frameworks that critically analyse the interplay among theory-informed policies, everyday practice and lived experience.

The promises and contradictions of diversity and inclusion work in universities

The lived experiences of historically marginalized faculty, staff, and students – including racialized and Indigenous scholars, women, the queer community, and people with disabilities – tell a story of exclusion and denial of opportunities in universities (Kobayashi, 2009; Tienda, 2013; Karakasoglu, 2014; Henry et al, 2017). Canadian and German data reveal the persistence of systemic barriers and implicit biases that lead to under-representation and precarity for equity-deserving groups (Karakasoglu, 2014; Henry et al, 2017; CAUT, 2018). Hegemonic whiteness and maleness persist in Eurocentric curricula, pedagogical approaches, hiring, promotion, tenure and research practices, and everyday interactions that render inclusivity and merit incompatible (Ahmed, 2012; Henry et al, 2017).

Spurred by an increasingly diverse student body, employment equity legislation, and empirical research detailing the experiences of community members, universities have embarked on equity, diversity, and inclusion (EDI) initiatives, bolstered by economic and social justice rationales (Shore et al, 2009; Karakasoglu, 2014, p 6) and often including the creation of policies and dedicated EDI administrative positions (Ahmed, 2012; Henry et al, 2017; Bradley et al, 2018). Yet, despite the promises of such policies, feminist and postcolonial research shows that doing diversity in universities is laden with contradictions. Policies have been critiqued for perpetually positioning under-represented groups as outsiders (Ahmed, 2012; Iverson, 2012) and for being inconsistent with the realities of daily practices of recruiting, hiring, and mentoring (Winters, 2014). EDI initiatives such as equal opportunity statements, diversity training, and hiring 'Chief Diversity Officers' have been demonstrated not to increase diversity (Dobbin and Kalev, 2011; Bradley et al, 2018). Indeed, critical analysis of university diversity policies points to white students and the universities themselves as the biggest beneficiaries of EDI initiatives, because intercultural competence is both a form of cultural capital and a status marker (Warikoo, 2016; Bradley et al, 2018).

Limited research has addressed the contradictions inherent in diversity policies through the experiences of students, staff, and faculty. Sara Ahmed (2012) analysed policies and conducted interviews with diversity officers in Australia and the United Kingdom, finding that the gap between the textual language of diversity and the lived experiences of individuals is wide. She notes that policy statements are mostly created without accompanying resources or follow-up actions, standing in for inclusion work that requires changing power relations or institutional structures and functioning as a form of performativity that actually hinders equity advancements. Shirley Ann Tate (2020, p 1154) describes the 'equality and diversity environments' of universities as 'zones of inaction forged through a proliferation of policy'.

She argues that EDI policies have displaced critical anti-racist work and have not decreased the racism, hostility, and delegitimization experienced by students of colour. Likewise, Henry et al (2017) found that outcomes for racialized and Indigenous faculty diverge from the intended goals of EDI policies. They argue that equity policies are poorly enforced in academia. Ahmed (2012) notes that when policies are toothless, people who raise discrimination issues are framed as the problem.

To consider these inherent contradictions and explore potential solutions, our approach in this chapter is grounded in the lived experiences of diversity and inclusion practices on our university campuses. Recognizing Ahmed's critique of EDI policies and Dorothy Smith's (2005) insight that texts mediate experience, we privilege instead participants' expert knowledge of their work and of policy as it is experienced daily (Smith, 1987, 2008). Through recounting experiences of their work and everyday life, the workshop provided participants with a sense of how their activities are connected with those of others while being mediated by EDI policy texts. Feminist policy analysts Allan et al (2010) and Ropers-Huilman et al (2017) suggest that powerful exclusionary discourses, and their silences, echo in organizational statements, with unanticipated consequences. These are revealed in people's accounts of their everyday work and student lives. These accounts alert us to the complex and often messy relationship between policy and practice, and to how, in an institutional context, praxis – an 'orientation to act that is grounded in deep contextualized knowledge of given circumstances' (Hardy and Melville, 2019) – can help in understanding how policies are enacted, embodied and experienced. A feminist approach to praxis insists that all actors have valuable knowledge to contribute to practice, and to understanding and changing the world (Stanley, 2013). Rather than analysing the policies themselves, this chapter then seeks to understand diversity and inclusivity praxis – the relationship between policy and the embodied work of diversity and inclusion, learning from the experiences of diverse and differently located campus community members doing the work.

The inclusivity workshop

The workshop was developed collaboratively by a Bremen–Guelph team over a span of six months. Fifty campus community members from both universities met in Guelph for two days in 2019 to share how they work to advance EDI agendas, with the goal of learning about practical actions that ensure all campus community members feel included. Through presentations and facilitated discussions, participants shared research- and experience-based knowledge. By including students, staff, faculty and administrators as co-creators of the workshop, participants explored how community members with different relationships to power can advance inclusion.

The workshop was designed around three themes identified as key sites for inclusivity work: governance, curriculum, and spaces. These themes anchored half-day sessions comprising team presentations followed by facilitated discussions designed to elicit learning from participants. The governance session addressed how inclusion relates to management and oversight of universities, including strategic planning, policy development, and institutional priorities. The curriculum session focused on how formal and informal learning objectives, programmes of study and course content are produced and experienced in the classroom, a key site of exclusion at universities. The spaces (and places) session dedicated time to exploring formal/informal, online/offline, and physical/abstract places and spaces as significant sites for making inclusion visible or invisible. A fourth and final session synthesized the knowledge presented, and identified plans for knowledge mobilization and action.

Workshop reflections

While the initial goal of the workshop was to share diversity and inclusivity practices at the two universities, participant discussions unexpectedly revolved around the tensions inherent in EDI work. To be clear, the emerging tensions were not points of conflict but instead were both creative and productive, revealing both the context for and the balancing act of doing diversity in the university environment.

Our analysis of our observations as participants, together with notes taken at each session, revealed emergent tensions in three categories: (1) who is doing the work of diversity and inclusion? (2) what kind of work needs to be done? and (3) how should that work be done to produce effective outcomes? These areas are not discrete; they necessarily bleed into each other. Together they help to reveal the complexity of university systems and some of the most powerful tensions that underlie attempts to make change.

Question 1: Who does the work?

At the workshop, productive tensions emerged around *who* is doing the work of fostering diversity and inclusivity: who should be doing the work? Who should be included? Who is ultimately responsible for the work? We could argue that this was the main tension in the room during the workshop, and the question of who was in the room shaped our reflections on the workshop outcomes.

The focus of EDI work (that is, who are we trying to include?) is shaped by historical and political national contexts. Canadian universities are steeped in a colonial past and an increasingly diverse population stemming from high immigration rates. Inclusion work is mandated for four federally defined target groups: women, Indigenous peoples, persons with disabilities, and members of 'visible minorities'. But Guelph participants also noted the university's necessary attention to fostering class diversity (for example, via first-generation university students and faculty [Jack, 2019]), along with sexual and gender diversities. German universities also grapple with a colonial past, along with an internal war history, the Holocaust, socioeconomic inequalities in the education system, and tensions around racism and immigration in Europe. Inclusion work at Bremen centres on women, sexual minorities, Muslim students, and other recent immigrants.

Historical exclusions and contemporary social movements tend to shape who is doing diversity work on Guelph and Bremen university campuses. Some of the challenges confronting those of us doing diversity work in universities concern questions about identity and representation, as people bring their own identities and intersections to the work of EDI and occupy power positions that may place them in opposition to each other. Although invitations were extended to diverse community members, it was predominantly (white) women of varying sexual orientations and queer men who accepted our invitation to participate in the workshop. Staff and faculty members were mainly from social sciences and humanities backgrounds, which we surmise to be due the focus on equity and social justice within those areas of study. While under-represented at our workshop, we did extend invitations to people doing this work in science, technology, engineering, and mathematics areas, where EDI needs may be different than those in the humanities and social sciences.

The tension concerning who is included (and who shows up), even within a group of people focused on inclusion work, emerged clearly in our workshop, and raised further questions around how people from dominant social groups can avoid either taking up too much space or not taking enough responsibility. Our workshop ended with a challenge from a Black faculty member who asked us to look around the room and see how few people of colour were involved. The (visible) identities of the participants reflected in part the tension of trying to include, yet not overload, under-represented community members. University administrators often make EDI yet another project that they expect minority scholars and staff to take on. Yet those of us who come to diversity work from positions of privilege are epistemically limited. Those of us who are white women (as many of the workshop participants were and all of the authors of this chapter are) may know our own experiences of marginalization – as women, perhaps as queer, and/or living with a disability – but we have not experienced what it is like to be on our campuses as people of colour. There may be major limitations to our knowledge or lived experience. Self-interest and privilege may work to block our understanding of access and justice in academic contexts. And yet, our positions of relative privilege also give us access to power where we can implement policies, programmes, and practices that those who have not (yet) had access to those positions cannot. How do we do the work without taking over?

One of the student presenters from Bremen used a mantra deriving from the German discourse on the inclusion of (dis)abled persons – 'nothing about us without us' – to highlight the importance of working with, rather than for, under-represented groups. Participants spent time discussing what it means to be an ally, and there was agreement that allies are valuable in activism by standing with members of under-represented groups. But these discussions frequently moved on to consider how to turn allies into *accomplices* who work to dismantle the existing structures of oppression, revealing connections to a second group of tensions that emerged in the workshop, around what kinds of work need to be done to create an inclusive university.

Question 2: What work needs to be done?

Workshop discussions revealed tensions around what kinds of actions we are taking, what issues have been in focus, what the emergent priorities are, and what kinds of change we are making when it comes to inclusion work. As discussed earlier, key priorities understandably differed, given the distinct national locations of the two university communities.

One aspect of the tension around what we are doing is the question of whether our actions are compelled or voluntary. Universities face increasing pressures from governments and research-granting agencies to include attention to EDI in hiring and funding decisions. University governance requires compliance with regulations or mandates that often involve time-consuming reporting activities. To be eligible for scarce federally funded research positions in Canada, universities must be accountable concerning equity targets. But regulatory reporting processes like these focus on diversity rather than inclusion. They ensure that under-represented groups are on campus, but do not address whether those people feel a sense of belonging once they arrive. As a result, many universities participate in voluntary programmes designed to broaden their progress towards EDI goals. Bremen has participated in the triannual Stifterverband's Diversity Audit in Germany since 2012, while Guelph has access to the Canadian government's Dimensions programme. Participation in such evaluative processes, compelled or otherwise, may leave little time for more innovative and action-oriented approaches to inclusion and ultimately may serve to create more texts (policies) that are sites of inaction and do little to change outcomes for under-represented people (Tate, 2020).

A second aspect of this tension is the question of whether universities are making changes that are systemic and structural, or merely symbolic. Some attempted changes are designed to raise awareness and institutionalize the celebration of difference. Bremen participants identified cultural dance showcases and hosting a campus *iftar* (breaking of the fast) during Ramadan. Such events are intended to raise visibility and encourage community members from under-represented groups to bring their whole selves to campus, encouraging demystification of cultural practices, rather than stereotyping and essentializing. However, such events can also be critiqued for highlighting diversity as exoticization and spectacle, and for being superficial or tokenistic. Bremen participants told us that migrants to Germany are perpetually positioned as 'others' and face severe challenges in society and in the university environment to be considered 'real' Germans. Watching a bhangra dance does not make structural inequality magically disappear for South Asian students. This is not to say that celebratory activities have no value to community members as empowering or consciousness raising, but workshop participants were concerned that inclusivity work also requires embedded changes to university systems and structures, reflecting their awareness of contradictions inherent in diversity policies. Cultural showcase events are also structured by dominant ideas that tacitly oppose European versus 'international' students and ways of knowing. A Guelph professor who identifies as Indigenous distinguished between *Indigenous inclusion* and the *Indigenization* of university spaces, where Indigenous ways of knowing, being, and doing are integrated into the university structure.

The kinds of campaigns that are constructed also reveal tensions around what we are doing to encourage inclusivity. Gender-equity work comes with decades of research, practices, and regulations that provide universities with guidance for action, while others, such as how to support Islamic students, may be newer. Bremen's diversity policy, including its commitment to refugee students, was described by a Bremen administrator as a 'litmus test' for the institution's willingness to transform. The tension between comprehensive or more specific diversity work was visible in Bremen and Guelph's different foci, with Guelph leaning towards ongoing, all-encompassing efforts to include many different groups of historically under-represented people. Examples included working with the Indigenous Task Force to create a 'grandmother's house' to foster connections between Indigenous students and the land, adding gender-inclusive washrooms, and creating a permanent room for the Guelph Black Students' Association. In contrast, Bremen has focused on high-profile campaigns that take turns highlighting specific groups, intended to educate the community and foster 'diversity mainstreaming'. An example is the 'GoDiverse!' programme, which used e-mail campaigns and workshops to encourage recruiting diverse staff members. Another 'Queering University' themed project, designed to create LGBTQ (lesbian, gay, bisexual, trans and queer) visibility on campus, included art installations, a lecture series and workshops for positive-space champions. Ultimately, the kinds of diversity work that universities choose to focus on may reinforce implicit assumptions around who is an insider or outsider on campus, who is already included versus who is presumed to be the 'other' (Ahmed, 2012), failing to measure outcomes for under-represented communities (Tate, 2020).

Question 3: How do we do the work?

In examining what our workshop revealed about *how* diversity and inclusion work is carried out in our institutions, two main tensions emerged: the top-down versus grassroots nature of the work, and the incremental versus revolutionary nature of the changes that occur or are desired.

Workshop presentations and discussions showed clearly that diversity and inclusion work is accomplished through both top-down and grassroots initiatives, and the interplay between them. As mentioned, administrators from both Guelph and Bremen described governance initiatives that are themselves embedded in broader mandates established and monitored by federal and regional governments, which are sometimes linked to funding commitments. Bremen University, for example, must follow German anti-discrimination laws and hosts the municipal office for anti-discrimination. Internally, both institutions approved new inclusion strategy documents in 2017 – the 'Fostering a Culture of Inclusion' framework at the University of Guelph (Ngobia, 2017) and 'Promoting and Shaping Diversity as Opportunity' at Bremen University (Universitat Bremen, 2017) – which set out institutional values, mandates, and structures to foster inclusion. Workshop participants noted the significance of clear, consistent, and vocal support for inclusion work from upper administration, and the effectiveness of top-down initiatives that are followed through with specific actions and resources. This might involve incorporating diversity work in employees' performance objectives and holding them accountable for outcomes. In this way diversity work is put into practice rather than being textually symbolic.

Diversity work on campuses also includes more grassroots, bottom-up movements. A student from Bremen shared an example of her involvement with a Muslim student club working with other faith-based clubs to establish a 'room of silence', available for prayer, worship, and individual retreat. Structuring spaces like this on campus makes the work of diversity visible and has material outcomes for campus community members. Faculty members from both universities talked about their own and colleagues' work to change their teaching practices to be more inclusive, such as using universal design to accommodate students with different learning needs, or incorporating different ways of knowing into their curriculum. In contrast to the planned, strategic inclusion work of institutional leadership for long-term goals, participants noted that these smaller-scale actions may feel insignificant or isolating for the people involved.

A second aspect of the tension around *how* diversity work is done reflects the speed and breadth at which progress is made. Workshop participants expressed the need for revolutionary, broad-scale structural and cultural change in addition to more incremental, step-by-step, and seemingly isolated changes that seem to be the norm. We explored this tension through integrative discussion questions in the final session of the workshop. For one discussion activity we asked: 'How do we facilitate the revolutionary, transformational, structural changes that are needed for our institutions to be leaders in diversity and inclusion?' One participant noted that we need to seek change that is ecological, not additive, drawing on Neil Postman's (1998, p 4) suggestion that a technological innovation 'does not add something; it changes everything'. Others suggested that the post-revolution university would be a place 'where everyone learns from each other', with intentional and focused co-learning across difference, and with a flatter, more nimble organizational structure. It was harder for participants to identify specific actions needed to accomplish the desired ecological change, but top-down initiatives were described as catalysts for productive, resistance-oriented actions. One participant noted that it is important to consider potential 'victims' of the revolution and to see their concerns as genuine. Who feels threatened? How can we work with them to gently move them towards being allies and accomplices in the transformation?

Participants also engaged in discussion about how to counter the seemingly glacial pace of change in universities despite the immediate needs of under-represented groups, responding to the question: 'What are the short-term or immediate actions we as individuals can take now?' Interestingly, there were many similarities between the responses to this question and to the question about facilitating revolutionary change. Suggestions included: facilitating intergenerational knowledge sharing, using a non-hierarchical approach, looking for allies and accomplices, working to create a culture of teaching and learning among peers, and being willing to take risks and being prepared to fail. Just as the tension between top-down and grassroots approaches indicates that both are required in diversity and inclusion work, both revolutionary and stepwise approaches are required for transformational change within universities. It was also noted that desired changes do not happen in isolation but, rather, within complex, messy systems, and will include resistance. Prospective students, parents, employers, as well as government stakeholders have expectations of what universities are and should be, some of which may be resistant to the kinds of transformational changes some workshop participants desired.

Conclusions

Members of university communities are working within all of the earlier tensions, seeking to create inclusive institutions. Through the workshop we were able to observe and then analyse inclusion practitioners grappling with policy, with 'usual' practices, with opportunity, and with their own experiences, demonstrating the value of a feminist praxis approach that can incorporate all of these. Focusing on the emergent tensions around what needs to be done, by whom, and how allows us to understand better the complexity of the policies, processes, structures, and practices that both facilitate and impede change. These three tensions are present in governance structures, in diversity spaces, and in graduate and undergraduate curricula across disciplines. Moreover, our bi-national workshop allowed participants to question and problematize practices and assumptions that they would have otherwise taken for granted within their own national context. The framing themes helped to give the workshop structure, in a context of diverse identities and priorities.

Our focus on *what* kind of work is being done echoes previous research revealing that (1) certain groups are perpetually positioned as outsiders and (2) diversity work is often a site of inaction, with policies standing in for real inclusion work (Ahmed, 2012; Tate, 2020). Yet we also heard examples illustrating that significant resources may be directed to inclusion work, including physical changes to campus. A major contribution of this chapter is the focus on *who* is doing the work and *how* it happens, both of which are not addressed in the existing literature. We learned of work happening in different spaces on campus and by people in different positions and with lived experience of marginalization, people of colour and allies. We also heard that the work is often prompted by grassroots initiatives rather than institutional policies. Our analysis points to a broader conception of diversity work to include informal kinds of organizing on campus, undertaken by a variety of actors.

While the literature subjects top-down diversity initiatives to critique, closer examination suggests that success also requires grassroots initiatives to achieve the kind of broad-scale institutional culture change that is being called for. It seems crucial for sustainability of these initiatives that university leadership and grassroots actors are in continuous exchange. Institutional frameworks and strategies are pointless if individuals do not do the work to bring them to fruition. But individuals and grassroots groups may not be successful without the support of administration. The Bremen 'room of silence', for example, could not have been established without the university administration providing student access to the space. At Guelph, the work of making curricula more inclusive is accomplished through interactions among administration, staff, and course instructors. Administrative processes also provide the policy context and staff resources to guide instructors in accommodating students with disabilities. Teaching support staff provide professional development to faculty in inclusive pedagogies and curriculum development. Faculty uptake of these opportunities and advocacy for additional support can catalyse further policy development and availability of staff and other resources.

Through the process of hosting the Inclusivity Workshop, we learned that the research literature contains little in the way of concrete solutions for how to create an inclusive university and that 'best practices' are ever evolving and constituted differently across space and time. Through the emergent tensions we learned that solutions and strategies are likely to need top-down *and* grassroots initiatives, incremental *and* revolutionary change, symbolic celebrations of difference *and* deep systemic alterations to our structures. And we learned that people can come together collectively to make those changes, but allies need to ensure that the voices of under-represented groups are strong and heeded. Workshop participants were keen to identify and take with them suggestions for moving forward in their day-to-day work lives and in broader campus discussions, and they pointed to the following practices as especially helpful and potentially productive:

- Inclusion cannot be the responsibility of one office. This work needs to be included in operations at all levels and in all units of the university.
- Privileged actors in the university community can draw on their privilege and decision-making power to work as accomplices in transformative change.
- Diversity and inclusion work needs to be diverse and inclusive, ensuring space for active involvement and leadership from those who are seeking to be fully included in our institutions.
- There are many possibilities for opening up space for this work and making connections across hierarchies and siloed departments and divisions.
- There is no magic solution that will make the campus inclusive, but creating an inviting context for the work of inclusion is a start.
- We should acknowledge our accomplishments, and the significant work that remains.

Diversity and inclusion work is transformation work. Achieving institutional transformation is not merely a matter of inviting others in and expecting the new arrivals to assimilate to existing institutional norms. Rather, true inclusion means being open to change and open to transformation.

References

Ahmed, Sara (2012) *On Being Included: Racism and Diversity in Institutional Life*. Durham: Duke University Press.

Allan, Elizabeth J., Iverson, Susan, and Ropers-Huilman, Rebecca (eds) (2010) *Reconstructing Policy Analysis in Higher Education*. New York: Routledge.

Bradley, Steven W., Garven, James R., Law, Wilson W., and West, James E. (2018) 'The impact of chief diversity officers on diverse faculty hiring', The National Bureau of Economic Research. Working Paper no. 24969. [online] Available from: https://bit.ly/3e85Hbm [accessed 15 April 2021].

CAUT (Canadian Association of University Teachers) (2018) 'Underrepresented and underpaid: diversity and Equity amongst Canada's postsecondary education teachers'. April. [online] Available from: https://bit.ly/3uOzhco [accessed 15 April 2021].

Dobbin, Frank, Kim, Soohan, and Kalev, Alexandra (2011) 'You can't always get what you need', American Sociological Review, 76 (3): 386–411.

Hardy, Ian and Melville, Wayne (2019) 'Policy as praxis: Senior educators' enactment of assessment policy reform', Power and Education, 11(1): 69–84.

Henry, Frances, Enakshi, Dua, James, Carl E., Kobayashi, Audrey, Li, Peter, Ramos Howard, and Smith, Melinda S. (2017) The Equity Myth: Racialization and Indigeneity at Canadian Universities. Vancouver: University of British Columbia Press.

Iverson, Susan V. (2012) 'Constructing outsiders: The discursive framing of access in university diversity policies', The Review of Higher Education, 35(2): 149–177.

Jack, Anthony Abraham (2019) The Privileged Poor: How Elite Colleges Are Failing Disadvantaged Students. Cambridge: Harvard University Press.

Karakasoglu, Yasmin (2014) 'Interculturality and diversity management at universities: Theoretical claims and practical challenges', Humboldt Ferngespräche Discussion Paper Series 3 (August): 1–25.

Kobayashi, Audrey (2009) 'Now you see them, how you see them: Women of colour in Canadian academia', in Frances Henry and Carol Tator (eds) Racism in the Canadian University: Demanding Social Justice, Inclusion, and Equity. Toronto: University of Toronto Press, pp 60–75.

Ngobia, Jane (2017) 'Fostering a culture of inclusion at the University of Guelph: An institutional imperative'. University of Guelph. [online] Available from: https://bit.ly/3e869GA [accessed 15 April 2021].

Postman, Neil (1998) 'Five things we need to know about technological change', Talk delivered in Denver, Colorado, 28 March. [online] Available from: https://bit.ly/3awOzev [accessed 15 April 2021].

Ropers-Huilman, Rebecca, Reinert, Leah, and Diamond, Kate (2017) 'Gender equity in Austrian university contexts: Constructions of power, knowledge and response-ability in the process of change', in Pamela L. Eddy, Kelly Ward, and Khwaja Tehmina (eds) Critical Approaches to Women and Gender in Higher Education. New York: Palgrave Macmillan, pp 191–214.

Shore, Lynn, Chung-Herrera, Beth, Dean, Michelle, Holcombe-Ehrhart, Karen, Jung, Don, Randel, Amy, and Singh, Gangaram (2009) 'Diversity in organizations: Where are we now and where are we going', Human Resource Management Review, 19: 117–133.

Smith, Dorothy (1987) *The Everyday World as Problematic: A Feminist Sociology.* Toronto: University of Toronto Press.

Smith, Dorothy (2005) *Institutional Ethnography: A Sociology for People.* Walnut Creek: AltaMira Press.

Smith, Dorothy (2008) 'From the 14th floor to the sidewalk: Writing sociology at ground level', *Sociological Inquiry*, 78: 417–422.

Stanley, Liz (2013) *Feminist Praxis: Research Theory and Epistemology in Feminist Sociology.* Abingdon: Routledge.

Tate, Shirley Ann (2020) 'The student of color attainment gap in higher education and the institutional culture of equality, diversity and inclusion', in Rosemary Papa (ed) *Handbook on Promoting Social Justice in Education.* New York: Springer, pp 1153–1171.

Tienda, Marta (2013) 'Diversity inclusion: promoting integration in higher education', *Educational Researcher*, 42(9): 467–475.

Universitat Bremen (2017) 'Promoting and shaping diversity as an opportunity'. [online] Available from: https://bit.ly/3gfSgc6 [accessed 15 April 2021].

Warikoo, Natasha (2016) *The Diversity Bargain and other Dilemmas on Race, Admissions and Meritocracy at Elite Universities.* Chicago: University of Chicago Press.

Winters, Mary-Frances (2014) 'From diversity to inclusion: An inclusion equation', in Bernardo M. Ferdman, and Barbara R. Deane (eds) *Diversity at Work: The Practice of Inclusion.* San Francisco: Jossey-Bass, pp 205–228.

PART II

Diversifying Curricula

6

How 'Diverse' is Your Reading List? Tools, Tips, and Challenges

Karen Schucan Bird

Introduction: The shifting context for curriculum reform in the United Kingdom

Around the world, there is a strong and growing imperative to develop inclusive and diverse reading lists in higher education. Such reform of syllabi constitutes a small but important step in the process of transforming university curricula. In the United Kingdom (UK), the content of curricula in higher education has long been a site for contestation (for example, Peters, 2018; Andrews, 2019), with the 2019–21 Black Lives Matters (BLM) campaigns underscoring the importance of reforming curricula as part of efforts to address racial inequalities and decolonise the university (Bhambra et al, 2018; Doku, 2020). In historical perspective, calls for reform have been anchored in a range of narratives. In the decade since 2010, developing global curricula was part of the 'internationalisation' of UK universities who sought to adopt an increasingly global outlook and develop syllabi fitting for the growing international student cohort (Luxon and Peelo, 2009; May and Spalding, 2014). Simultaneously, the growth of the widening participation agenda, with a focus on equal opportunities for UK-domiciled students, highlighted the need for curricula to foster success for all students, irrelevant of background (Bowl, 2018). In more recent years, the drive towards 'equality' has gradually been replaced with an agenda based on 'diversity', and then 'inclusion,' and so mirroring the discursive shifts observed in other organisations (Oswick and Noon, 2014; Bowl, 2018; Brewis, 2019). While the drivers for curriculum reform have shifted, institutional responses of UK universities have long been subject to critique for inserting perspectives into syllabi without challenging mainstream content or practices (Robson, 2015; Clifford and Montgomery, 2017), recognising historical inequalities (Ahmed, 2007), or questioning the neoliberal frameworks within which such strategies sit (Gyamera and Burke, 2018). It is only more recently that the agenda for curriculum change has been shaped in line with a 'transformational' approach that challenges 'traditional views and assumptions; encourages new ways of thinking; and reconceptualises the field in light of new knowledge, scholarship and ways of knowing' (Kitano, 1997, p 23). Current calls for decolonisation often fit within this framing by highlighting that curricula are deeply implicated in the processes of producing/reproducing inequalities, while holding the potential for transforming higher education and delivering societal change more widely (Heleta, 2016; Le Grange, 2016; Luckett and Shay, 2017; Andrews, 2019).

The interrogation of reading lists, as an initial step towards curriculum transformation, has attracted growing attention from UK university students, staff, and institutions. Student-led movements have questioned the dominance of Eurocentric and male authors on university reading lists and called for an overhaul of their syllabi (for example, #WhyIsMyCurriculumWhite, Alternative Reading List Project, #decolonisemycurriculum). Academic staff have begun to empirically analyse the composition of reading lists, with a focus on the authorship of recommended readings (for example, Colgan, 2017; Phull et al, 2019), and institutional toolkits are emerging to encourage individual staff to do just that (Ward and Gale, 2016; Decolonising SOAS Working Group, 2018; UCL, 2018; UUK and NUS, 2019a). This chapter considers four toolkits, together with lessons from a social science case study (reported in Schucan Bird and Pitman, 2020), to identify practical recommendations for students and staff who are interested in reviewing their own syllabi, with a particular emphasis on authorship.

A social science case study and four toolkits

This chapter draws lessons from a case study that examined the gender, ethnicity, and geographical location of all authors included on a reading list for a post-graduate module on social science research methods. The project was undertaken at a research-intensive university in the UK, with the work constituting part of, and funded by, the local 'Liberating the Curriculum' initiative (a working group that aims to advance inclusivity in higher education curricula). The team consisted of one British female academic of European descent and one international male post-graduate student of Middle Eastern descent. This staff–student partnership collected and analysed data about the gender, ethnicity, and geographical affiliation of all authors included on the specified reading list. The project found an equal proportion of female and male authors were included on the reading list, with the majority categorised as non-BME (Black or Minority Ethnic) and affiliated to universities in Europe, North America, or Australasia. The process undertaken by the team to identify and categorise the demographic characteristics of the authors constitutes the basis of the recommendations set out in this chapter. To complement these and explore institutional approaches towards inclusive curriculum reform, four toolkits will also be considered. These toolkits aim to promote curricula that are inclusive (UCL, 2018) or decolonised (Decolonising SOAS Working Group, 2018), target particular inequalities such as the BME attainment gap (UUK and NUS, 2019a), or advance the issues of particular groups in higher education, that is, LGBTQ (lesvian, gay, bisexual, trans and queer) (Ward and Gale, 2016).

Ten tips for reviewing the authors on reading lists

1. Use theoretical tools

Reviewing the authors listed on syllabi is becoming an increasingly popular method for exploring bias and exclusion, principally in terms of gender and ethnicity, in teaching materials (for example, Phull et al, 2019; UUK and NUS, 2019b). However, such analysis is meaningful only when a theoretical framework is used to guide the project and interpret the findings. A reading list dominated by male authors, for example, is not inherently problematic but requires theory to diagnose and justify the critique. There are a variety of theoretical frameworks within which to situate an analysis of curricula vis-à-vis reading lists, that recognise the dominance of Eurocentric and masculinist knowledge structures (for example, Tickner, 2013; de Sousa Santos, 2018). Such assumptions form the basis of some toolkits (that is, Decolonising SOAS Working Group, 2018), but not all.

The case study invoked the concept of *representation* (Pitkin, 1972) to recognise and analyse the reading list as a representative device. This theoretical framework guided the research practice: deciding which author characteristics were most salient, the nature of the analysis, and the types of inferences that could be drawn. Understanding the reading list as a representative tool allowed the team to draw meaningful, theoretically robust conclusions about how far the syllabi represented the student or scholarly body in terms of gender, ethnicity, and geographical affiliation. The concept of representation provided an underpinning theoretical rationale for problematising the dominance of particular authors, for example, non-BME authors from the global North, when the student and staff community is changing and becoming increasingly diverse.

2. Engage students

Staff–student collaborations arguably chime with an agenda for genuinely inclusive or transformative curricula (Mercer-Mapstone and Bovill, 2019; Wijaya Mulya, 2019). Yet, there is a dearth of institutional schemes that utilise student–staff collaboration for curriculum reform (Mercer-Mapstone and Bovill, 2019), and the engagement of students in the *process* of interrogating curricula/reading lists is typically either absent from toolkits (UCL, 2018) or framed in relatively vague terms: 'Talk to students about what kinds of content they would like to see addressed' (Decolonising SOAS Working Group, 2018, p 10). The case study was undertaken collaboratively by a staff–student team, drawing on the student's expertise as both a representative of the wider student cohort (having attended the module and utilised the reading list under scrutiny) and a co-researcher. Collaboration was invaluable, enabling student views to shape the research, draw meaningful inferences from the findings, and engage with wider issues about curriculum design (Bovill et al, 2011). As there is limited understanding of student views of, or reactions to, diversity in curricula (Wolff, 2016), any attempt to examine a reading list should necessarily engage with local, discipline-specific student cohorts. In doing so, student opportunities for engagement should be meaningful and appropriately rewarded as part of a truly inclusive approach (Mercer-Mapstone and Bovill, 2019; Cook-Sather, 2020). The team learned that funding for student (and staff) time can facilitate this process in the short term. As students move through or out of the university, however, it is more difficult to facilitate engagement in the longer term.

3. Engage staff

While staff are contributing to numerous initiatives pertaining to diversity in reading lists (UUK and NUS, 2019b), there is also a history of resistance to such agendas within academia (Last, 2019; D. Stokes, 2019). Many institutional toolkits recognise that 'discussion is key to change' (UUK; and NUS, 2019b, p 9), and so engaging staff, generating awareness, and facilitating conversations is integral to the work of inclusion (Ward and Gale, 2016; Decolonising SOAS Working Group, 2018; UUK and NUS, 2019b). The case study did seek to engage staff in the project, but only at the end of the project via a presentation of the findings. Both members of the team were pleasantly surprised by the level of staff interest in the project, but also recognised that conversations about diversity in the curriculum can create discomfort and/or resistance. On reflection, the team decided that early and regular engagement with staff would have been preferable to encourage longer-term discussions and promote wider change across the department. Such engagement would allow colleagues, as recognised by a toolkit, 'to engage with these issues proactively, to share their experiences and ideas, to challenge, debate and revise the ideas and to identify where their own teaching can be transformed' (Decolonising SOAS Working Group, 2018, p 21).

4. Be reflexive

Reflexivity has played a central role in debates about curriculum reform. Engaging with issues of diversity means that individuals become 'embroiled in an embodied struggle' occupying raced and gendered spaces (Azumah Dennis, 2018, p 193). In practice, this means acknowledging and exploring the interaction between individual social locations and the wider structures that are subject to critique (hooks, 1994; Luckett and Shay, 2017; Azumah Dennis, 2018; Last, 2019). The team endeavoured to actively reflect on the racialized, gendered, and ranked position of both staff and student. The team acknowledged that the positionality of each member influenced their research priorities, methodological approach, and interpretations of the findings. For example, the staff collaborator held a particular interest in gender and knowledge production that shaped the project and its methods. Having experienced post-graduate study in the UK as international student, the student member approached the study and interpreted the findings through a lens of student belonging. Toolkits and guidance for staff, however, rarely encourage such reflexivity. The focus remains solely on the way in which the teaching content relates to a particular 'orientation to the world' (Decolonising SOAS Working Group, 2018).

5. Seek resources

Published examples of reading list initiatives, while mainly small scale, suggest that projects are time and resource intensive (UUK and NUS, 2019b; Schucan Bird and Pitman, 2020). In the case study, the team took between 10 and 15 minutes to review each author on the reading list (n=144), which amounted to four days just for the data-collection stage. Funding for the project included student time but did not extend to staff involvement or longer-term activities, for example, dissemination. Therefore, the staff member undertook the project in her own time in order to be an active partner and facilitate meaningful staff–student collaboration. While some toolkits acknowledge the 'time intensive' nature of curriculum reform and the need for dedicated resources (Decolonising SOAS Working Group, 2018, p 21), others frame the activities as teaching practices that could be integrated into the existing academic cycle (UCL, 2018). 'Formally integrated and properly resourced opportunities' are needed within our institutions and across the sector (UUK and NUS, 2019b, p 8) in order to recognise the time and intellectual investment required for curriculum reform and inclusive approaches.

6. Determine which author characteristics are salient

Existing reviews of reading lists, including the featured case study, have tended to focus on the gender, geographical location, and ethnicity of authors (for example, in political science Colgan, 2017; Mngomezulu and Hadebe, 2018; Phull et al, 2019). While existing reviews of reading lists present a useful starting point, there remain a range of other categories that could (and should?) be interrogated. The Equality Act 2010 in England and Wales identifies nine characteristics that warrant protection from discrimination and harassment in higher education (age, disability, gender reassignment, pregnancy and maternity, race, religion or belief, sex, sexual orientation, marriage or civil partnership). Should an assessment of reading lists consider all nine characteristics? A growing body of literature contends that it should: critical disability studies (Goodley, 2013) and queer theorists (Smith and Lee, 2015), for example, argue that disability and sexuality should be considered. Further, there could also be additional characteristics beyond the Equality Act, such as social class, which warrant exploration. Deciding on which vectors of difference to interrogate is difficult, and there is a lack of advice on such matters. Toolkits and guidance tend to be broad, prompting teaching staff to consider the 'demographic profile of authors on the syllabus/programme' (Decolonising SOAS Working Group, 2018, p 9) without stipulating which demographic features to consider (or how). The case study decided to focus on the gender, geographical location, and ethnicity of authors in line with the interests of the team, the theoretical framework, and the wider debates that were occurring at the time (such as #WhyIsMyCurriculumWhite and #decolonisemycurriculum). Pragmatism also played a role, as it appeared, on first glance, that it would be relatively straightforward to collect and analyse data on these characteristics.

7. Collect and manage data

The process of reviewing a reading list requires an explicit and systematic approach to collecting and managing data about each author and/or publication. A simple spreadsheet that contains all references, including authors, is recommended. The reading list used for the case study was relatively short, with 57 publications and 144 different authors, but still required an orderly approach to data management. Each publication was listed, together with the author(s) and associated information. The spreadsheet became long and somewhat unwieldly, but the team also became familiar with the individual publications and each author as the data collection progressed.

Following the creation of a spreadsheet, it is then necessary to decide on the most appropriate system for identifying and classifying the data about each author. What information or sources should be used to provide data on, for example, the sex/gender of the author? How should sex/gender of the author be categorised? Such questions are not straightforward and need careful consideration. The team engaged in a series of discussions to arrive at the methods outlined later. Unfortunately, toolkits for developing diverse/inclusive/decolonised curricula do not tend to offer fine-grained methodological detail or guidance on these issues.

The case study examined the gender, ethnicity, and geographical location of each author, manually collecting data from a range of sources to do so. There are also a range of studies that have employed machine-learning techniques to classify individuals' ethnicity or gender by their names (West et al, 2013; Freeman and Huang, 2015; AlShebli et al, 2018). While this approach can analyse vast amounts of data with potentially high levels of accuracy (AlShebli et al, 2018), such approaches are also seen to disguise and normalise racial inequity (Gillborn et al, 2018). The manual collection of data was adopted, with data sources primarily including the publication itself together with institutional websites or online professional platforms (such as ResearchGate or LinkedIn). Other sources, such as personal sites or social media entries, were occasionally chanced upon, but the team considered these to be less ethical sources of data.

The identification and classification of data on the author's geographical location was most straightforward and was based on the author's university affiliation, determined by the contact details stipulated on the publication. The team found that identifying an author's gender and ethnicity, however, was more challenging in both conceptual and pragmatic terms.

The case study categorised the gender sex of each author as 'female'/ 'male'/'unclear'. While such binary categories are increasingly recognised as inadequate for capturing diverse gender and sexual identities (Hines, 2006; Ward and Gale, 2016), the team was influenced by the methods used by previous studies (Schucan Bird, 2011; Eigenberg and Whalley, 2015) and driven by pragmatism. This approach meant that it was possible to deduce and categorise the sex/gender of the author via first name and pronouns.

The team was faced with similar challenges in codifying the ethnicity of authors. While existing studies of academic authorship have tended to use ethnic groupings (Freeman and Huang, 2015; AlShebli et al, 2018), there is no consensus on the most appropriate terms to use for the scientific study of ethnicity and race (Bhopal, 2004). Overarching categories such as 'Black or Minority Ethnic' or 'White' are somewhat 'blunt' instruments that are unable to take into consideration the nuances and locally defined populations (Bhopal, 2004; Song, 2018). Further, there is virulent debate about whether a terminology of 'race' should also be used to meaningfully measure difference (Roth, 2016; Song, 2018). Following complex debate, the team decided to utilise categories that had been defined by an independent and well-respected body in the UK, the Institute of Race Relations. This body refers to 'BME' as the 'terminology normally used in the UK to describe people of non-white descent'. Decisions about authors' ethnicity were based on photographs and surnames. While extrapolating demographics from photographs is relatively unproblematised in other studies (for example, Eigenberg and Whalley, 2015), this approach meant that the findings were mainly based on assumptions and demographic proxies, with limited possibilities for ensuring accuracy (Sloan, 2017; Mügge et al, 2018). In hindsight, the team decided that a more robust and ethical approach to data collection would involve contact with the individual themselves (Sloan, 2017) or with wider scholars in the same field (Dickersin et al, 1998) to verify the data/classification associated with each author. Indeed, the team began to feel uncomfortable when making assumptions and applying rigid, broad categories to individual authors without their knowledge. Further, this process seemed to take place in opposition to current scholarly thought that recognises that categories of ethnicity and gender are imprecise and fluid (Bhopal, 2004; Roth, 2016).

8. Analyse data

On completion of the data collection, the team had a large spreadsheet listing all of the publications and authors on the reading list together with the coding for their gender, ethnicity, and geographical location. Initially, descriptive statistics were calculated to encompass the total numbers of authors for each category. The analysis was then be guided by the theoretical framework. In the case study, the gender, ethnicity, and geographical location of the authors were compared to the same characteristics of the wider scholarly community in the field and/or the local student populations. This intended to consider whether the reading list was an accurate representation of student or staff bodies. While potentially useful, this analysis was hindered by a lack of data about student or staff demographics at location, national, or international levels. The team also endeavoured to analyse intersectionality and authorship, but with small numbers of authors for each category (for example, female, BME authors) it was difficult to draw meaningful inferences.

In analysing the data, the team also recognised that authorship patterns and expectations vary across disciplines. Single authorship is most prominent in some academic fields, such as the humanities, whereas multiple authorship is typical of others, such as medical and natural sciences (Helgesson and Eriksson, 2019). To recognise the greater importance attributed to single or first authors in the social sciences, the team undertook sub-analysis of single-authored papers (n=10) and publications with co-authoring teams (=47). This allowed the analysis to explore whether particular groups were equally present in the most prestigious roles (first or sole authors) − for example, female authors and their male colleagues.

9. Consider ethical issues

A number of ethical and data protection issues were raised in the process of reviewing the authorship of a reading list. As mentioned earlier, the team felt uncomfortable collecting data and making judgements about individuals without their knowledge or consent. The case study did not seek informed consent from the authors on the reading list but endeavoured to use publicly available information. The team assumed that data derived from documents, text, or observations taking place in public online space may not require consent (Hudson and Bruckman, 2004; Wilkinson and Thelwall, 2011). Collecting data on an author's geographical affiliation was seen to be relatively straightforward, in ethical terms, as this information was intentionally public (Willis, 2019). Collecting data about an author's gender and ethnicity, however, generated concerns about informed consent, as such data/categorisation is not explicitly presented as public information. On the whole, toolkits and guidance for staff do not consider the potential ethical concerns of curriculum reviews. There was one exception (Ward and Gale, 2016) that briefly considered the ethical implications associated with applying identities/categories to populations who do not self-identify with that category. Greater discussion is required to develop an ethical approach that thinks through these complex issues.

The case study also highlights ethical concerns around anonymity. The centrality of personal demographics and author identities in the project makes the issue of anonymity particularly complex. As Wilkinson and Thelwall (2011) suggest, revealing the identity of an individual may simply involve the transference of identity from one public space (online) to another (academic presentation or publication). Yet, referring to named individuals when drawing inferences about diversity and exclusion may be problematic and seen to vilify particular scholars. Careful and ethical approaches are paramount.

10. Get started ...

Reviewing the authors on reading lists is fraught with conceptual and methodological difficulties and, so, understandably, teaching staff may shy away from such practices for fear of failure or criticism (Last, 2019). Yet, critical reflection on reading lists also offers scope for curriculum innovation and the potential for wider educational change (hooks, 1994; Luckett and Shay, 2017). Recognising that syllabi are personal, partial, and fluid teaching tools may be a useful starting point. Reading lists allow teaching staff to 'imprint and construct their values and identity and beliefs into a given programme' (P. Stokes and Martin, 2008, p 121). They are inherently partial, representing 'an official selection that structures knowledge in ways that privilege a particular construction of knowledge and the history of knowledge' (Peters, 2018, p 267). Teaching staff and students can critically engage with their own reading lists to reflect on how these represent the field and associated scholars.

References

Ahmed, Sara (2007) 'The language of diversity', *Ethnic and Racial Studies*, 30(2): 235–256.

AlShebli, Bedoor K., Rahwan, Talal, and Woon, Wei Lee (2018) 'The preeminence of ethnic diversity in scientific collaboration', *Nature Communications*, 9(1): 5163.

Andrews, Kehinde (2019) 'Blackness, empire and migration: How Black studies transforms the curriculum', *Area*, 52(4): 701–707.

Azumah Dennis, C. (2018) 'Decolonising education: A pedagogic intervention', in Gurminder K. Bhambra, Dalia Gebrial, and Kerem Nişancıoğlu (eds) *Decolonising the University*. London: Pluto Press.

Bhambra, Gurminder K., Gebrial, Dalia, and Nişancıoğlu, Kerem (2018) 'Introduction: Decolonising the university?', in Gurminder K. Bhambra, Dalia Gebrial, and Kerem Nişancıoğlu (eds) *Decolonising the University*. London: Pluto Press, pp 1–15.

Bhopal, Raj (2004) 'Glossary of terms relating to ethnicity and race: For reflection and debate', *Journal of Epidemiology and Community Health*, 58(6): 441–445.

Bovill, Catherine, Cook-Sather, Alison, and Felten, Peter (2011) 'Students as co-creators of teaching approaches, course design, and curricula: Implications for academic developers', *International Journal for Academic Development*, 16(2): 133–145.

Bowl, Marion (2018) 'Differentiation, distinction, and equality – or diversity? The language of the marketised university: an England, New Zealand comparison', *Studies in Higher Education*, 43(4): 671–688.

Brewis, Deborah N. (2019) 'Duality and fallibility in practices of the self: The "inclusive subject" in diversity training', *Organization Studies*, 40(1): 93–114.

Clifford, Valerie, and Montgomery, Catherine (2017) 'Designing an internationationalised curriculum for higher education: Embracing the local and the global citizen', *Higher Education Research and Development*, 36(6): 1138–1151.

Colgan, Jeff (2017) 'Gender bias in international relations graduate education? New evidence from syllabi', *PS: Political Science and Politics*, 50(02): 456–460.

Cook-Sather, Alison (2020) 'Respecting voices: How the co-creation of teaching and learning can support academic staff, underrepresented students, and equitable practices', *Higher Education*, 79(5): 885–901.

de Sousa Santos, Boaventura (2018) *The End of the Cognitive Empire: The Coming of Age of Epistemologies of the South*. Durham: Duke University Press.

Decolonising SOAS Working Group (2018) Decolonising SOAS Learning and Teaching Toolkit for Programme and Module Convenors, *SOAS*. [online] Available from: https://bit.ly/32rE1si [accessed 19 April 2021].

Dickersin, Kay, Fredman, Lisa, Flegal, Katherine. M., Scott, Jane D., and Crawley, Barbara (1998) 'Is there a sex bias in choosing editors? Epidemiology journals as an example', *JAMA*, 280(3): 260.

Doku, Amatey (2020, July 8) Black Lives Matter: Taking action to tackle racism across HE. [online] Available from: https://bit.ly/3tDIvIE [accessed 19 April 2021].

Eigenberg, Helen M., and Whalley, Elizabeth (2015) 'Gender and publication patterns: Female authorship is increasing, but is there gender parity?', *Women and Criminal Justice*, 25(1–2): 130–144.

Freeman, Richard B., and Huang, Wei (2015) 'Collaborating with people like me: Ethnic coauthorship within the United States', *Journal of Labor Economics*, 33(S1): S289–S318.

Gillborn, David, Warmington, Paul, and Demack, Sean (2018) 'QuantCrit: Education, policy, "Big Data" and principles for a critical race theory of statistics', *Race Ethnicity and Education*, 21(2): 158–179.

Goodley, Dan (2013) 'Dis/entangling critical disability studies', *Disability and Society*, 28(5): 631–644.

Gyamera, Gifty O., and Burke, Penny J. (2018) 'Neoliberalism and curriculum in higher education: A post-colonial analysis', *Teaching in Higher Education*, 23(4): 450–467.

Heleta, Savo (2016) 'Decolonisation of higher education: Dismantling epistemic violence and Eurocentrism in South Africa', *Transformation in Higher Education*, 1(1): 1–8.

Helgesson, Gert, and Eriksson, Stefan (2019) 'Authorship order', *Learned Publishing*, 32(2): 106–112.

Hines, Sally (2006) 'What's the difference? Bringing particularity to Queer studies of transgender', *Journal of Gender Studies*, 15(1): 49–66.

hooks, bell (1994) *Teaching to Transgress: Education as the Practice of Freedom*. New York: Routledge.

Hudson, James M., and Bruckman, Amy (2004) ' "Go away": Participant objections to being studied and the ethics of chatroom research', *The Information Society*, 20(2): 127–139.

Kitano, Margie (1997) 'What a course will look like after multicultural change', in Margie Kitano and Ann Morey (eds) *Multicultural Course Transformation in Higher Education: A Broader Truth*. np: Pearson, pp 18–34.

Last, Angela (2019) 'Internationalisation and interdisciplinarity: Sharing across Boundaries?', in Gurminder K. Bhambra, Dalia Gebrial, and Kerem Nişancıoğlu (eds) *Decolonising the University*. London: Pluto Press, pp 208–230.

Le Grange, Lesley (2016) 'Decolonising the university curriculum', *South African Journal of Higher Education*, 30(2): 1–12.

Luckett, Kathy, and Shay, Suellen (2017) 'Reframing the curriculum: A transformative approach', *Critical Studies in Education*, 61(1): 50–65.

Luxon, Tony, and Peelo, Moira (2009) 'Internationalisation: Its implications for curriculum design and course development in UK higher education', *Innovations in Education and Teaching International*, 46(1): 51–60.

May, Helen, and Spalding, Nikki (2014) *Internationalising Higher Education Framework*. York: Higher Education Academy.

Mercer-Mapstone, Lucy, and Bovill, Catherine (2019) 'Equity and diversity in institutional approaches to student–staff partnership schemes in higher education'. *Studies in Higher Education*, 45(12): 2541–2557.

Mngomezulu, Bhekki R., and Hadebe, Sakhile (2018) 'What would the decolonisation of a political science curriculum entail? Lessons to be learnt from the East African experience at the Federal University of East Africa', *Politikon*, 45(1): 66–80.

Mügge, Lisa, Montoya, Celeste, Emejulu, Akwugo, and Weldon, S. Laurel (2018) 'Intersectionality and the politics of knowledge production', *European Journal of Politics and Gender*, 1(1): 17–36.

Oswick, Cliff, and Noon, Mike (2014) 'Discourses of diversity, equality and inclusion: Trenchant formulations or transient fashions?', *British Journal of Management*, 25(1): 23–39.

Peters, Michael A. (2018) 'Why is my curriculum White? A brief genealogy of resistance', in Jason Arday and Heidi Safia Mirza (eds) *Dismantling Race in Higher Education: Racism, Whiteness and Decolonising the Academy*. London: Palgrave Macmillan, pp 253–270.

Phull, Kiran, Ciflikli, Gokhan, and Meibauer, Gustav (2019) 'Gender and bias in the International Relations curriculum: Insights from reading lists', *European Journal of International Relations*, 25(2): 383–407.

Pitkin, Hannah F. (1972) *The Concept of Representation* (1st paperback edn, [Nachdr.]). Berkeley: University of California Press.

Robson, Sue (2015) 'Internationalisation of the curriculum: Challenges and opportunities', *Journal of Perspectives in Applied Academic Practice*, 3(3): 50–52.

Roth, Wendy D. (2016) 'The multiple dimensions of race', *Ethnic and Racial Studies*, 39(8): 1310–1338.

Schucan Bird, Karen (2011) 'Do women publish fewer journal articles than men? Sex differences in publication productivity in the social sciences', *British Journal of Sociology of Education*, 32(6): 921–937.

Schucan Bird, Karen and Pitman, Lesley (2020) 'How diverse is your reading list? Exploring issues of representation and decolonisation in the UK', *Higher Education*, 79(5): 903–920.

Sloan, Luke (2017) 'Social Science "Lite"? Deriving demographic proxies', in Luke Sloan and Anabel Quan-Haase (eds) *The SAGE Handbook of Social Media Research Methods*. Thousand Oaks, CA: SAGE, pp 90–104.

Smith, Nicola J., and Lee, Donna (2015) 'What's queer about political science?' *The British Journal of Politics and International Relations*, 17(1): 49–63.

Song, Miri (2018) 'Why we still need to talk about race', *Ethnic and Racial Studies*, 41(6): 1131–1145.

Stokes, Doug (2019) 'Universities should resist calls to "decolonise the curriculum"', *The Spectator*. [online] Available from: https://bit.ly/3n0e SP3 [accessed 19 April 2021].

Stokes, Peter, and Martin, Lindsey (2008) 'Reading lists: A study of tutor and student perceptions, expectations and realities', *Studies in Higher Education*, 33(2): 113–125.

Tickner, Arlene B. (2013) 'Core, periphery and (neo)imperialist International Relations', *European Journal of International Relations*, 19(3): 627–646.

UCL (University College London) (2018) *Inclusive Curriculum Healthcheck*. *UCL*. [online] Available from: https://bit.ly/3twmDyA [accessed 19 April 2021].

UUK (Universities UK), and NUS (National Union of Students) (2019a) 'Black, Asian, and Minority Ethnic Student Attainment at UK Universities: #Closingthegap', *UUK*. [online] Available from https://bit.ly/3rr010A [accessed 19 April 2021].

UUK, and NUS (2019b) 'Black, Asian, and Minority Ethnic Student Attainment at UK Universities: Case Studies', *UUK*. [online] Available from: https://bit.ly/32sU1KN [accessed 19 April 2021].

Ward, Nikki, and Gale, Nicola (2016) *LGBTQ-Inclusivity in the Higher Education Curriculum: A Best Practice Guide*. University of Birmingham. [online] Available from: https://bit.ly/3tyTe74 [accessed 19 April 2021].

West, Jevin D., Jacquet, Jennifer, King, Molly M., Correll, Shelley J., and Bergstrom, Carl T. (2013) 'The role of gender in scholarly authorship', *PLoS ONE*, 8(7), e66212.

Wijaya Mulya, Tegun (2019) 'Contesting the neoliberalisation of higher education through student–faculty partnership', *International Journal for Academic Development*, 24(1): 86–90.

Wilkinson, Davin and Thelwall, Mike (2011) 'Researching personal information on the public web: Methods and ethics', *Social Science Computer Review*, 29(4): 387–401.

Willis, Roxana (2019) 'Observations online: Finding the ethical boundaries of Facebook research', *Research Ethics*, 15(1): 1–17.

Wolff, Ernst (2016) 'Four questions on curriculum development in contemporary South Africa', *South African Journal of Philosophy*, 35(4): 444–459.

7

Pluralised Realities: Reviewing Reading Lists to Make Them More Culturally Sensitive

Dave S.P. Thomas

The aim of creating distance in relation to the Eurocentric tradition is to open analytical spaces for realities that are 'surprising' because they are new or have been ignored or made invisible, that is, deemed non-existent by the Eurocentric critical tradition ... keeping distance does not mean discarding the rich Eurocentric critical tradition and throwing it into the dustbin of history. ... It means including it in a much broader landscape of epistemological and political possibilities. It means exercising hermeneutics of suspicion regarding its 'foundational truths' by uncovering what lies below their 'face value'. It means giving special attention to the suppressed or marginalized smaller traditions within the big Western tradition. (De Sousa Santos, 2014, p 44)

True global history is only possible to the extent that both Ethnocentrism and Eurocentric anti-Eurocentrism, both Occidentalism and orientalism are superseded. Such history is more accurate on the epistemological level and more progressive on the social, political and cultural. Only this kind of history will allow the world to recognize itself in its infinite diversity. (Jack Goody, as cited in De Sousa Santos, 2014, p 100)

Introduction

Most Westerners think that the world's first university was founded in Bologna in 1088 CE. They are wrong, Al-Qarawiyyin University in Fes el-Bali, Morocco, was founded 170 years earlier, in 859, by Fatima al-Fihri. UNESCO (nd) considers it the oldest existing, continuously operating, degree-granting university in the world. Its library housed a huge collection of manuscripts, including a 9th-century Qur'an. It taught medicine, mathematics, English literature, and Maliki law (one of the four schools of Islamic jurisprudence), plus many other subjects. Nalanda University in India was established even earlier, in 415 CE. It provides the first example of what we now think of as university-level higher education (Bhattacharyya and Guha, 2018). Gundishapur University in Iran (531 CE–832 CE) was the most important medical centre and higher learning institution in the world during the 6th and 7th centuries (Azizi, 2008), with a pivotal role in the history of mathematics as well as a teaching speciality of philosophy, architecture, and geometry; the library had 259 rooms and contained approximately 400,000 books (Zamiri, 1995, p 64). Nalanda and Gundishapur are long closed, but al-Azhar University, established in Cairo, Egypt, in 972 CE, is still active, and is one of the oldest functioning universities in the world.

Compared to these, European universities are relative newcomers: Bologna (1088); Oxford (1096–1167); Salamanca (1134); Paris (1160); Cambridge (1209); and Harvard (1636). They are old, but their temporal pre-eminence is a myth. It would be plausible to conclude that universities originated in the global South and were merely copied by the Western world.

Within higher education institutions (HEIs), the conventional notion of students 'reading for a degree' has become more complicated in the light of globalisation, technological advancements, and massification of higher education. The curriculum is often presented as being colour blind, meritocratic, and a neutral resource, with little appreciation for indigenous approaches to knowing and non-Western knowledge systems. This unchallenged paradigm is hugely problematic, particularly because the purpose of the university has been remodelled in the ever changing, commercially driven landscape of higher education (HE). We have seen the emergence of the student-consumer (Nixon et al, 2018), who is now rejecting the ideals of the neoliberal university and calling for a decolonised curriculum (Peters, 2018; Thomas and Jivraj, 2020) that accounts for the ecology of knowledges (De Sousa Santos, 2014) that encapsulates a diverse range of knowledge systems. As a central feature of the curriculum, the reading list objectively sets out the terrain of study for the student through a selection of core readings (classics) and additional or supplementary reading. Students are then expected to acquiesce by consuming the recommended material, trusting in its objectivity and non–maleficence. But to what extent are faculty the gatekeepers of the Western self-presentation of the university knowledge systems by way of Anglo-American, Eurocentric curricula? How are these ideologies operationalised through the curriculum within the reading lists?

Budd Hall and Rajesh Tandon (2017), in highlighting the limitations in understanding of what constitutes knowledge in universities globally, write:

> knowledge in the universities of our world represents a very small proportion of the global treasury of knowledge. ... Higher education institutions today exclude many of the diverse knowledge systems in the world, including those of Indigenous peoples and excluded racial groups, and those excluded on the basis of gender, class or sexuality. (Hall and Tandon, 2017, pp 6–7)

This chapter aims to casts a fresh light on such perceptions, expectations, and realities as they relate to the reading lists in HEIs. It foregrounds theoretical questions about the role of 'Whiteness' in maintaining epistemic inequality, whereby disavowing knowledge systems that emanate from the global South. I commence with a desire to challenge certain types of epistemologies. I seek to disturb grounds upon which critics contrast; specifically, similar to Robbie Shilliam (2019), I aim to excavate a 'genealogy of academic debates that sought to assess the effects of an increased proximity of Black presence to empire's White spaces' (epistemologically and physically) (Shilliam, 2019, p 4). In reflecting, I will use critical race theory (CRT) in an integrated way as a theoretical and methodological framework, because it amplifies my voice and affords me, as a scholar of colour, the lens and authority to 'speak back' about epistemic injustice in a way that other theoretical tools hitherto delimited me (Crenshaw, 1991). The use of CRT also facilitates an analysis and articulation of how structural inequalities pattern society in shaping the experiences of people who are racialised as 'other' (Ladson-Billings and Tate, 1995). In an attempt to deconstruct and give life to some of the theoretical analyses outlined within this chapter, I will demonstrate how a pedagogical intervention that promoted staff–student interaction highlighted the extent to which epistemic injustice and epistemic violence are operationalised through the reading lists.

Throughout the chapter, I use an integrated approach to intersperse theoretical understandings with qualitative data from focus groups that formed part of a review of the reading lists at a higher education institution in the south-east of England.

The project

In order to develop a deeper understanding of the extent to which Whiteness maintains structural advantage or epistemic privilege and hegemony through the dissemination of the reading lists, I employed three students to assist me on the project (in the capacity of research assistants). It was essential to collaborate with students as co-producers of knowledge on this project because they were the 'consumers' of the curriculum. Firstly, the reading lists of all programmes that were taught across the school (recommended and additional reading) were obtained from the respective module convenors. These were then amalgamated to form a database and analysed as part of a desk-based review. As a fundamental part of the desk-based reading list review, it was essential to ascertain the demographic characteristics of the authors; specifically, I was interested in determining their ethnicity, nationality, and gender. This was done by conducting a web-based search of internet platforms (for example, institutional staff profile pages, publishers' websites, social media accounts, blogs, and so on); in some cases, authors were contacted directly by e-mail or telephone and asked how they identified in terms of ethnicity, nationality, and gender, in the absence of identifiable demographic information on public web-based platforms. This data-collection method was used in the absence of a more robust, established method of ascertaining the demographic characteristics of the authors. These data were analysed using Microsoft Excel, from which we produced infographics to depict the demographic representation of authors who were presented on the reading lists of respective modules, programmes, and school as a whole.

Secondly, research assistants conducted two focus groups with 15 students (from a range of racialised backgrounds). The questions that guided the focus groups were based around broad themes relating to the curriculum (for example, 'To what extent are you able to explore/challenge ideas relating to race in lectures and seminars?') and reading lists (for example, 'To what extent do you consider the demographic characteristics of the authors on your reading lists?' and 'Is there representation of authors from a diverse range of demographic backgrounds on your reading lists?'). Specifically, I sought to gain the perspectives of students because they had experiences of engaging with the curriculum from the perspective of a 'learner'.

Additionally, I gained the perspectives of three members of faculty by way of a short questionnaire. The questionnaires contained open-ended questions that sought to understand their perspectives on the function and purpose of the reading lists and the extent to which they ensured that diversity was represented on their respective reading lists. This was an important aspect of the data-collection process because it allowed me to gain a holistic understanding of the variations that may exist between students' and staffs' perspectives about the reading lists.

Fourthly, each module convenor was sent data from the analyses of their reading lists. The data were analysed intersectionally and the results were displayed according to the ethnic background and gender of the author. I sought to understand the extent to which the demographic representation of authors on the reading lists might be associated with (dis) engagement from the reading lists by students, and the extent to which this could be redressed through staff/student collaboration to introduce knowledge systems from the global South within the reading lists. In this sense, knowledge systems relate to a socio-ecologically robust repository of knowledge based on knowing and doing that emanates from different cultures and at different times. Western self-presentation of the origins of university learning remains a myth.

The findings from the desk-based review, focus groups, and questionnaires revealed three analytic conclusions: (1) epistemic racism was a normal feature of the curriculum, whereby White scholars/authors dominated the reading lists, except perhaps in those specific areas that racism assumes the specialty of non-White scholars (for example, John McWhorter would be read for his work on Black creoles (McWhorter, 2000), but not for his work on second-language acquisition or general linguistics (McWhorter, 2014)); (2) there is an interaction of racism and power that serves to maintain hegemony, whereby the scholarship and knowledge systems of authors from the global South are not perceived as authentic knowledge, worthy to be included within the canon as classics (for example, the work of Chancellor Williams (1987) that catalogues the destruction of Black civilisation remains obscure in the canon of history); and (3) Westernised knowledge systems are over-represented on the reading lists, whereby almost all of the contents of the reading lists emanate from Euro-American literature.

Throughout this chapter, I use the research findings to illuminate how a pedagogic intervention (reading list review) was operationalised to promote staff–student partnerships and co-creation of knowledge. First, I turn to epistemic racism/sexism as a means of exploring the geopolitics and body-politics of knowledge and rationalising the dominance of Westernised scholarship in the canons of thought. Epistemic racism/sexism recognises the production of theory by White/male Western subjects as authentic knowledge (see Grosfoguel, 2012). Second, I outline how 'Whiteness' is used as a means of promoting epistemic injustice. Third, I advance an argument that, when analysed intersectionally, the reading lists may promote an apartheid of knowledge, subsequently having an adverse impact on students' interest, engagement with the curriculum, and academic outcomes due to its lack of diversity. I further highlight some key considerations when developing staff–student relations in reviewing reading lists.

Epistemic racism/sexism and Whiteness

Since reading lists, as an essential component of HE curricula, set out the terrain of study for the learners, who then respond by producing assignments for assessment or sit examinations, I borrow two of Ramon Grosfoguel's (2012) questions to explore epistemic racism and how this may pose barriers to the presentation of knowledge systems from the global South within the curriculum:

1. How is it possible that the canon of thought in all the disciplines of the social sciences and humanities in the Westernized university [in the modern university] is based on the knowledge produced by a few men from five countries in the Western world (Italy, France, England, Germany and the United States)?
2. How is it possible that men from these five countries achieved such an epistemic privilege to the point that their knowledge today is considered superior over the knowledge of the rest of the world?

To begin an answer, we must note that the final conquest of Al-Andalus in the late 16th century was to become a key turning point in the distribution and authentication of 'authentic' systems of knowledge, as it accompanied by what Boaventura de Sousa Santos (2007) has called epistemicide – the killing of knowledge systems. For example, it is thought that one such method used in the conquest was the burning of libraries. The circumstances behind the destruction of the library in Cordoba are not clear, however, according to Grosfoguel (2012):

> the library of Cordoba that housed around 500,000 books at a time when the largest library of Christian Europe did not have more than 1000 books; this was burned in the 13th century. Many other libraries had the same destiny during the conquest of Al-Andalus, until the final burning of more than 250,000 books of the Granada library by Cardenal Cisneros in the early 16th century. These methods were extrapolated to the Americas. Thus, the same happened with the indigenous 'códices' which was the written practice used by Amerindians, Mayans, Inca and Aztec to archive knowledge. Thousands of 'códices' were also burned, destroying indigenous knowledges in the Americas. Genocide and epistemicide went together in the process of conquest in both the Americas and Al-Andalus. (de Sousa Santos, 2007, p 79)

I am of the opinion that epistemic racism/sexism developed from the four interlinking genocides of the 16th century, which provided socio-historic conditions (see Dussel, 1993; Grosfoguel, 2013). By amalgamating four distinct stories of epistemicide that are often treated as separate historical processes, we can see a pattern of suppressing non-European knowledge.

The four genocides/epistemicides were: (1) against Muslims and Jews in the conquest of Al-Andalus in the name of 'purity of blood'; (2) against indigenous peoples first in the Americas and then in Asia; (3) against African people with the captive trade (slave trade) and their enslavement in the Americas; and (4) against women who practised and transmitted Indo-European knowledge in Europe, burned alive accused of being witches (Grosfoguel, 2013, p 77). It was these conquests that shifted the power of earlier dominant Islamic centres of intellectual power to Europe. Arguably, the conquests were both military and epistemological/ideological. The oral knowledge systems of Africa, primarily practised by women, were silenced and African slaves were portrayed as non-human, incapable of Western-style thought. These philosophies were maintained by many in those times, and aligned with those of esteemed Western scholars, such as Hegel, whose damaging opinion that 'among negroes, it is the case that consciousness has not attained even the intuition of any sort of objectivity … the negro is man as beast' (Lectures, 218, quoted in Dussel, 1993). These historic events and philosophies have served to justify the exclusion of non-Western scholars' scholarship from the canon and have wronged them specifically in their capacity as knowers. Miranda Fricker (2010) calls this epistemic injustice.

Commenting on the 'Whiteness' of the reading lists and normalcy of epistemic racism, one of the focus group participants stated:

'I didn't notice the race of the authors. I don't really look at author's names, I just focus on their opinions. We're kind of in a time when we can't think, or we are supposed to think like we are not racist anymore … you don't get judged anymore because of your race.' (White, female student)

This quote highlights the permanence of Whiteness, and the myth of meritocracy that is normalised to the point where 'it is unthinkable that such an ugly word such as [racism] could be directed at a genteel, educated and liberal [set of dons who curate the curriculum]' (Back, 2004, p 2). Another respondent conceded that it was inevitable that most of the authors on their reading lists would be White men:

'In an article that I read, some White guy was just saying that most books are written by White men anyway, so you can only see it from their view point.' (Black, female student)

The preceding quotes are indicative of the centrality of epistemic racism, whereby Whiteness is viewed as ordinary and natural because it is so deeply entrenched within the curriculum. This may be also be indicative of how faculty may be complicit in the maintenance of epistemic racism through the lack of representation of knowledge systems from the global South in their curriculum by way of their reading lists.

I will now outline how 'Whiteness' is used as a location of structural advantage to maintain hegemony and promote epistemic injustice. 'One of the most powerful and dangerous aspects of Whiteness is that many (possibly the majority) White people have no awareness of Whiteness as a construction, let alone their own role in sustaining and playing out the inequities at the heart of Whiteness' (Gillborn, 2005, p 9).

Although White identities are socially constructed and lived, White as an ethnicity or identity has retained a status of 'race-lessness' (Frankenberg, 1993; Ahmed, 2004). The issue here is not just the Western denigration of people of colour and the societies from which their ancestors came. It also involves the creation of 'Whiteness' as an unmarked social category that nonetheless maintains social, political, and epistemic privilege and power. In relation to the curriculum, the persistence of Whiteness (the disavowal of knowledge systems from the global South) may be seen as a precursor to White supremacy. Neely Fuller Jr maintains that 'if you do not understand White supremacy [racism + power] ... everything else that you understand will only confuse you' (Fuller, 1984, A). An example of White supremacy is seen in the curricula and reading lists, where theory and the canon keep in place Black/White opposition (Tate, 2016).

There was a collective feeling among focus group participants that, on investigation of their reading lists, the authors all seemed to be White males. On accessing the resources, participants also recognised the diminished status afforded to some authors on the reading lists, where in cases where diverse authors were present, they were listed as 'additional reading' on the reading list, as opposed to 'mandatory/required reading':

'I found that it is normal for Black people and people of colour to be the subject of research and not the researchers. It almost makes me think that being a researcher is an unrealistic aspiration.' (Black, female student)

'[S]tudents hold the recommendations of the lecturers in high regard. Therefore, if a reading list only consists of scholars from one ethnic and national background, it presents the idea that only those perspectives are truths or facts and decreases the potential for critical thinking that is often encouraged at university level.' (Black, male student)

These excerpts demonstrate how a dearth of diverse perspectives on the reading lists may inadvertently send subliminal messages to students. This may serve to promote epistemic injustice due to the lack of understanding of the impact of these subliminal messages on students' aspirations, and overall well-being due to the historic exclusion of non-Western knowledge systems from the curriculum of HEIs and equal recognition as knowers.

Among module convenors, there was a consensus that their reading lists (core and additional reading) were primarily comprised of White, British authors. One convenor rationalised this by hypothesising that it might be due to quality assurance:

> 'I always use the best available research in my teaching. I agree that there is a lack of diversity on my reading lists, but this may be because the pool of quality research is so small in my discipline.' (White, female academic)

There was also an admission by the lecturers that the lack of diversity in the curriculum and reading lists was common knowledge and that more needs to be done to address this problem:

> 'I agree that the seminal texts are mostly from White European/Anglo-American scholars but you have to understand that these sources are seen as the best ones. There are not many scholars from the global South that write about research methods. Maybe we need to be thinking about how we incorporate other more diverse scholars who write in this area on the reading lists.' (White, female academic)

Alarmingly, there is a dearth of expansive or potent literature that explores reading lists from a cultural, sociological, or political perspective. If Whiteness is seen as a precursor to White supremacy, to what extent do Western universities unwittingly perpetuate White supremacy through their reading lists?

Theorising race, gender, and intersectionality in relation to 'authentic knowledge'

In order to understand how race and gender are approached in the process of creating reading lists, I advance another argument, that reading lists in their current format may promote an apartheid of knowledge. An apartheid of knowledge in this context relates to the climate of separation between what is considered 'legitimate' knowledge and 'illegitimate' knowledge in academia (see Delgado Bernal and Villalpando, 2002; Villalpando and Delgado Bernal, 2002). The institutional concerns around 'race', racialised gendered issues, and its intersections in society may be reproduced in the HE curriculum in general and reading lists in particular. Oppression cannot be neatly dissected or explicitly categorised (Bell, 1992). Kimberle Crenshaw (1989) rearticulated work by Black feminist scholars such as Patricia Hill Collins, Angela Davis, and Audrey Lorde in emphasising the intersectional salience of 'race' and gender with related identities and forms of oppression.

She critiqued the use of single-axis frameworks that compartmentalise 'race' and gender as mutually exclusive categories of experience and analysis. This compartmentalisation has served to distort and discredit the multidimensionality of Black women's experiences, thus erasing them from practice, policy, and theory (Crenshaw, 1989; Mirza, 1997).

Returning to the focus groups responses, the next excerpts demonstrate the overwhelming importance of considering intersectionality when curating the curriculum and subsequent reading lists, because of its ability to trigger and sustain interest in the subject. There was a consensus among participants that the demographic characteristics of the author were important in terms of promoting (dis)engagement:

'If there was a book or paper on the reading list where someone was talking about their educational experience and they were White, middle class and male, how much could I connect with that? Their experiences are not the same as mine. But I find that a paper that is written by a woman who is working class and talks about things from her perspective, then I would be more likely to read her work.' (Mixed heritage, female student)

'[S]ometimes it is not as clear cut as that. There's almost a bias sometimes in the way some authors address some issues. For example, some authors would rather talk about issues relating to "class" than race. Even when they talk about race it is always from a male perspective.' (Black, female student)

These quotes correlate with the conception of intersectionality (intersections of race, class, and gender in this case) (Crenshaw, 1989). While accepting that issues of race and class were discussed by the author, there was a lack of confidence that the author's positionality would enable the students to understand the demographic nuances. The perspectives presented in these quotes serve as a call to action to neutralise dominant epistemologies that serve to promote and maintain ethnocentrism.

Conclusion

As I have written elsewhere (Thomas, 2020), there are ten key considerations when conducting a reading list review, among them the importance of reflecting on your epistemic practices; noticing your engagement with paradigms, discourses, and theories relating to epistemology, ontology, and pedagogy; developing familiarity with legislation, policies, and practices concerning equality, diversity, and inclusivity; the importance of adopting a critical approach to analysing quantitative data; and so on. I shall not describe these here. Instead, I will focus on the importance of developing healthy staff–student relations as a fundamental part of the process.

There is a 'circle of fear' that compromises positive staff–student relationships in the academy. The term 'circle of fear' is commonly used in healthcare to quantify the acrimonious relationships between Black communities and health services. In an academic context, I contend that it relates to a circle that impacts negatively on the engagement of students with staff/university services and vice versa. Within this circle, students may mistrust and often become wary of staff, while staff are often wary of students (particularly Black male students). The cycle is fuelled by stereotypes, misconceptions, misunderstandings, and often microaggressions and overt racism. This may result in social distancing between staff and students, thus having an adverse effect on the students' overall experiences within the academy. In developing staff–student relations, one should endeavour to combat the 'circle of fear' and adopt an assets-based approach to empowering students to become partners in learning.

In developing staff–student relations when reviewing the reading lists, I was mindful of the potential 'circle of fear' and thought it prudent to create an environment conducive to the development of rapport and trust. In doing this, I relinquished power and acknowledged the students' contributions to the co-creation of knowledge. I explicitly acknowledged this in a manner that Mary Rowe (2008) calls microaffirmation. I was also mindful of the general student perception of the professor, academic, or member of staff as the 'font of all knowledge' from whom they, as 'empty vessels', should be eternally grateful to be filled. This was particularly evident among first-year undergraduate students, who often declared that they accepted the reading lists at face value, unconcerned with the demographic background of the authors. This corroborates with what I call normalised epistemic racism, prompted by the epistemicide described earlier in this chapter (de Sousa Santos, 2007). Therefore, in line with the CRT tenet of counter-storytelling (Solórzano and Yosso, 2002), I invited the student researchers to contribute reflections on their initial/current perceptions of the reading lists and the process of reviewing them, as well as make recommendations as to how these reading lists could be developed to be more inclusive. This served to amplify their voices and recognise their perspectives as 'legitimate knowledge'. These recommendations formed the basis of my end-of-project report.

An assets-based approach to staff–student relations promotes capacity and connectedness and builds social capital through the use of students' pre-existing knowledge, skills, and lived experiences. The assets perspective has been proven to impact on positive factors that nurture health and well-being (Foot, 2012). The assets-based approach serves to redress the legacy of epistemic racism/sexism and the apartheid in knowledge by legitimising the 'outsider' perspective. In building staff–student relations, it is important to recognise students' lived experiences as 'legitimate' knowledge, as articulated by Gloria Ladson-Billings, writing on racialised discourses and ethnic epistemologies (Ladson-Billings, 2000). This has also proven to be an essential strategy in the co-creation of knowledge by enabling a shared vision and understanding of positions of inclusion and exclusion through the employment of liminal perspectives. Therefore, an assets-based approach to developing staff–student relations requires power-sharing and a reimagination of students as co-producers of knowledge in order to realise new intellectual dispositions.

There is an urgent need for a concerted, race-conscious, intersectional analysis of reading lists in HE curricula in order to examine the patterns of (in)visibility, inclusion, and exclusion. I contend that the 'colour blindness' that suggests that reading lists are curated to present race-/gender-neutral perspectives are likely to heighten patterns of discrimination and hegemony that are produced within the curriculum. Redressing those inequalities requires an approach that engages a politics of intersectionality, encourages different ways of thinking and theorising, and encourages the multiplicity of complexities and dynamic nature of power relations and oppressions (Brah and Phoenix, 2004, as cited in Rankin-Wright et al, 2019). A review of the reading lists should not be perceived as a myopic approach to improving body count through identity politics but, rather, as a catalyst for more sustainable institutional conversation and strategy to redress structural inequalities in promoting transformational change. In the rapidly changing HE sector, HEIs will need to look beyond their seemingly 'colour blind' lenses and cross the 'colour line' that defined the 20th century, in order to meet the expectations and realities of their ever-increasingly diverse student cohorts. Meeting these expectations may serve as a catalyst to promote healthy staff–student relations. Decentring Europe from current understandings of the world within the HE curriculum will take time. However, this process of decentring needs to start with proactive initiatives that explicitly interrogate current epistemologies and the Eurocentric canon, then deliberately aim to achieve epistemic amelioration and ultimately pluriversity – a process of knowledge production that is receptive of epistemic diversity (Mbembe, 2015).

References

Ahmed, Sara (2004) 'Declarations of whiteness: the non-performativity of anti-racism', *Borderlands*, 3: 1–15.

Azizi, Mohammed-Hossein (2008) 'Gondishapur school of medicine: The most important medical center in antiquity', *Archives of Iranian Medicine*, 11: 116–119.

Back, Les (2004) 'Ivory towers? The academy and racism', in Ian Law, Deborah Phillips, and Laura Turney (eds) *Institutional Racism in Higher Education*. Stoke on Trent: Trentham Books, pp 1–6.

Bell, Derrick (1992) *Faces at the Bottom of the Well*. New York: Basic Books.

Bhattacharyya, S., and Guha, D. (2018) 'Nature & Quality of world higher education in reference to Nalanda, Gundishapur, Al-Qarawiyyin and Al-Azhar: 415 A.D. – 1200 A.D.', *International Journal of Research in Social Sciences*, 8(11): 2249–2496.

Brah, Avtar, and Phoenix, Ann (2004) 'Ain't I a woman? Revisiting intersectionality', *Journal of International Women's Studies*, 5: 75–86.

Crenshaw, Kimberle (1989) 'Demarginalizing the intersection of race and sex: A Black feminist critique of antidiscrimination doctrine, feminist theory and antiracist politics'. *University of Chicago Legal Forum*. [online] Available from: https://bit.ly/3s4EJXU [accessed 18 March 2021].

Crenshaw, Kimberlé W. (1991) 'Mapping the margins: Intersectionality, identity politics, and violence against women of color', *Stanford Law Review*, 43(6): 1241–1299.

de Sousa Santos, Boaventura (2007) 'Beyond abyssal thinking: From global lines to ecologies of knowledge', *Eurozine*, 33: 45–89.

de Sousa Santos, Boaventura (2014) *Epistemologies of the South: Justice against Epistemicide*. London and New York: Routledge.

Delgado Bernal, Dolores, and Villalpando, Octavio (2002) 'An apartheid of knowledge in academia: The struggle over the "legitimate" knowledge of faculty of color', *Equity and Excellence in Education*, 35: 169–180.

Dussel, Enrique (1993) 'Eurocentrism and modernity', *Boundary 2: An International Journal of Literature and Culture*, 20: 65–76.

Foot, Jane (2012) 'What makes us healthy? The asset approach in practice: Evidence, action, evaluation'. [online] Available from: http://www.janefoot.co.uk/downloads/files/healthy%20FINAL%20FINAL.pdf [accessed 4 January 2022].

Frankenberg, Ruth (1993) *White Women, Race Matters: The Social Construction of Whiteness*. Minnesota: University of Minesota Press.

Fricker, Miranda (2010) *Epistemic Injustice: Power and the Ethics of Knowing*. Oxford, UK: Oxford University Press.

Fuller, Neely (1984) *The United Independent Compensatory Code System Concept: A Compensatory Counter-Racist Code*. New Jersey: NFJ Productions.

Gillborn, David (2005) 'Education policy as an act of white supremacy: Whiteness, critical race theory and education reform', *Journal of Education Policy*, 20: 485–505.

Grosfoguel, Ramon (2012) 'The dilemmas of ethnic studies in the United States between liberal multiculturalism, identity politics, disciplinary colonization, and decolonial epistemologies', *Human Architecture: Journal of Sociology of Self-Knowledge*, 10(1): 81–89.

Grosfoguel, Ramon (2013) 'The structure of knowledge in Westernized universities: Epistemic racism/sexism and the four genocides/epistemicides of the long 16th century', *Human Architecture: Journal of Sociology of Self-Knowledge*, 11(1): 73–90.

Hall, Budd L, and Tandon, Rajesh (2017) 'Decolonization of knowledge, epistemicide', *Research for All*, 1(1): 6–19.

Ladson-Billings, Gloria (2000) 'Racialised discourses and ethnic epistemologies', in Norman K. Denzin and Yvonne S. Lincoln (eds) *Handbook of Qualitative Research* (2nd edn). London and New Delhi: Sage Publications, pp 257–277.

Ladson-Billings, Gloria, and Tate, William F. (1995) 'Toward a critical race theory of education', *Teachers College Record*, 97: 47–58.

Mbembe, Achille J. (2015) 'Decolonizing knowledge and the question of the archive', *Wits Institute for Social and Economic Research (WISER), University of the Witwatersrand*. [online] Available from: https://bit.ly/3s7i eBx [accessed 18 March 2021].

McWhorter, John H. (2000) *The Missing Spanish Creoles: Recovering the Birth of Plantation Contact Languages*. Berkeley: University of California Press.

McWhorter, John H. (2014) *The Language Hoax: Why the World Looks the Same in Any Language*. New York: Oxford University Press.

Mirza, Heidi Safia (ed) (1997) *Black British Feminism*. London: Routledge.

Nixon, Elizabeth, Scullion, Richard, and Hearn, Robert (2018) 'Her majesty the student: marketised higher education and the narcissistic (dis)satisfactions of the student-consumer', *Studies in Higher Education*, 43: 927–943.

Peters, Michael A. (2018) 'Why is my curriculum white? A brief genealogy of resistance', in Jason Arday and Heidi Safia Mirza (eds) *Dismantling Race in Higher Education: Racism, Whiteness and Decolonising the Academy*. London: Palgrave Macmillan, pp 253–270.

Rankin-Wright, Alexandra J., Hylton, Kevin, and Norman, Leanne (2019) 'Critical race theory and black feminist insights into "race" and gender equality', *Ethnic and Racial Studies*, 43(7): 1111–1129

Rowe, Mary (2008) 'Micro-affirmations and micro-inequities', *Journal of the International Ombudsman Association*, 1(1): 45–48.

Shilliam, Robbie (2019) 'Behind the Rhodes statue: Black complacency and the imperial academy', *History of Human Sciences*, 20: 1–25.

Solórzano, Daniel G., and Yosso, Tara J. (2002) 'Critical race methodology: Counter-storytelling as an analytical framework for education research', *Qualitative Inquiry*, 8(1): 23–44.

Tate, Shirley Anne (2016) '"I can't put my finger on it": Racism's touch', *Ethnicities*, 16(1): 68–85.

Thomas, Dave S.P. (2020) 'Democracy, diversity and decolonisation: Staff-student partnerships in a reading list review', *Advance HE*. [online] Available from: https://bit.ly/38VxU36 [accessed 8 January 2020].

Thomas, Dave S.P., and Jivraj, Suhraiya (eds) (2020) *Towards Decolonising the University: A Kaleidoscope for Empowered Action*. Oxford, UK: Counterpress.

UNESCO (nd) 'Medina of Fez'. *World Heritage List*. [online] Available from: https://whc.unesco.org/en/list/170/ [accessed 10 March 2021].

Villalpando, Octavio, and Delgado Bernal, Dolores (2002) 'A critical race theory analysis of barriers that impede the success of faculty of colour', in William A. Smith, Philip G. Altbach, and Kofi Lomotey (eds) *The Racial Crisis in American Higher Education: Continuing Challenges for the Twenty-First Century*. New York: State University of New York Press, pp 243–269.

Williams, Chancellor (1987) *Destruction of Black Civilization: Great Issues of a Race from 4500BC to 2000AD* (2nd edn). Chicago: Third World Press.

Zamiri, Mohammed H. (1995) *History of Education and Learning in Iran and Islam*. Shiraz: Rahgosha Publication.

8

Decolonizing Research Methods: Practices, Challenges, and Opportunities

Sara Ewing

Introduction

Raising and addressing decolonizing perspectives and approaches through every stage of the research process, regardless of discipline, creates numerous opportunities and challenges. It is fundamentally based on the reconsideration of the concepts and priorities of academic practices in higher education (HE), including their links with research, curriculum development and teaching. A key feature of this project is exploring pedagogical approaches that explicitly solicit, incorporate, and validate individual experiences and research interests. Classroom encounters are thus reconceptualized as ones which engender emotional, intellectual, conceptual, and cognitive transformations (Takacs, 2002), all of which impact on the choices students make in their own research practices. Incorporating disciplinary conventions and interdisciplinary imagination expands the relevance and impact of these efforts. The reciprocal influence between research and curriculum serves to create, disseminate, and share knowledge, so the ultimate aim is to galvanize research, curricular, and pedagogical reforms that better represent and include the social, economic, and political concerns of Goldsmiths' diverse student body and community, creating an experience of belonging and aspiration.

Goldsmiths is a public university located in south-east London that is known for its emphasis on creative, cultural, and political subjects, and which has a strong and enduring reputation for radical curricula and research. The liberal HE on offer at Goldsmiths is predicated on a publicly stated encouragement and acceptance of the diversity that decolonization both implies and demands. However, a failure to adequately engage with meaningful definitions of difference and the dialogue it requires obfuscates the norms and mechanisms of power that underpin relationships in academia. The 2018–23 Goldsmiths Strategic Plan (2018) claims that 'students will continue to have a voice in developing and diversifying our curriculum and we will continue to engage with the Goldsmiths Students' Union's "Liberate My Degree" campaign, ensuring that programme developments are informed by a range of voices, experiences, and global perspectives'. This declaration of priorities can be seen as an instantiation of what Sara Ahmed (2012) calls the performativity of valuing diversity as an official act, since the institution itself does not act on these stated goals. Instead, the practical implementation of 'liberation' is left to academics, who must be interested, motivated, and free to make decisions and take supporting action. Such freedom requires secure contracts and flexible roles, which are increasingly scarce in the neoliberal university model. Furthermore, the emphasis on diversity presumes that staff and students prioritize tolerance and acceptance when discussing both theory and experience (Brown, 2006), an unwarranted belief (Gabriel and Tate, 2017). By uncritically employing the concept of diversity and failing to consciously reflect on our own biases, we may continue to rely on the normative misrepresentation that education is neutral, thereby naturalizing cultural hierarchies in both research and pedagogy. This can be seen as a 'recolonization of social relations' (Balibar, 2004, p 41) which reinforces endemic assumptions and conventions of academic knowledge and thus pre-empts radical change.

The Black and Asian Minority Ethnic Attainment gap and the Goldsmiths Anti-Racist Action occupation have highlighted an institutional failure to consider a range of pedagogies and curricula that would be more inclusive of a wider range of student backgrounds, experiences, and perspectives (Akel, 2019). In their current state, many curricula advantage some students while disadvantaging others, reproducing racially and ethnically based social and political inequalities in the classroom. This represents continuity in the colonial educational strategy, a process that Ngũgĩ wa Thiong'o (1986, p 3) asserts 'annihilate[s] a people's belief in their names, in their languages, in their environment, in their heritage of struggle, in their unity, in their capacities and ultimately in themselves. … It makes them want to identify with that which is furthest removed from themselves.' The Eurocentrism of curricula, and its origins in research, is embedded in the institutional legitimacy of HE in the UK. Problematizing these traditions can construct the necessary foundations for 'dismantling power relations, social hierarchies and cultural hegemonies that currently underpin the canons, the assumed norms and values of inherited curricula' (Luckett and Shay, 2020, p 53). Reimagining more inclusive and representative participation in the practices of research, curricula, and pedagogy can serve to implement transformative change. The Decolonizing Research Methods (DRM) project attempts to address each of these facets of HE academic practices.

Motivations and origins

The DRM classes were motivated by my experience of teaching English for Academic Purposes (EAP) at Goldsmiths. EAP is an academic discipline focused on the linguistic and discursive conventions and practices specific to academic contexts (Li, 2020). The target population in EAP has traditionally been international students, although it has grown to include widening-participation students, often defined as mature or from non-traditional backgrounds. EAP provision emphasizes the use of academic English as a tool for meeting disciplinary and institutional requirements, particularly through acculturating students to independent researching and writing processes that underpin written assessment in UK HE. This acculturation takes place through learning about and utilizing the academic discourses that are considered acceptable, legitimate, and necessary in their discipline, which are predominantly Eurocentric. Discourses are not simply ideas, discussions, or communication events, but 'ways of being in the world, or *forms* of life which integrate words, acts, values, beliefs, attitudes, social identities' (Gee, 1996, p 127), a definition that emphasizes the shared activities and exchanges that make up HE experiences. These social interactions create opportunities for students to conform to or resist institutionally promoted knowledge and practices by how they plan and conduct their study, research, and assessment, thereby constructing and situating their academic and personal identities in relation to institutional expectations.

Traditional standards of determining academic validity are based on the selection, organization, and presentation of persuasive arguments. An academic argument is a logically structured integration of theory, context, and examples supported by credible evidence. Assessments of academic credibility include the perceived legitimacy of the source of the evidence, as well as its significance and relevance to both the discipline and the student's argument. Linda Tuhiwai Smith (2012, p 38) argues that this evaluative process privileges and validates Eurocentric ideas, values, and world-views, while simultaneously rendering non-Eurocentric approaches, perspectives, and contexts invisible – a dynamic which reinforces the authority of Eurocentric theorizing and empirical research as the only legitimate basis for knowledge. Consequently, students are expected to assimilate to this dominant academic culture, and those who do not are seen as deficient. Such an ascription of deficit 'works to reproduce colonial binaries and maintain social hierarchies – us and them, the educated and uneducated … the prepared and the under-prepared, the advantaged and the disadvantaged, white and black' (Luckett and Shay, 2020, p 58). By these means, Western education becomes aspirational, not in a personal goal-oriented way, but in a way in which student success is oriented to an institution whose interest lies in maintaining its own research legitimacy and dominance.

The motivation for initiating the DRM project emerged from the experience of teaching in this institutional context: a module called Critical Moments in Western Thought (CMWT), and a series of academic writing classes for MA students in the Institute for Creative and Cultural Entrepreneurship (ICCE). CMWT classes are taught to international Graduate Diploma students hoping to progress onto an MA degree in a wide range of departments and programmes. Each week across the autumn and spring terms introduces a different theoretical perspective, including rationalism, modern political concepts, values, and feminism. The module was developed in order to familiarize students with the foundations of theory and practice that are considered to be essential for engaging in academic study, writing, and research at Goldsmiths, regardless of discipline. As their summative assessment, students must write a researched essay related to one of module themes. ICCE students, a combination of international and home students, are likewise assessed through an essay for their core module called 'Theories of Capital', which focuses on a wide range of socioeconomic conditions and relationships. Many of these students have decades of work experience but have never written an academic essay; others have produced academic writing only in a language other than English. The focus of the first two DRM classes was created in response to the theoretical and contextual foundations of these modules.

Two key themes that are often considered to construct legitimacy in Western academic research are 'The Enlightenment' and 'History'. Firstly, The Enlightenment established the principles for valid, reliable, and rigorous research practices, especially the reliance on rational evaluation of empirical evidence to develop an objective understanding of the physical and social world (Hall and Gieben, 1992). This is the implicit basis for the ways in which students are expected to gather and analyse evidence, then use it to construct written arguments. Secondly, history is seen as an objective collection of facts about the linear progression of human development and civilization, and therefore a neutral and mutually recognized means of contextualizing arguments. Empirical and historical data is presented in terms of the natural, inevitable evolution of humanity which informed and justified the civilizing mission of colonization (Mignolo, 2011). As such, a decolonial critique of Enlightenment and historical foundations asserts that, rather than these ideas simply being disseminated, they must be questioned and reinterpreted in context. Through the contributions of participants' ideas, experiences, contexts, and research interests during these first two workshops, eight additional themes (Borders, Religion, Language, Education, Gender, Capitalism, Democracy, and Progress) were co-created to complete a standard 10-week module, an example of decolonizing pedagogy in practice.

Pedagogy and praxis

Research methods are systematic strategies and tools used to conduct research, including formulating research questions, selecting research subjects, collecting and analysing data, drawing conclusions, and applying results (Tuhiwai Smith, 2012). Traditional research methods privilege discrete and transferrable measures that rely on prior research, conceptual precedent, and perceived disciplinary value. This has a generative effect on the way in which research becomes redirected towards pre-existing centres of power, thus disregarding or delegitimizing other systems of values, knowledge, culture, and practice (Datta, 2018). In contrast, decolonial thinking anchors the exploration of research in the embodied experience of the marginalized, those who exist in the periphery or on the border, what Enrique Dussel (1995, p 137) calls 'the reason of the Other'. The production and exchange of knowledge can thus be considered a means to acknowledge and validate the liminal space in which ideas and identities are formed. This approach delinks the construction of knowledge from the colonial matrix of classification and domination. As such, a decolonizing response to a Eurocentric research paradigm requires the careful deconstruction of the social and conceptual hierarchies that underpin Western epistemology.

The Western canon of research consists of a foundation of core conceptual and contextual assumptions that determine what is relevant or comprehensible in a particular discipline, and what is not. This theoretical framework influences what is included in programme curricula and also restricts what is considered a legitimate basis for discussion in the classroom. Boaventura de Sousa Santos (2007, p 45) asserts that these disciplinary foundations construct a social reality which also produces an invisible Other, a relationship of inclusion and exclusion that is embodied by students (Akel, 2019) rather than remaining in the abstract spaces of academic theorizing. As bell hooks (1994, p 82) argues,

> racism, sexism and class elitism shape the structure of classrooms, creating a lived reality of insider versus outsider that is predetermined, often in place before any class discussion begins. There is rarely any need for marginalized groups to bring this binary opposition into the classroom because it is usually already operating.

In consideration of this embodied context, DRM classes are based on affirmative pedagogical strategies that reinforce all students' right to be present, to speak and to be heard. Decolonization requires not only continually unlearning and relearning our identities as educators and researchers, but also actively taking responsibility for the experiences of students when they engage with spaces of learning and researching (Datta, 2018, p 1). This can be seen as necessary intervention into the unquestioned hierarchies of social identities, relationships, and classifications of knowledge that bind pedagogy and research practices.

Decolonization is understood in myriad ways in a wide range of contexts, but in HE it can be defined as 'an expression of the changing geopolitics of knowledge whereby the modern epistemological framework for knowing and understanding the world is no longer interpreted as universal and unbound by geo-historical and biographical contexts' (Baker, 2012, p 2). This reconceptualizes the production, reception, and application of knowledge as highly contextual and subjective. Subjectivity is itself an ongoing negotiation between individual agency and endemic power hierarchies in society. In this sense, academic subjectivities can be seen as the consequence of colonial impositions of superiority and inferiority as established through the criteria of Eurocentric knowledge (Mignolo and Tlostanova, 2016, p 131). The imperial epistemological foundations of Western academia implicitly invalidate discourses that challenge the singularized narrative of Western history, and consequently silence the memories and experiences of marginalized groups (Meneses, 2016, p 126). Decolonizing pedagogy and praxis, on the other hand, intentionally create an inclusive and participatory space that does not privilege one set of experiences or ways of theorizing over others. They are teaching and learning strategies and practices which enable a recognition of both the broader societal structures of colonization and their implications for interactions in the classrooms and research of any discipline (Regan, 2010), facilitating activities that disrupt unequal power dynamics and encourage an active exploration of possibilities for change.

Affect and co-production

Both teaching and learning are composed of multiple and interrelated affective encounters which are intellectual, emotional, and entwined with power. Affective pedagogy is an ethical framework that unsettles the boundaries of traditional systems of knowledge construction and exchange. This requires more than finding, acknowledging, and rearranging previously constructed pieces of knowledge; it is a means of consciously reflecting on the possibilities of 'increasing our capacity to act and be in the world [in relation to] knowledge, ethics, and pedagogy' (Springgay, 2011, p 68). In the DRM classes, students and teacher alike analyse the connections between their sociocultural positions and their orientation toward systems of knowledge, naming our own attitudes, values, assumptions, and passions (Takacs, 2002). We then examine these values through discussions with classmates and by reflecting on how disciplinary and experiential biases impact on the choices we make in these discussions and in our own research. As such, the classes become creative spaces of personal and intellectual growth and activity, rather than a place to receive content, instructions, and tools. This pedagogical orientation exemplifies the core principles of decolonization in this context, as designing or conducting a class in a way that tells students how or what to think is the antithesis of a decolonizing pedagogy (Tejada, 2008, p 30). The success of these loosely structured interactions requires the acceptance of a fundamental reciprocity between the students and the teacher.

DRM classes deliberately avoid a classroom structure of 'tell and practise', a standard pedagogical approach which positions the lecturer as the source of relevant and significant ideas, contexts, and examples (Chun, 2015). Indeed, I do not use prepared talking points, acting instead as a facilitator who provides directed tasks to provoke engagement with and discussion about the theme. This student-centred format offers an opportunity to collaboratively develop the focus, trajectory, breadth, and depth of the content, or to co-produce the class. Because the learning outcomes are not tied to a particular plan that I have prepared in advance, they instead emerge from the 'interactive work [that] takes place among the participants and leads to the creation of a whole range of learning opportunities, many of which are perhaps unexpected' (Slimani, 2001, p 87). Shifting the dynamic in this way requires transparent attention to issues of identity, agency, anxiety, and implicit power relations, which challenges and reorients expectations about what *should* be taking place in the classroom. This renunciation of expectations requires me to critically reflect on my relationship with others both inside and outside the classroom and university (Meneley and Young, 2005) in a way that confronts my own attachment to being perceived as having disciplinary expertise. Endemic power relations connected to perceptions of knowing or not knowing, understanding or not understanding, must be highlighted, deconstructed, and reconceptualized rather than perpetuated. With all participants assuming equal roles in the negotiated meaning-making processes, the classroom becomes a space which reaffirms our capacity to think and act in relation to knowledge and the world without the constraints of the presumption of expertise.

Each class begins with students spending five minutes independently generating their own initial ideas about that week's theme in response to guiding questions. For example, in the 'Borders' class, students are asked to write down in as much detail as possible what information they think someone would need to know in order to understand where they are from, interpreting that instruction as broadly or narrowly as they choose. They are then given ten minutes to exchange their thoughts with a small group before returning to share with the whole class. In this case, students examine ideas about geography alongside complex layers of identity, belonging, and exclusion, including family, class, race, political ideology, language, and embodiment. The most fruitful, engaging, and surprising discussions often come from this initial task, as students feel free to simply talk about what they think, have experienced, know, or to reconsider what they have previously learned or been taught. These ideas and discussions frame the remainder of the class. Students are then directed to read and discuss an anecdote about a particular human experience of borders (Anzaldua, 2012), and to relate their response to the initial discussion. Building these connections prompts a recognition and elaboration of the crossovers in experiences that defy territorial boundaries. Only when this foundation is established are they asked to read an academic text that explores the power dynamics embedded in the geopolitics, body-politics, and ego-politics of knowledge (Grosfoguel, 2007). With this academic conceptualization, they can then tie their own prior knowledge to a new theoretical framework of 'knowing' and understanding the world. As bell hooks (1994, p 84) explains, '[i]f experience is already invoked in the classroom as a way of knowing that coexists in a non-hierarchical way with other ways of knowing, then it lessens the possibility that it can be used to silence'. As such, rather than creating distance from their own subjectivity through the abstraction of theory, engagement with academic texts is situated in the lived experiences of the students and can thus become both personally and academically meaningful.

Encouraging and embedding decolonial critique

Decolonial critique provokes engagement with, and understanding and application of, new ideas and contexts by going beneath the surface of concepts and theories – an approach that is embedded in every DRM class. This process includes describing situations and experiences, considering different perspectives, developing explanations and interpretations, establishing connections between ideas, and identifying consequences of actions and interactions (Ritchard et al, 2011, pp 11–13). Highlighting and deconstructing the world in this way enables the recognition of uncritical assumptions of shared social and conceptual meaning and value that underpin research practices. Active curiosity thus enables the formation of a critique of colonial epistemological frameworks and embedded hierarchies that comprise disciplinary knowledge and legitimate research in HE. It also opens up the possibilities of understanding how the range of individual identities and experiences intersect in various ways, depending on the sociocultural context (Anzaldua, 2012). The intersecting experiences and consequences of oppression based on social identities such as race, ethnicity, class, gender, and sexuality must be acknowledged through an interdisciplinary approach to decolonizing research methods. Renewing understanding of non-Eurocentric identities, relationships, institutions, and processes offers the possibility of a cognitive transformation that confronts resignation to injustice, intolerance, and inequality (Battiste and Henderson, 2009).

Linking the experience in the classroom to practical choices in individual research projects is a key element of this project. After each class, students are encouraged to connect the classroom discussion to their own area of interest and study. For example:

- *Enlightenment*: Create a concept map to categorize and organize ideas about research and colonialism based on their own interpretation in the context of their own research interest or emphasis.
- *History*: Interrogate context, participation, and impact. Who makes decisions about this? Who is affected by this and how? What is an alternative? Where can we see this in the real world? Where are there similar concepts/situations? When would this cause a problem? Why are people influenced by this? Why has it been this way for so long?
- *Borders*: Create your own alternative map related to some aspect of your discipline or research interest. How does representing boundaries differently help you to see your topic, theoretical, practical, or both, in a new way?
- *Religion*: Review the classifications and hierarchies of your discipline embedded in the Dewey Decimal System. How are these recreated in your programme, on your reading lists, and in the real world? Develop an alternative hierarchy of categories based specifically on your research topic or question.

Each of these tasks encourages students to consolidate their thinking about ideas and relationships, establish relevant links, and retrieve particular points for use in their own research and writing. Including individual identities, experiences, and meaning-making in the deconstruction of commonly accepted conceptual categories and classifications reorients students to what can be valid contributions in their discipline, and motivates them to apply these outputs to their own research practices. Students have responded to these activities by commenting that they have broadened their own perception of what is possible to conceptualize and research in their discipline, and that it has thus impacted on the ways in which they have developed their research questions, approach, focus, and analysis. They have expressed feeling empowered to trust and assert their own voice in what they had previously experienced as a narrow, exclusionary, and elitist academic environment. Students have implemented these strategies in research projects in subjects as diverse as psychotherapy, public policy, visual cultures, youth and community work, international development, and entrepreneurship. In my own practice, I have applied decolonial critique to embedded academic skills provision in a range of programmes, including Arts Management, Tourism and Cultural Policy, and Law.

In EAP, embedded practice means integrating academic research and writing strategies with discipline-specific theories and practices. Similarly,

I have embedded decolonizing approaches into different programme modules by combining decolonizing pedagogies and texts with academic skills and module content. The purpose of this integrated effort is to enable students to 'actively engage in a conceptualization from whence they can actively negotiate and/or reject the particular understandings, historical interpretations, and theorizations' (Tejada, 2008, p 29) of their programme. As such, they are encouraged to assert opinions, wonder and ask questions, listen to their classmates' views, uncover complexity, and relate academic theories to their own personal lives. At the same time, they are learning the conventions and expectations of their assessments and realizing that these approaches are not mutually exclusive.

One of the more substantial embedding projects is integrating decolonizing approaches into three guest lectures on the first-year core module '21st Century Legal Skills' in the Department of Law at Goldsmiths. These classes aim to develop critical reading and writing skills within the subject of law. They refer to ideas and assessments from other core modules, but also involve discussing attitudes, assumptions, motivations, and values related to their theoretical and practical contexts. Rather than focusing on traditional legal texts, they instead use decolonizing texts to deconstruct moral, ethical, and epistemological positions that underpin legal research and study. For example, the critical reading class begins with a discussion based on students' own backgrounds and experiences. They are initially asked to explain what the law is, who benefits from it, and who is harmed by it, generating ideas about the prevention of harm, relationships between authority and agency, the regulation and enforcement of behaviour, and the imposition of a universal moral and ethical order on disparate sociocultural practices, all of which they contextualize using examples from their own backgrounds. They then transition to reading an article that considers international law and human rights to be a continuity of colonial domination (Anghie, 2016). The students are prompted to link these ideas to their initial discussion, highlighting specific parallels and relevant examples. The subsequent lecture on critical writing strategies integrates these perspectives into teaching essay structure, consolidating the importance of deconstructing conceptual assumptions and applications in order to develop an informed, coherent, and original argument. This approach reflects the innovative nature of the programme and facilitates critical research and writing practices that normalize decolonial thinking at the very start of the degree programme. In a discipline that is often perceived as rigid, students are also able to reclaim a degree of intellectual agency by incorporating and reflecting on a wide range of academic and non-academic experiences, which constitutes an 'emergence of consciousness and critical intervention in reality' (Freire, 1997, p 62). This is a challenge that also pervades the development of curricula and reading lists.

'Liberate our Library'

The motivation for the selection of reading and visual materials for each DRM and embedded class is to facilitate decolonial critique by incorporating a wide range of types of resources, including poetry, artwork, renderings of maps, personal narratives, and academic theorizing. These choices reflect the desire to incorporate and validate modes of communication and voices that are traditionally excluded from the classroom due to predetermined perceptions of what and who constitute legitimate academic research. Linda Tuhiwai Smith (2012, p 37) explains that, '[w]hen I read texts ... I frequently have to orientate myself to a text world in which the centre of academic knowledge is either in Britain, the United States or Western Europe; in which words such as "we", "us", "our", "I" actually exclude me'. This is an experience shared by many students and academics alike (Gabriel and Tate, 2017), and is a key focus of the National Union of Students' (NUS) aim to 'Liberate my Degree' (UUK and NUS, 2019). Decolonial thinking offers counternarratives whose point of origin is in previously colonized territories, including South Asia, Africa, and South America, presenting the possibility of multiple possible narratives based on locally constructed and validated meanings, which are equally legitimate ways of being in and understanding the world. For these reasons, all materials that are selected for each class are produced by people whose 'site of enunciation' (Mignolo, 2011), or situated knowledge, is in the global South. This inclusive representation confronts the supposed truth-telling power of curricula that are based almost entirely in the global North.

Finding appropriate and accessible readings for DRM classes has been a significant challenge, in part because non-Eurocentric theories, perspectives, and experiences do not form a substantial part of most curricula in the Western world, and may indeed not be readily available through libraries or their online resource subscriptions. To begin remediating these deficits, endemic in almost every department at Goldsmiths (Akel, 2019), we established a working group called 'Liberate our Library' in June 2018. The objectives of this group attend to both the physical and intellectual organization of knowledge in the university by drawing on the expertise of a wide range of roles. The EAP lecturer convenes the DRM class series, focusing on pedagogical and methodological decolonization. Subject librarians facilitate Resistance Researching workshops, which interrogate how resources are classified, organized, and accessed in the library. The Discovery librarian has dedicated a separate budget to expanding the availability of decolonizing resources, and actively encourages students and members of staff to make suggestions for purchases. The Reading List librarian develops interactive reading lists, as they do for degree modules, which collate and provide links to decolonizing resources. The Systems and Digital Assets Team has added tags to the library's online catalogue search function, meaning that students can explicitly search for decolonizing resources just as they search for other resources related to their discipline. The Student Union Liberation Officer advocates particular actions on behalf of students. Together, these efforts offer an intervention into how epistemological presumptions and precedent impact on the ways in which students access and interact with representations of knowledge.

Conclusion

Developing communities of practice is essential to advancing decolonizing efforts. There is demand and space for underpinning the deconstruction and reconstruction of disciplinary foundations with practical and embedded decolonizing research strategies. The reach and impact of the DRM project can be extended by offering training to academic members of staff. These trainings focus on three key areas:

- What is happening in the classroom with regard to what and who are represented and discussed in lectures and seminars, and in what ways.
- Rethinking the foundations of disciplines, including the concepts, theories, and themes of reading lists. This also explores what is deemed alternative or 'Other' in relation to what is considered core or essential, and how this reinforces and perpetuates disciplinary, institutional, and colonial hierarchies of legitimacy.
- Encouraging decolonial critique in independent research, including developing activities which integrate not only disciplinary conventions of academic research but also individualized and decolonizing contexts and purposes.

In these ways, the responsibility for the prioritization and implementation of decolonizing efforts can be shared more equitably and can thus be cascaded to all students more effectively.

Treating research, curricular, and pedagogical agency as processes enables an analysis of institutional interactions that accounts for the discursive actions and power structures that comprise and maintain the HE institution. Analysing interactional production in this way can highlight the methods that are used to 'demonstrate complicity with, negotiate or resist institutional agendas' (Benwell and Stokoe, 2006, p 89). The DRM project involves a number of different and developing initiatives that encourage and enable Goldsmiths' students and staff to resist the structures of power that naturalize and enact a Eurocentric research paradigm. In the DRM module, a space is offered in which participants can isolate, articulate, and reconceptualize the foundations of academic theorizing, discussions, and writing by incorporating both personal and decolonizing experiences and perspectives. Engagement with diverse opinions and perspectives on multiple topics facilitates experiential and interdisciplinary contributions which enhance both learning and teaching. Decolonial critique is encouraged through both the design of each class and the supplementary exercises that facilitate students' ability to independently link decolonial critique to their own research interests. Embedding decolonizing perspectives with academic skills and module content integrates this critique into the fulfilment of assessment expectations. Collaborations with students and staff in different roles merge previously siloed individual streams of work in order to offer strategic and coherent goal-oriented practices. The DRM project reconsiders classifications of knowledge, reimagines social identities and relationships, and destabilizes the racial, ethnic, and cultural hierarchies that are built into the basic assumptions of research practices. This is the purpose of HE: a means by which new knowledges and ways of thinking are constructed, rather than a means by which existing knowledges are perpetuated and reified. Disrupting the organization of systems is pivotal, including the structure of curricula, the expectations and dynamics of classroom interactions, and the ways in which research is designed and validated. By doing so, decolonizing approaches to research, curricula, and pedagogy can move toward becoming normalized as a central and expected feature of the student experience, rather than remaining an optional, peripheral extra.

References

Ahmed, Sara (2012) *On Being Included: Racism and Diversity in Institutional Life*. London: Duke University Press.

Akel, Sofia (2019) *Insider-Outsider: The Role of Race in Shaping the Experiences of Black and Minority Ethnic Students*. London: Goldsmiths.

Anghie, Antony (2016) 'Imperialism and international legal theory', in Anne Orford and Florian Hoffman (eds) *The Oxford Handbook of the Theory of International Law*. Oxford: Oxford University Press, pp 1–18.

Anzaldua, Gloria (2012) *Borderlands/La Frontera: The New Mestiza* (2nd edn). San Francisco: Aunt Lute Books.

Baker, Michael (2012) 'Decolonial education: meanings, contexts and possibilities', in *Interpreting, Researching and Transforming Colonial/Imperial Legacies in Education*, American Educational Studies Association, Annual Conference Seattle. [online] Available from: https://bit.ly/3stvPTN [accessed 22 November 2019].

Balibar, Etienne (2004) *We, the People of Europe: Reflections on Transnational Citizenship*. Oxford: Princeton University Press.

Battiste, Marie and Henderson, James Youngblood (2009) 'Naturalizing indigenous knowledge in Eurocentric education', *Canadian Journal of Native Education*, 32(1): 5–18.

Benwell, Bethan and Stokoe, Elizabeth (2006) *Discourse and Identity*. Edinburgh: Edinburgh University Press.

Brown, Wendy (2006) *Regulating Aversion: Tolerance in the Age of Identity and Empire*. Princeton, NJ: Princeton University Press.

Chun, Christian (2015) *Power and Meaning Making in an EAP Classroom: Engaging with the Everyday*. Bristol: Multilingual Matters.

Datta, Ranjan (2018) 'Decolonizing both researcher and research and its effectiveness in indigenous research', *Research Ethics*, 14(2): 1–24.

de Sousa Santos, Boaventura (2007) *Another Knowledge is Possible*. London: Verso.

Dussel, Enrique (1995) *The Invention of the Americas: Eclipse of 'the Other' and the Myth of Modernity*. New York: Continuum.

Freire, Paolo (1997) *Pedagogy of the Oppressed*. New York: Continuum.

Gabriel, Deborah and Tate, Shirley Ann (eds) (2017) *Inside the Ivory Tower: Narratives of Women of Colour Surviving and Thriving in British Academia*. London: Trentham.

Gee, John Paul (1996) *Social Linguistics and Literacies: Ideology in Discourses* (2nd edn). London: Taylor and Francis.

Goldsmiths (2018) 'Strategic plan'. [online] Available from: https://bit.ly/3lWMzR5 [accessed 24 November 2018].

Grosfoguel, Ramon (2007) 'The epistemic decolonial turn', *Cultural Studies*, 21: 2–3, 211–223.

Hall, Stuart and Gieben, Bram (eds) (1992) *Formations of Modernity*. Cambridge: Polity.

hooks, bell (1994) *Teaching to Transgress: Education as the Practice of Freedom*. London: Routledge.

Li, Yulong (2020) *Educational Change amongst English Language College Teachers in China*. Singapore: Springer.

Luckett, Kathy, and Shay, Suellen (2020) 'Reframing the curriculum: a transformative approach', *Critical Studies in Education*, 61(1): 50–65.

Meneley, Anne and Young, Donna (eds) (2005) *Auto-enthnographies: The Anthropology of Academic Practices*. Ontario, Canada: Broadview.

Meneses, Maria Paula (2016) 'Images outside the mirror: Mozambique and Portugal in world history', in Antonia Darder, Peter Mayo, and Joao Paraskeve (eds) *International Critical Pedagogy Reader*. London: Routledge, pp 118–128.

Mignolo, Walter (2011) 'Geopolitics of sensing and knowing: On (de) coloniality, border thinking and epistemic disobedience', *Postcolonial Studies*, 14(3): 273–283.

Mignolo, Walter and Tlostanova, Madina (2016) 'Theorizing from the borders', in Antonia Darder, Peter Mayo, and Joao Paraskeve (eds) *International Critical Pedagogy Reader*. London: Routledge, pp 129–135.

Ngũgĩ, wa Thiong'o (1986) *Decolonising the Mind: The Politics of Language in African Literature*. Suffolk: James Currey.

Regan, Paulette (2010) *Unsettling the Settler Within: Indian Residential Schools, Truth Telling, and Reconciliation in Canada*. Vancouver: University of British Columbia Press.

Ritchard, Ron, Church, Mark, and Morrison, Karin (2011) *Making Thinking Visible: How to Promote Engagement, Understanding and Independence for all Learners*. Cambridge, MA: Harvard University Press.

Slimani, Assia (2001) 'Evaluation of classroom interaction', in Christopher Candlin and Neil Mercer (eds) *English Language Teaching in its Social Context*. London: Routledge, pp 287–305.

Springgay, Stephanie (2011) 'The ethico-aesthetics of affect and a sensational pedagogy', *Journal of the Canadian Association for Curriculum Studies*, 9(1): 66–82.

Takacs, David (2002) 'Pedagogies for social change', *Social Justice*, 29(4): 168–181.

Tejada, Carlos (2008 'Dancing with the dilemmas of a decolonizing pedagogy', *Radical History Review*, 102: 27–31.

Tuhiwai Smith, Linda (2012) *Decolonizing Methodologies: Research and Indigenous Peoples*. London: Zed Books.

Universities UK (UUK) and National Union of Students (NUS) (2019) *Black and Minority Ethnic Student Attainment at UK Universities:#Closing the Gap*. [online] Available from: https://bit.ly/3rr010A [accessed 11 November 2019].

9

Towards an Intersectional Feminist Pedagogy of Gender-Based Violence

Denise Buiten, Ellen Finlay, and Rosemary Hancock

Denise: Students were pouring out the door of my first-year sociology class after a lecture on gender-based violence. A soft-spoken female student approached me, her male friend lingering behind her near the exit. Glancing back at him, she gingerly asked me: 'We were wondering, what about male victims of domestic violence? You barely spoke of them, but aren't they victims too?'

This was not the first time I had encountered this question. Many of the student essays I read on gender-based violence have, over the years, raised questions about the silence around male victims. Some more confident students had raised their hands in class to ask this question directly. What struck me in this instance, however, were two things.

First, neither of the students had felt comfortable raising the question in our two-hour class, and the male student seemed particularly reluctant to articulate the question himself. I wondered how many other students in that class left with similar questions gone unasked, and how those questions might have tugged uncomfortably at – or even undermined – their perception of the relevance of feminist theories of violence I presented. Had students left feeling resistant to a gendered account of violence because of this perceived silence? Were there male students with experiences of domestic or sexual violence who left with their experiences unaccounted for? What was the cost of not explicitly addressing these experiences, and, if I had, would I have pulled focus from the important question of gendered violence against women?

Second, it struck me that, of all the 'what about' questions I receive when teaching gendered violence, raising the experiences of male victims is the most common. Far less frequently, for example, am I asked about the unique experiences of non-binary or transgender people, people living with disabilities, or racial minorities. The pattern in 'what about' questions has always reflected the dynamics and make-up of my classroom: male students are present in numbers that command a symbolic quorum to make questions about male experience speakable – even if tentatively. Other minority students in the classroom do not.

Introduction

All three authors, who teach units on gender-based violence (GBV) in a social justice programme at an Australian university, have experienced similar questions and concerns to those expressed in Denise's story. Her account exemplifies three concerns regarding diversity, inclusive learning, and the teaching of GBV which we aim to address in this chapter. These are: student resistance to the importance of gender in shaping violence; the silences (re)produced by non-intersectional accounts of violence; and the tendency for classrooms to reproduce their own social arrangement and power relations, thus constructing knowledge in hierarchical and exclusive ways.

Our argument is that, although it presents challenges, teaching GBV through an intersectional feminist approach is the best method to address the issues raised in Denise's account. Such an approach is central to the way that we, as university teachers, try to 'do diversity' within our classrooms. By speaking to a wider range of student experiences, we can create a classroom that is more inclusive and reflective of diversity.

Further, classrooms are a space of knowledge (re)production, where the existing silences and knowledge hierarchies around GBV make some forms of violence more visible than others. Interrogating these silences and hierarchies is central to producing more inclusive understandings of violence. This can shape students' attitudes and actions far beyond the classroom. We are deeply influenced in this work by critical and transformative pedagogies, by scholars such as Freire (1970), Shor (Shor and Freire, 1987), and hooks (1994), who position the classroom as a political space where society is either reproduced or transformed. In the context of teaching GBV, effective use of critical and transformative pedagogy means that our classes are not simply about imparting knowledge of GBV. They become 'a vehicle for emancipation' (Cowden and Singh, 2013) from the social structures and norms that *cause* GBV.

It is important to outline what it means – and does not mean – to include a feminist intersectional lens in learning and teaching on GBV. First, as we will show, an intersectional lens contributes to understanding the complex interplay of social forces and identities in constituting gendered violence. This lens does not mean the silencing of gender as a key component of various forms of violence, nor does it challenge the systemic and patterned forms of violence that target women. Rather, it 'recognises that women have an elevated risk of victimisation when structural and institutional forms of violence overlap' (Lange and Young, 2019, p 12). An intersectional feminist approach can also account for violence against men and boys, but in a way that understands masculinity as socially contingent, hierarchically co-constituted by other social vectors, and operating within a patriarchal and hegemonic context (Connell and Messerschmidt, 2005). An intersectional feminist lens also enables an examination of the structural conditions that construct vulnerabilities to violence, supporting its perpetration and the extent to which it is subject to impunity (Lange and Young, 2019). It further considers the ways that sexual violence reproduces other forms of inequality (Armstrong et al, 2018). It is a lens, therefore, that is to be applied to all aspects of GBV.

In the remainder of this chapter, we first examine the three key issues already identified regarding the teaching of GBV. We then consider some key areas that exemplify the importance of intersectionality to teaching GBV: race and class; sexuality; and violence against men. This is not to suggest that these areas exhaust the range of intersections relevant to GBV; on the contrary, various others such as (dis)ability and age are of central importance. For the sake of brevity, we have selected only three examples that we believe highlight the theoretical and pedagogical urgency of adopting an intersectional feminist approach to teaching and learning in this space. After outlining some of the risks and challenges of teaching GBV through a feminist intersectional lens, we propose some key principles to guide the implementation of this approach in the classroom.

Beyond resistance, towards inclusion

Gendered understandings of sexual and domestic violence may have a decades-long heritage in feminism, but they have become prominent in mainstream public, media, and policy discourse only since 2006 (Murray and Powell, 2009; Hawley et al, 2018). In Australia, as elsewhere, there is a great deal of resistance to reframing violence as gendered (Murray and Powell, 2009; Hawley et al, 2018). We see this resistance in our classrooms when we teach feminist accounts of GBV. A structural account of GBV can be jarring and uncomfortable for both male and female students, particularly when the evidence of these patterns does not reflect students' personal experiences of violence (Lange and Young, 2019). It may also challenge particular students to confront difficult questions about their own positionality in relation to patriarchal power – an experience that can be deeply discomforting, even threatening. The presence of both an individualised, psychologically focused discourse of violence and trauma (Lange and Young, 2019) and a tendency among some students to eschew identity politics in favour of individualism (McQueeny, 2016) encourages many students to resist structural accounts of GBV. This fuels exceptionalism and 'what-aboutism' in our classrooms.

Resistance to gendered accounts of violence also comes from another quarter; some students are dissatisfied by a perceived reductionism in the representation of gender in the teaching of GBV. Some gendered accounts of violence may reduce gender relations to a two-dimensional caricature: between homogenised 'men' and 'women', with male dangerousness and female vulnerability the defining feature (Hollander, 2001). These accounts fail to recognise both the varied and complex gendered experiences of violence and students' own 'expanded vocabularies of gender identity/expression' (Bragg et al, 2018, p 420). As contemporary feminism has become increasingly connected to a broader intersectional agenda (Evans, 2016; McQueeny, 2016), so theories of GBV need to be sufficiently nuanced to manage complexity and be relevant to the experiences of young people.

We argue that using an intersectional feminist approach to teaching GBV means both that students will be more likely to deeply engage with the topic in class and that their learning will also better reflect the current state of scholarship on GBV. The primacy of binary, homogenising conceptualisations of violence as by men against women (Sokoloff and Dupont, 2005) does not reflect the growing body of research that shows how gender is central to many forms of violence, but in ways that are varied, complex, and overlap with a range of social vectors such as sexuality, race, class, or (dis)ability. For example, the ground-breaking work of Crenshaw (1991) and Hill Collins (1993) points to the ways that interlocking social categories and power systems are implicated in how violence is produced and received. Intersectionality also helps us to understand the way masculinity is intertwined with other social categories. It highlights the impact this has on male violence (for example, Salo, 2006; Buiten and Naidoo, 2016).

This more nuanced portrayal of GBV can speak to a wider range of student experiences, while creating a classroom that is responsive to real diversity, both among students and in the world beyond the classroom. Reductive explanations of GBV may silence and exclude the experiences of diverse students. If we are to take seriously the claim that the classroom can be a space for social transformation, then the classroom must itself prefiguratively model recognition and inclusion of diversity.

In addition to creating a more inclusive experience for those within the classroom, it is important to consider pedagogies in terms of their broader transformative potential. Higher education classrooms are sites of knowledge (re)production, often in ways with consequences for the application of knowledge beyond the classroom. Critical and transformative pedagogies that model diversity and inclusion are therefore not only about creating transformative classrooms, but about harnessing education towards a more inclusive and diverse world. In our predominantly white, middle-class Australian university, it is noteworthy that 'what about' questions arise more regularly in respect to more privileged and represented identities present in the classroom, usually manifesting in the question 'what about men?' Far less frequently will students raise the experiences of gender-diverse, elderly, or disabled people. This reflects the tendency for classrooms to engage with and reproduce knowledge that mirrors the experiences and frames of reference of the dominant group in the classroom. With this in mind, the following three sections outline a research-informed case for why we should recognise intersectionality as central to constituting GBV.

The intersectional nature of gender-based violence

This section will examine three key areas that call attention to the significance of intersectionality for understanding GBV. As outlined earlier, there are many other social vectors of significance to GBV; the discussion here is not exhaustive but is intended to demonstrate the imperative of considering interlocking social forces in constructing gendered violence.

Race, class, and gender-based violence

Indigenous, third world, and black feminists have shown the tendency of western feminisms to claim universality, despite presenting the world from their own, partial perspectives (for example hooks, 1984, 1989; Mohanty, 1988; Moreton-Robinson, 2000). This is also the case for feminist writing on GBV.

> The assumed race and class neutrality [of anti-gender-based violence movements] led to the erasure of low-income women and women of colour from the dominant view … it has divorced racism from sexism … and invited a discourse regarding gender violence without attention to the class dimensions of patriarchy and white domination. (Richie, 2000, p 1135)

When constituted so reductively, the study of gender can overlook important systemic racialised and classed factors that manifest specific types of GBV. For instance, evidence suggests that violence against women disproportionately affects women in low-income areas and communities (Sokolof and Dupont, 2005; Phipps, 2009). Rather than GBV being absent from higher-income communities, poverty and socioeconomic status creates specific vulnerabilities to violence for women, including economic dependencies, resource availability, and level of exposure to violent crime (Humphreys, 2007). Socioeconomic status shapes attitudes towards women's worth and safety in ways that put them at increased risk. De Alba (2010), for example, has drawn connections between the devaluation of poor women's labour in Mexico under free trade and high levels of GBV and impunity. Because social class is linked to notions of respectability, middle-class women can be constructed as more believable, 'ideal' victims, and middle-class perpetrators as less likely to receive convictions or heavy sentences (Crenshaw, 1991; Phipps, 2009). Class dynamics also contribute to violence against middle- and upper-class women, with idealised gender norms that are part of performing class discouraging women from speaking out about violence, or encouraging economic dependency (Shows and Gerstel, 2009). Privileged entitlement can also act as social protection for perpetrators (Humphreys, 2007). Economic mobility, such as women transitioning into employment or increasing their earning capacity, can also lead to spikes in GBV (see, for example, Naved and Persson, 2005; Krishnan et al, 2010; Cao et al, 2014). When economic power is constructed as masculine and desirable, but is eroding or inaccessible for some men, violence represents opportunities to reinforce gendered dominance (for example, Moffett, 2006; Salo, 2006).

For women of colour, GBV is uniquely shaped by experiences of racism and stereotypes about racial and ethnic communities (Humphries, 2007). For example, stereotypes of Asian women as hyper-feminine (Pyke and Johnson, 2003) or hyper-sexualised and exotic (Woan, 2008) contribute to their sexual fetishisation and exploitation. Assumptions about, and othering representations of, African women's bodies have a long history of inflicting harm on black women (Lewis, 2011). This includes assumptions about black women's sexual 'excess' and the ways racism and misogyny intersect to render black women as objects for seizure by white patriarchy (Lewis, 2011).

Class and race compound to produce GBV in a way that cannot be fully comprehended when examined through discrete categories. In South Africa, for example, high levels of GBV can be understood only at the intersection of multiple social forces. British colonisation and apartheid rendered violence an integral part of the social landscape, created racialised economic inequalities, and intersected with the patriarchal structures of both white and black societies to create conditions for rates of GBV among the highest in the world (Gqola, 2007).

Sexuality and gender-based violence

In conventional narratives, heterosexuality is 'the rubric through which' GBV is understood (Harris, 2017, p 274). Queer sexuality and gender, and queer peoples' experiences of violence, complicate these conventional narratives and explanatory frameworks, and challenge who can be subjected to, or perpetrate, GBV. For example, people who do not conform to binary gender norms are subject to violence, even if it does not sit neatly within heterosexist accounts. Judith Butler (2007) describes a young man with a feminine walking style who was thrown off a bridge by a group of men because of his femininity; although both the victim and the perpetrators were men, the violence is nonetheless gendered, linked to the victim's failure to conform to normative masculinity. Yet, where violence does not follow the heterosexual 'script' as in this example, it may be treated as instances of homophobia and divorced from strategies to tackle GBV (Haynes and DeShong, 2017).

Violence also occurs within queer relationships (Ristock, 2002), with some research suggesting that intimate partner violence within queer relationships may be an outcome of 'minority stress' (Dank et al, 2014; Whitton et al, 2019). In these cases, gender is implicated within violence, but constituted through a complex network of gendered norms, structures, and power relations rather than by virtue of membership in a binary gender category. Violence within relationships consisting of two women can confound legislation and policy, which are often structured in ways that make 'women's violence against other women … barely intelligible' (Harris, 2017, p 273). An intersectional approach to GBV can challenge these silences around who can be subject to violence, and the diverse ways in which violence can be gendered.

The experiences of gender nonconforming, trans, and intersex people also bring our attention to institutional harms obscured by narrow framings of GBV. For example, trans people may receive substandard healthcare (Lanham et al, 2019), a violence that may not be direct and interpersonal but that exemplifies structural violence on the basis of gender (nonconformity). Seen through this prism, GBV 'also references the structures and discourses that enable those acts' (Harris and Hanchey, 2014, p 323).

Heterosexist narratives of GBV that essentialise women as primarily passive or submissive objects of desire and men as dominant and sexually aggressive can normalise acts of GBV. In the long -run, essentialisms legitimise rape and violence because 'these everyday taken-for-granted normative forms of heterosexuality work as the cultural scaffolding of rape' (Gavey, 2013, p 2). When constructed in binary terms 'gender' as a category of analysis can in this way re-essentialise GBV. Accounting for diverse gendered and sexual and experiences therefore forms part of the process of dismantling the naturalised assumptions that undergird many forms of violence. It also has implications for the affective dimensions of education, particularly for gender nonconforming students in our classrooms. We need to ensure that knowledge (re)produced in this space does not silence or minimise violence against queer people.

Violence against men and the importance of intersectionality

Feminist accounts of GBV have typically excluded violence against men in their analyses (Javaid, 2016). While feminist theories have the capacity to account for gendered forms of violence against men, such violence has not received much scholarly attention to date. This is, in many respects, for good reason. Challenging both the historical silencing of women's experiences and the privileging of men's experiences has been central to the feminist movement. By focusing on violence against women in its myriad forms, early feminist theorists of GBV such as Brownmiller (1976), MacKinnon (1979), and Kelly (1988) established violence as distinctly gendered and showed the connections between overt physical violence and more insidious everyday violations and gender norms. However, omitting men's experiences entirely is problematic, both in terms of fuelling resistance to (and misunderstandings of) feminist accounts of GBV and in terms of excluding the diverse experiences of violence among males – including trans men, gay men, men in war zones, children, and more (for example Carpenter, 2006; True, 2010; Javaid, 2017). Further, it silences how gender norms and homophobia operate to deny, and make less visible, the rape of men (see, for example, Gear, 2007).

Hegemonic masculinity is in many senses aspirational and inaccessible to most men (Connell, 1995; Connell and Messerschmidt, 2005); it does not reflect the complex experiences of most boys and men (Paechter, 2019). When examined from an intersectional perspective, a range of social vectors constitute experiences of masculinity and position men and boys differentially in respect to GBV along dimensions from class, race, and sexuality to expressions of femininity. This is not to suggest that masculinity is not dominant or connected to power in cultural or structural terms; instead, it is to suggest that how and in what contexts masculinity is connected to power is complex and intersectional.

Providing a sociological account that retains a feminist lens while discussing men and boys' experiences of GBV in the classroom can have a number of benefits. Centring gendered theorisations of patriarchy in intersectional terms 'enables for a distinction between individual men on the one hand, and the structures of hegemony on the other' (Javaid, 2016, p 285). It reconfigures male supremacy as a structural condition and positions it as the enemy, rather than framing male-committed violence as innate and inevitable (Javaid, 2016). This shifts the classroom conversation to the social drivers of violence.

Challenges in teaching a feminist intersectional account of gender-based violence

As outlined earlier, an intersectional feminist approach to teaching GBV is considered theoretically, pragmatically, and ethically important. However, such an approach does present some challenges.

Individualising

The tremendous variety of experiences of GBV that are integral to an intersectional feminist account is taken, by some students, as evidence of *individual* rather than *structural* causes. Challenging homogenised accounts of violence, and drawing attention to a range of experiences, often elicits responses such as 'it really depends on the individual' or 'it just shows that everyone is different and has their own experiences'. This is part of an increasingly neoliberal discourse that focuses on individual responsibilities over collective ones (Coker, 2016). One of the challenges of teaching in this way is to account for diversity and complexity while maintaining a structural, feminist-informed framework of analysis.

Othering

Teaching GBV from an intersectional perspective requires us to explore a diverse range of subjectivities and experiences, which can run the risk of 'othering' and voyeurism of marginalised social groups. Given that students (and teachers) bring a range of implicit frames regarding violence and social categories to the classroom, and that our middle-class Australian student body sometimes lacks diversity, it is possible that intersectional analyses can awaken and give space to these implicit frames and stereotypes as has been found in other contexts (Bertram and Crowley, 2012). A privileged classed and racialised feminist lens can (re)construct stereotypes of an 'other' – defined in opposition to an (assumed) liberated white first-world self (Mohanty, 1988). When case studies are geographically or culturally distant from students' own experiences, they may reductively situate the cause and culpability for violence in 'culture', obscuring questions of power connected to gendered historical, colonial, and economic relations (Weissman, 2010). Often, when examining GBV in their own experience or in the dominant culture, 'culture' is not easily problematised (Sokoloff and Dupont, 2005); this results in reinscribing such cultures in neutral terms. Representations of violence against gender and sexual minorities can also be sensationalised and 'invite public voyeurism' (Haynes and DeShong, 2017, p 115), thus constituting a second kind of violence against survivor-victims, and framing them as deviant and perpetuating discrimination and violence towards queer people. The second key challenge we have found, therefore, is to include diverse narratives of violence in a way that does not feed othering or voyeuristic practices.

Complexity, depth, and time

University teaching is constrained by time: classes run for two or three hours per week, teachers may be on precarious contracts, students may be juggling study with work, and only one or two weeks may be allocated to teach GBV in some courses. Given that many students come to university with little knowledge of structural analyses of gender and power, care and attention is required to unpack violence in intersectional terms. McQueeny (2016, p 1466), for example, proposes a layered approached to teaching GBV with an intersectional lens, 'focusing on one system at a time, [and] building up a framework that incorporates the simultaneity of privileges and oppressions'. It can be difficult to teach GBV in a way that systematically addresses complexity and nuance, is adequately sensitive to the emotionally demanding nature of the topic, and still fits within the constraints of a standard university course.

Principles for an intersectional feminist approach to gender-based violence

In response to these challenges we suggest, as a starting point, some key principles for teaching gender-based violence through an intersectional feminist lens.

Model positive diversity

Diversity of experiences needs to be included, being mindful of the ways in which they are presented. This would include case studies that both mirror the social identities of those within the class and go beyond them in non-judgemental and non-voyeuristic ways. Part of achieving this is to model and draw attention to the need for inclusive language and concepts – for example, avoiding 'us' and 'them' language. Educators can also remind students that they do not know the full range of experiences and identities of other class members, modelling talking about diverse experiences of violence in a way that does not assume their otherness. Further, incorporating diverse texts and authors in class, avoiding a reliance only on elite-authored texts, is part of positively modelling diversity.

Focus on structure

Placing structure at the centre of analysis also helps to avoid othering and social voyeurism, encouraging students to identify 'structural inequalities that may sustain or inform experiences of abuse' (Coker, 2016, p 1429). A *structural* intersectional framework is also important to resist neoliberal tendencies towards individualisation (Coker, 2016). *Diversity* of experiences should be accounted for alongside *patterns* that help to signal the social and structural causes.

Remember privilege

Intersectionality as a theory accounts for both marginalisation *and* privilege. It must not be a lens applied only to marginalised groups or wielded as a tool for voyeurism. Narratives and case studies of violence experienced from within the dominant culture therefore need to be interrogated with the same attention to intersectional factors, for example by considering the role of 'middle-class' values and structures in supporting GBV. Further, intersectionality includes interrogating how privilege operates to render particular forms of violence more/less visible, to legitimise the experiences of some survivors over others, or to foster impunity to violence.

Make a sustained commitment

A feminist intersectional pedagogy requires commitment and time. Establishing a robust structural and intersectional lens is not something that can be achieved in one or two classes. Instead, it something that requires an integrated, whole-of-curriculum approach, and sustained commitment to build over time.

Create a supportive environment

It is essential to encourage a classroom environment that promotes critical dialogue, while providing a supportive and safe space for students. Drawing on Friere, Wagner (2005) highlights that in anti-racist pedagogies the aim is not to master the critique of racism and whiteness but to encourage students to move beyond comfort, towards thinking and speaking in terms that create risk and seal collaborative learning. This means creating a classroom space in which students feel safe to ask the burning questions, but also feel secure enough to have their assumptions challenged. As the story at the beginning of this chapter shows, it is only when students and teachers can ask the difficult questions and have the difficult discussions that a feminist understanding of gender will be of use and value to all students in the classroom and beyond.

References

Armstrong, Elizabeth A., Gleckman-Krut, Miriam, and Johnson, Lanora (2018) 'Silence, power, and inequality: An intersectional approach to sexual violence', *Annual Review of Sociology*, 44: 99–122.

Bertram, Corrine C., and Crowley, M. Sue (2012) 'Teaching about sexual violence in higher education: Moving from concern to conscious resistance', *Frontiers: Journal of Women's Studies*, 33(1): 63–82.

Bragg, Sara, Renold, Emma, Ringrose, Jessica, and Jackson, Carolyn (2018) '"More than boy, girl, male, female": Exploring young people's views on gender diversity within and beyond school contexts', *Sex Education*, 18(4): 420–434.

Brownmiller, Susan (1976) *Against Our Will: Men, Women and Rape*. Harmondsworth: Penguin.

Buiten, Denise, and Naidoo, Kammila (2016) 'Framing the problem of rape in South Africa: Gender, race, class and state histories', *Current Sociology*, 64(4): 535–550.

Butler, Judith (2007) *Phylosophe* [Video File]. [online] Available from: https://bit.ly/3r3q6Tq [accessed 20 March 2021].

Cao, Yu-Ping, Yang, Shi-Chang, Wang, Guo-Qiang, and Zhang, Ya-Lin (2014) 'Sociodemographic characteristics of domestic violence in China: A population case-control study', *Journal of Interpersonal Violence*, 29(4): 683–706.

Carpenter, R. Charli (2006) 'Recognizing gender-based violence against civilian men and boys in conflict situations', *Security Dialogue*, 37(1): 83–103.

Coker, Donna (2016) 'Domestic violence and social justice: A structural intersectional framework for teaching about domestic violence', *Violence Against Women*, 22(12): 1426–1437.

Connell, Raewyn W. (1995) *Gender and Power*. Cambridge: Polity Press.

Connell, Raewyn W., and Messerschmidt, James W. (2005) 'Hegemonic masculinity: Rethinking the concept', *Gender and Society*, 19(6): 829–859.

Cowden, Stephen, and Singh, Gurnam (2013) *Acts of Knowing: Critical Pedagogy In, Against and Beyond the University*. London: Bloomsbury.

Crenshaw, Kimberlé W. (1991) 'Mapping the margins: Intersectionality, identity politics, and violence against women of color', *Stanford Law Review*, 43(6): 1241–1299.

Dank, Meredith, Lachman, Pamela, Zweig, Janine M., Yahner, Jennifer (2014) 'Dating violence experiences of lesbian, gay, bisexual, and transgender youth', *Journal of Youth and Adolescence*, 43(5): 846–857.

de Alba, Alicia Gaspar (2010) 'Poor brown female: The miller's compensation for "free" trade', in Alicia Gaspar de Alba and Georgina Guzmane (eds) *Making a Killing: Femicide, Free Trade, and la Frontera*. Austin: University of Texas, pp 63–94.

Evans, Elizabeth (2016) 'What makes a (third) wave? How and why the third-wave narrative works for contemporary feminists', *International Feminist Journal of Politics*, 18(3): 409–428.

Freire, Paulo (1970) *Pedagogy of the Oppressed*. New York: Herder and Herder.

Gavey, Nicola (2013) *Just Sex? The Cultural Scaffolding of Rape*. New York: Routledge.

Gear, Sasha (2007) 'Behind the bars of masculinity: Male rape and homophobia in and about South African men's prisons', *Sexualities*, 10(2): 209–227.

Gqola, Pumla Dindeo (2007) 'How the "cult of femininity" and violent masculinities support endemic gender-based violence in contemporary South Africa', *African Identities*, 5(1): 111–124.

Harris, Kate Lockwood (2017) 'Re-situating organizational knowledge: Violence, intersectionality and the privilege of partial perspective', *Human Relations*, 70(3): 262–285.

Harris, Kate Lockwood, and Hanchey, Jenna N. (2014) '(De)stabilizing sexual violence discourse: Masculinization of victimhood, organizational blame, and liable imperialism', *Communication and Critical/Cultural Studies*, 11(4): 322–341.

Hawley, Erin, Clifford, Katrina, and Konkes, Claire (2018) 'The "Rosie Batty effect" and the framing of family violence in Australian news media', *Journalism Studies*, 19(15): 2304–2323.

Haynes, Tonya, and DeShong, Hallman A.F. (2017) 'Queering feminist approaches to gender-based violence in the anglophone Caribbean', *Social and Economic Studies*, 66(1): 105–131.

Hill Collins, Patricia (1993) 'Toward a new vision: Race, class, and gender as categories of analysis and connection', *Race, Sex and Class*, 1(1): 25–45.

Hollander, Jocelyn A. (2001) 'Vulnerability and dangerousness: The construction of gender through conversation about violence', *Gender and Society*, 15(1): 83–109.

hooks, bell (1984) *Feminist Theory: From Margin to Centre*. Cambridge: South End Press.

hooks, bell (1989) *Talking Back: Thinking Feminist, Thinking Black*. Boston: South End Press.

hooks, bell (1994) *Teaching to Transgress: Education as the Practice of Freedom*. New York: Routledge.

Humphreys, Cathy (2007) 'A health inequalities perspective on violence against women', *Health and Social Care in the Community*, 15(2): 120–127.

Javaid, Aliraza (2016) 'Feminism, masculinity and male rape: Bringing male rape "out of the closet"', *Journal of Gender Studies*, 25(3): 283–293.

Javaid, Aliraza (2017) 'In the shadows: Making sense of gay male rape victims' silence, suffering, and invisibility', *International Journal of Sexual Health*, 29(4): 279–291.

Kelly, Liz (1988) *Surviving Sexual Violence*. Minneapolis: University of Minnesota Press.

Krishnan, Suneeta, Rocca, Corinne H., Hubbard, Alan E., Subbiah, Kalyani, Edmeades, Jeffrey, and Padian, Nancy (2010) 'Do changes in spousal employment status lead to domestic violence? Insights from a prospective study in Bangalore, India', *Social Science and Medicine*, 70(1): 136–143.

Lange, Elizabeth, and Young, Susan (2019) 'Gender-based violence as difficult knowledge: Pedagogies for rebalancing the masculine and the feminine', *International Journal of Lifelong Education*, 38(2): 301–326.

Lanham, Michele, Ridgeway, Kathleen, Dayton, Robyn, Castillo, Britany M., Brennan, Claire, Davis, Dirk A., Emmanuel, Dadrina, Morales, Giuliana. J., Cheririser, Clifford, Rodriguez, Brandy, Cooke, Juana, Santi, Karin, and Evens, Emily (2019) '"We're going to leave you for last, because of how you are": Transgender women's experiences of gender-based violence in healthcare, education, and police encounters in Latin America and the Caribbean', *Violence and Gender*, 6(1): 37–46.

Lewis, Desiree (2011) 'Representing African Sexualities', in Sylvia Tamale (ed) *African Sexualities: A Reader*. Cape Town: Pambazuka Press pp 199–216.

MacKinnon, Catherine A. (1979) *Sexual Harassment of Working Women: A Case of Sex Discrimination*. New Haven: Yale University Press.

McQueeney, Krista (2016) 'Teaching domestic violence in the new millennium: Intersectionality as framework for social change', *Violence Against Women,* 22(12): 1463–1475.

Moffett, Helen (2006) ' "These women, they force us to rape them": Rape as narrative of social control in post-apartheid South Africa', *Journal of Southern African Studies*, 32(1): 129–144.

Mohanty, Chandra Talpade (1988) 'Under western eyes: Feminist scholarship and colonial discourses', *Feminist Review*, 30: 61–88.

Moreton-Robinson, Aileen (2000) *Talkin' up to the White Woman: Aboriginal Women and Feminism*. St Lucia, Qld: University of Queensland Press.

Murray, Suellen, and Powell, Anastasia (2009) 'What's the problem? Australian public policy constructions of domestic and family violence', *Violence Against Women*, 15(5): 532–552.

Naved, Ruchira Tabassum, and Persson, Lars Ake (2005) 'Factors associated with spousal physical violence against women in Bangladesh', *Studies in Family Planning*, 36(4): 289–300.

Paechter, Carrie (2019) 'Where are the feminine boys? Interrogating the positions of feminised masculinities in research on gender and childhood', *Journal of Gender Studies*, 28(8): 906–917.

Phipps, Alison (2009) 'Rape and respectability: Ideas about sexual violence and social class', *Sociology*, 43(4): 667–683.

Pyke, Karen. D., and Johnson, Denise L. (2003) 'Asian American women and racialized femininities: "Doing" gender across cultural worlds', *Gender and Society*, 17(1): 33–53.

Richie, Beth E. (2000) 'A black feminist reflection on the antiviolence movement', *Signs*, 25(4): 1133–1137.

Ristock, Janice Lynn (2002) *No More Secrets: Violence in Lesbian Relationships*. New York: Routledge.

Salo, Elaine (2006) '"Mans is Ma Soe": Ganging practices in Manenburg, South Africa, and the ideologies of masculinity, gender and generational relations', in Edna G. Bay, and Donald L. Donham (eds) *States of Violence: Politics, Youth and Memory in Contemporary Africa*. Charlottesville: University of Virginia Press, pp 148–178.

Shor, Ira, and Frerie, Paulo (1987) *A Pedagogy for Liberation: Dialogues on Transforming Educators*. Massachusetts: Bergin and Garvey.

Shows, Carla, and Gerstel, Naomi (2009) 'Fathering, class, and gender: A comparison of physicians and emergency medical technicians', *Gender and Society*, 23(2): 161–187.

Sokoloff, Natalie J., and Dupont, Ida (2005) 'Domestic violence at the intersections of race, class, and gender: Challenges and contributions to understanding violence against marginalized women in diverse communities', *Violence Against Women*, 11(1): 38–64.

True, Jacqui (2010) 'The political economy of violence against women: A feminist international relations perspective', *Australian Feminist Law Journal*, 32(1): 39–59.

Wagner, Anne E. (2005) 'Unsettling the academy: Working through the challenges of anti-racist pedagogy', *Race Ethnicity and Education*, 8(3): 261–275.

Weissman, Deborah M. (2010) 'Global economics and their progenies: Theorizing femicide in context', in Rose-Linda Fregoso and Cynthia L. Bejarano (eds) *Terrorizing Women: Feminicide in the Américas*. Durham NC: Duke University Press, pp 225–242.

Whitton, Sarah W., Dyar, Christine, Mustanski, Brian, and Newcomb, Michael E. (2019) 'Intimate partner violence experiences of sexual and gender minority adolescents and young adults assigned female at birth', *Psychology of Women Quarterly*, 43(2): 232–249.

Woan, Sunny (2008) 'White sexual imperialism: A theory of Asian feminist jurisprudence', *Washington and Lee Journal of Civil Rights and Social Justice*, 14(2): 275–301.

PART III

Diversifying Research and Scholarship

10

How Would a World Sociology Think? Towards Intellectual Inclusion

James Spickard

It is no secret that sociology was born in early 19th-century Europe and assumed its present intellectual form in the mid-20th-century United States (US). It was a new science, intended to uncover the ways that society shapes human life. As Anthony Giddens (1976) noted, however, the early sociologists assumed, falsely, that Europe was the leading edge of world history. Marx, Durkheim, Weber, and others sought to understand the origins and consequences of industrialization, of the growth of capitalism, of increasing social inequality, and of the breakdown of traditional mores – all of which were European concerns. Giddens argued that much of this work "is an attempt to rethink the foundations of liberalism in conditions in which liberal individualism and its base in social theory, namely, utilitarian philosophy ... were manifestly inappropriate" (1976, pp 725–726). The founders thus concentrated their sociology on matters that explained their own situation. They underplayed the role of colonialism in European ascendance, and they took their new discipline's core ideas from their own culture.

Mainstream American sociologists, working later and in the context of growing US world dominance, assumed that these core ideas would explain the rest of the world. They saw history as the gradual 'Westernization' of traditional societies (Rostow, 1971), a process that involved intellectual as well as material development. Sociologists expected those societies' elites to discard their 'traditional' views of the world and assume 'modern' ones (Inkeles and Smith, 1974). Even those few who did not highlight industrialization and modernity, such as W.E.B. Du Bois, used European concepts to understand the world.[1]

Some sociological theorists have wrestled with newer ways to describe contemporary 'modernity': "late" (Giddens, 1991), "post" (Jameson, 1991), "liquid" (Bauman, 2000), "reflexive" (Beck et al, 1994), or other (Foucault, 1977). All, however, centre their attention on the global North. Even sociologists inspired by Marx's emphasis on the interplay between class structure and ideology treat the North as the hub of the contemporary world system (for example, Wallerstein, 2004; Burawoy, 2015). All use concepts native to European and American intellectual traditions to explain the world.

As V.Y. Mudimbe (1988, p 15) put it, "epistemological ethnocentrism" is "the belief that scientifically there is nothing to be learned from 'them' unless it is already 'ours' or comes out of 'us'." Most European and American sociology is epistemologically ethnocentric in this sense.

What does this look like in practice? Like most scholarly disciplines, sociology has a series of default views of its subject matters. These vary by sociological subdiscipline, and they change over time. Early sociologists of race, for example, thought that race was a biological fact (Morris, 2007) and only later came to recognize that 'race' is a social construct (Omi and Winant, 2015) – albeit one that can kill you. Access to computer analysis in the 1970s shifted American sociology toward the use of survey techniques, which measure individual attitudes and actions, and away from neighborhood analysis, which stresses how people's interactions get channelled by particular social structures (Anderson and Massey, 2001).

My own subdiscipline, the sociology of religion, is no different (Spickard, 2017, pp 21–43). With few exceptions, it treats all religions as if they were organized into the equivalent of 'churches,' staffed by the equivalent of 'clergy,' focused on 'sacred texts,' and 'beliefs,' and concerned with personal and social morality. These elements are all central to Western Christianity, which locates 'the sacred' either in the sacraments (which means in church life) or in the inward relationship between the soul and God. It views religion as promulgating rules for living a (supposedly) 'holy' life. Sociology thus centers its understanding of religion on things that Christianity finds important: church participation, individual religiosity, and whether people follow their church leaders' moral advice. As a result, sociologists collect church membership figures, count church attendance, and ask people about their religious and moral beliefs and behavior. They argue at length about whether religions are growing or dying, based on these statistics (for example, Finke and Stark, 2005; Bruce, 2011). Even sociologists of New Age religions, which are at best informally organized, count adherents and collect people's beliefs about 'spirituality,' 'the supernatural,' and so on (for example, Heelas, 1996). They define these things in traditional Euro-American terms. The sociology of religion's default view makes Western Christianity the intellectual model for religions everywhere.[2]

What does this ignore about religious life? What aspects of religion escape a conceptual net based on organizations, leaders, texts, beliefs, and morality? I explored three possibilities in *Alternative Sociologies of Religion* (2017), each of which identified concepts from a non-Western society that illuminate an overlooked aspect of contemporary religious life.

In what follows, I shall summarize two of these possibilities, to show what Euro-American sociology can learn by seeing the world through other civilizations' eyes. The first is from ancient China and is specific to the sociological study of religion. The second is from 14th-century North Africa and speaks to the sociological study of both religion and ethnicity. I lack space here to explore the third, a set of Navajo ideas that can help sociologists to better understand collective experiences.

These alternative views are steps toward creating a truly world sociology. Including such ideas has the potential to transform – and improve – the field.

A Confucian sociology of the sacred

I am clearly not the first scholar to accuse sociology of imposing Euro-American models of religion on other societies (for example, Chidester, 1996; Masuzawa, 2005). Those societies responded in various ways. India's intellectuals embraced this plan, because revisioning their society's varied temples and festivals as 'Hinduism' put India on a par with Europe as a source of a world religion (Beyer, 2006, pp 188–224). Chinese intellectuals, on the other hand, argued that Confucianism is a philosophy of living, not a *zongjiao* or 'sectarian teaching' (Beyer, 2006, p 230). They used that invented word to describe European religions, which they saw as factional, partisan, and disturbing to the social order. Confucianism was none of these, so these intellectuals portrayed China as irreligious.

Confucianism does, however, have a well-established sense of the sacred – one that complements but does not duplicate the Euro-American definition. On a philosophical level, it is embodied in a set of concepts that orient people toward each other and toward the universe. On a practical level, it promotes a set of household activities that maintain the social relations that Confucian thinking holds dear.

Confucianism finds the sacred in the maintenance of social ties. Confucian philosophy is all about groups and group living, and a person's most essential duty is to act with due regard for the group, despite one's own feelings as an individual. Individuals matter, but they do so not because they are sacred, but because the human self is the spot where social ties come together. Those ties are more important than is the individual person who embodies them.

Henry Rosemont (1991, pp 71–73) invites us to experience this in the difference between how we introduce ourselves as Confucians and as Westerners. Imitating him in the Western mode,

> I am Jim Spickard, Emeritus Professor of Sociology at the University of Redlands, Past-President of the of the International Sociological Association's Research Committee on the Sociology of Religion, and President of the Association for the Sociology of Religion. I teach and write about social theory, the sociology of religion, and research design. I have published six books and over 75 journal articles and book chapters. My next book is about what is happening to religion in the contemporary world.

Clearly, this introduction is all about me. It presents me as an individual, and it focuses on my personal accomplishments. In this, it mirrors other aspects of Euro-American culture, such as the Protestant image of the individual standing alone before God and the importance of individual human rights in Euro-American secular law (Spickard, 2002).

In contrast, here I am as a Confucian:

> I am Jim Spickard, son of Donald Spickard and Mary Alice Adkins, grandson of Vernon and Mildred Spickard and of Russell and Mary Adkins. I am brother to Paul Spickard, husband to Meredith McGuire, father to Janaki and Dmitri Spickard-Keeler, grandfather to Benjamin Spickard Chiarello. My teachers included George Spindler, Trent Schroyer, Charles McCoy, and James McClendon. My students include Aaron Olive, Javier Espinoza, Maggie Smith, and Julia Pazzi Clements.

This Confucian introduction emphasizes that I am shaped by those around me. My parents, grandparents, and natal family formed my core personality. My marriage made me a different person, as did having children. My teachers shaped me, as did my students and friends. I am simply different as the result of these relationships than I would have been without them. This is a great insight into my individuality.

These introductions display what each of these two cultures finds sacred about the self. For the West – especially in the US – it is the individual person. For classic Confucianism, on the other hand, it was the nest of relationships. One maintained those relationships through lǐ, the practice of ritual propriety; this lǐ was the source of dé (virtue). In Confucian philosophy, maintaining the sacredness of relationships is our chief duty.

Classic Confucians practiced lǐ on two levels (Spickard, 2017, pp 83–93). One was 'ancestor worship,' which involved maintaining shrines to one's departed forebears (Lakos, 2010). These reminded people of the importance of family and lineage. 'Worshiping' ancestors – who were not seen as gods – reminded people who they were: son or daughter of X, grandson or granddaughter of Y, and so on. Doing so acknowledged the sacredness of the relationships that shape us.

Confucians also practiced *lǐ* on a political level, through the idea of 'the mandate of heaven.' This stressed the importance of right relationships between a ruler and the people (*min*). The ruler had to care for the *min*, to protect and organize them. Otherwise, Heaven (*tiān*) would bring disasters, which signaled that it was time for new leaders to arise. Ruling was a matter of connection, not simply of power.

Both 'ancestor worship' and 'the mandate of heaven' are relational. For Confucians, human flourishing is not an individual matter but a community responsibility. Attention to that community through proper regard for others (*lǐ*) is thus a sacred act. *Dé*, or virtue, results from and also feeds this process.

How might we use these insights to expand the sociology of religion? What kinds of questions would a Confucian sociologist ask about religious life? Here is one that is seldom asked in Euro-American sociology: "Who maintains the sacred relationships that make religions possible?" Put in Confucian terms, "Who practices the *lǐ* that creates the *dé* on which Western Christianity depends?"

In American and British church life, which are largely centered on local congregations, this has historically been women.

Many scholars have demonstrated women's importance in local religious communities, despite Euro-American Christianity's still-patriarchal nature. Penny Marler (2008) highlighted their importance by showing that changes in women's involvement in both American and English congregations can explain most of the last century's religious decline. Abby Day (2017) showed how Anglican parishes in the United Kingdom depend on unpaid work by now-elderly women; their passing will make it much harder for those parishes to sustain their mission. Food historian Daniel Sack (2000) described the role that church suppers have long played in the life of White Protestant congregations in the American Midwest. Those weekly or monthly church meals have tied US congregations together – a tie that has loosened with the growing need for middle-class women to work outside the home. African American congregations also depend on women's "kitchen ministry" (Dodson and Gilkes, 1995). In fact, women are central to African American religious life, from cooking for the congregation to women's choirs, to accompanying the bereaved, to keeping the pastor fed and on track. African American churches are not the male-pastor-centered patriarchies oft imagined (see Gilkes, 2000).

Women's religious contributions work a bit differently in the low-income Catholic parishes on San Antonio, Texas's largely Mexican American West Side. There, women's influence happens outside of the clergy-led parishes, in such events as the neighborhood *pastores* (Christmas plays) that women sponsor as their personal thanks to *El Niño Dios* ("the Child God"), who has intervened to save a relative from gangs or drugs, delivered them from legal troubles, and so on (Flores, 1995). The plays are performed in backyards and driveways, and the women cook with their relatives and friends to feed the cast and the audience. To quote sociologist Ana María Díaz-Stevens (1994, p 26),

> It is there, in the kitchen, where the women of the household and other women from the extended family and community often gather and, over a cup of café con leche, reminisce about the past, give each other counsel and consolations, discuss the events of the community, and plan for family and community celebrations which most often are also religious celebrations.

Flores (1994, p 177) wrote that such events "function to ... gather those present into a common social body by building on experiences that affect everyone." Simply put, the events create community. Local people see them as an important part of religious life – often more important than Sunday Mass.

A Confucian sociologist would highlight this as a core part of Mexican American religion. Mainstream sociology of religion, on the other hand, has mostly ignored it because it happens outside of church control.[3]

In short, a Confucian sociology of religion would see religion as embedded in relationships, whether or not they happen under church auspices. It would focus less on individual 'morality' and more on communal 'right action.' It would focus on the interplay between *lǐ* and *dé*, ritual propriety and virtue. It would ask who maintains the relationships that make the religious community possible.

Euro-American sociology of religion does not ask these questions. Instead, it asks about beliefs, conversions, and organizational structures. These speak to men's experiences – one reason why the sociology of religion has long focused on men's lives (Woodhead, 2008).

I can imagine a society in which men might maintain the relationships that sustain communal religious life, but that is not the dominant Euro-American pattern. Contemporary sociology's default view of religion makes women an afterthought rather than putting them at center stage. Their role in religious life is much more visible from a Confucian perspective.

Tribes and cities: a view from 14th-century North Africa

I shall treat my second example more briefly. It comes from the *Muqaddimah* or "Introduction" to the *Kitāb al-'Ibar* ("Book of History") by the

14th-century Tunisian polymath Walī al-Dīn Abū Zayd 'Abd ar-Raḥmān Ibn Muḥammad Ibn Khaldūn (1377). That work was an encyclopedic account of the Arab conquests and of the rise and fall of its dynasties and kingdoms ranging from Iran to Moorish Spain. It was also the first sociopolitical analysis of a multi-ethnic, multi-religious society. Despite its long importance in the Arab world, Ibn Khaldūn's work has only recently begun to penetrate sociology (see Alatas, 2006, 2011). There are two reasons. First, Euro-American sociologists have assumed that 14th-century society has nothing to teach them about the modern industrial and post-industrial eras. Second, they have also assumed that Khaldūn's chief topics, ethnicity and religion, would fade as societies modernize. Reality has proved them wrong. Our world is full of religious and ethnic conflict, to which Khaldūn's insights are highly relevant.

Like any good sociologist, Ibn Khaldūn did not just recount events; he teased out the regularities and forces that shaped them. The most important of these were dynamics of al 'aṣabiyyah, a term usually translated as "group-feeling," "esprit de corps," or "spirit of kinship." The term comes from the Arabic root 'aṣab, "to bind." It is a force for social solidarity. Societies with well-developed 'aṣabiyyah are strong and capable; those with weak 'aṣabiyyah are easily conquered. The Muqaddimah outlines the aspects of social life that strengthen and weaken this group-feeling. The rest of the Kitāb al-'Ibar applies this analysis to the pre-Islamic Mediterranean world, to early Arab and Eastern Muslim history, and to the kingdoms of Muslim Spain and North-Western Africa.

Ibn Khaldūn built his work around three key ideas. The first was his observation that the nomadic peoples of this region have repeatedly conquered settled peoples since at least Roman times. They overrun cities and either sack their wealth or become their rulers. Both choices lead them to settle down, becoming civilized themselves. He argued that they typically maintain their strength for three generations, by which time they have lost their group-feeling and are easy prey for the next nomads to arrive.

The second idea is the reason for this: that nomads live a rougher, more dangerous life than do city dwellers; as a result, they must rely on their kin or tribe for safety. This develops more group-feeling (al 'aṣabiyyah) and a greater willingness to sacrifice themselves for others. City people, however, depend on walls and hired police for safety, not on kin. They lose the habit of sacrificing for others' sake. Their group-feeling declines. Al 'aṣabiyyah thus varies with the practical requirements of people's lives.

The third idea stems from the first two. Nomads have great group-feeling, but it does not extend beyond their kin and tribe. This makes it harder for them to unite with other nomads, and harder still to carry out a sustained campaign. Nomad armies succumb to factional fighting because they cannot generalize their al 'aṣabiyyah widely. The most prominent exception, wrote

Khaldūn, was the expansion of Islam. He argued that Islam generated a shared loyalty to God and a sense of divine mission that overcame lesser group-feelings and united people toward a common purpose. Other religions could presumably do the same.

I have described this elsewhere as a center-focused theory of group solidarity (Spickard, 2017, pp 135–157). In Khaldūn's view, groups are held together by common feeling, ties, and purpose. This differs from edge-focused theories, which argue that groups are formed by conflict with outsiders (Thye and Lawler, 2002). Scholars of ethnic relations divide into these two camps, with proponents of ethnic primordialism arguing for center-focused ties (see Ignatieff, 1993) and proponents of conflict-based solidarity arguing for edge-focused ones (Barth, 1966). The same is true for scholars of religion. Are religions stronger when they tie people tightly together (for example, Iannaccone, 1994)? Or does that happen when religions feel they are under attack (for example, Smith, 1998)? Ibn Khaldūn's work speaks to the scholarly conversations on both topics.

European and American sociologists have typically put ethnicity and religion into separate conceptual boxes. Ibn Khaldūn, on the other hand, saw ethnic and religious 'aṣabiyyah as more alike than different. He acknowledged both that group-feelings vary from situation to situation and that they can operate either separately or together. Rather than assuming that they have little to do with each other, a Khaldūnian sociologist would want to examine the details of their entanglements.

A few scholars have done so. McGuire (1981, pp 166–179), Ignatieff (1993, pp 213–249), and Mitchell (2005) have each explored the relationship between ethnicity and religion in the Northern Ireland "troubles." Tambiah (1992) has explored it in Sri Lanka's civil war. Sells (2003) and I (Spickard, 2017, pp 159–173) have explored it in the civil war in Bosnia. These cases are different, and Ibn Khaldūn's approach is not always the most fruitful. Yet it does need to be part of the sociological conversation.

In fact, his approach might well shed light on two recent events for which standard sociology has no easy explanation. The first was the rise of the Islamic State (ISIS) in mid-2010s Iraq and Syria. There, a militant religious movement united certain ethnic groups in opposition to others – 'ethnicity' being defined in some cases by religious divisions. On the one hand, there is evidence to support Roy's (2004) suggestion that religion played a very Khaldūnian role in radicalizing "deterritorialized Muslim elites" to fight for a new anti-Western ummah. On the other hand, Wilson (2015) found that some ISIS fighters were very edge oriented in their retribution against Iraqi Shiites. We could learn a lot by examining how religious and ethnic solidarities interacted in this setting.

The second case is the astounding support that Donald Trump received from Evangelical Christians, both in the 2016 presidential election and afterwards. Was this part of America's religious "culture wars" (Hunter, 1991), with 'conservative' Christians reading Trump as a modern-day King Cyrus delivering them from their enemies (Stewart, 2019)? Or was it a White people's revolt to take back 'their' country from uppity minorities, immigrants, and liberal elites (Rubin, 2020)? Probably both. A Khaldūnian sociology might tell us something about how these two factors intertwine.

These two cases should remind sociologists that religion is not just a matter of belief, morality, and formal organizations. It is also a matter of how people connect to one another.

The point

The point here is not that classic Confucianism offers us a complete sociology of religion, nor that Ibn Khaldūn has the skeleton key to unlocking the politics of a multi-ethnic, multi-religious society. It is that Euro-American sociology has something to learn from each of them. The sociologies of the global North typically imagine that they are universal when they are not. Concepts from other intellectual traditions do more than just fill in the gaps; they force a re-examination and a reshaping of sociology's default views. Adding *lǐ* and *dé, al ʿaṣabiyyah*, the Navajo concept of *hózhǫ* (Spickard, 2017), the Nahuatl *tecoatlaxope* (Maduro, 1993), the Yoruba distinction between *aṣuwada* and *aṣuwa* (Akiwowo, 1986), and other ideas to sociology does not just stir exotic tastes in a basically Euro-American intellectual stew (Harding, 1995). It potentially decenters Euro-American sociology by forcing it to see its blind spots and to embrace change. Ideas from the global South can make sociology more applicable to the entire world.

The point of this chapter is that sociologists everywhere can learn from one another and can borrow each other's concepts to improve their understanding. As Michael Okyerefo argues, doing so well "would engender a symbiosis of ideas in our globalizing world, a cross-fertilization of epistemologies in a transnational circulation or exchange of knowledge that is indigenous to different societies, but meant for the benefit of humanity" (2018, p 33).

Martin Albrow (1997) argued that it is now impossible to understand events in one part of the world without reference to what happens elsewhere. Societies, cultures, and civilizations mutually shape each other even as the after-effects of the colonial era still affect how that shaping occurs. If we want to understand the world as it is and is coming to be, we must overcome intellectual ethnocentrism.

Notes

[1] For an account of Du Bois's grounding in 19th-century European ideas, see Appiah (1992, 2014). On American sociology's suppression of Du Bois's ideas, see Morris (2007, 2017).

[2] I lack space for nuance. See Beyer (2006) for a subtle and thorough treatment.

³ This has begun to change because of the work of Latino sociologists (Stevens-Arroyo and Díaz-Stevens, 1994) and advocates of the 'lived religion' approach to religious life (McGuire, 2008).

References

Akiwowo, Akinsola A. (1986) 'Contributions to the sociology of knowledge from an African oral poetry', *International Sociology*, 1(4): 343–358.

Alatas, Syed Farid (2006) 'Ibn Khaldun and contemporary sociology', *International Sociology*, 21(6): 782–795.

Alatas, Syed Farid (2011) 'Ibn Khaldûn', in George Ritzer and Jeffrey Stepnisky (eds) *The Wiley-Blackwell Companion to Major Social Theorists*. Oxford: Blackwell, pp 12–29.

Albrow, Martin (1997) *The Global Age: State and Society Beyond Modernity*. Stanford: Stanford University Press.

Anderson, Elijah, and Massey, Douglas S. (2001) 'The sociology of race in the United States', in Elijah Anderson and Douglas S. Massey (eds) *Problem of the Century: Racial Stratification in the United State*. New York: Russell Sage, pp 3–12.

Appiah, Kwame Anthony (1992) 'Illusions of race', in *In My Father's House: Africa in the Philosophy of Culture*. New York: Oxford University Press, pp 28–46.

Appiah, Kwame Anthony (2014) *Lines of Descent: W.E.B. Du Bois and the Emergence of Identity*. Cambridge: Harvard University Press.

Barth, Fredrik (ed) (1966) *Ethnic Groups and Boundaries: The Social Organization of Cultural Difference*. London: RAIGBI.

Bauman, Zygmunt (2000) *Liquid Modernity*. Cambridge: Polity Press.

Beck, Ulrich, Giddens, Anthony, and Lash, Scott (1994) *Reflexive Modernization: Politics, Tradition, and Aesthetics in the Modern Social Order*. Stanford: Stanford University Press.

Beyer, Peter F. (2006) *Religions in Global Society*. New York: Routledge.

Bruce, Steve (2011) *Secularization: In Defence of an Unfashionable Theory*. Oxford: Oxford University Press.

Burawoy, Michael (2015) 'Facing an unequal world', *Current Sociology*, 63(1): 5–34.

Chidester, David (1996) *Savage Systems: Colonialism and Comparative Religion in Southern Africa*. Charlottesville: University Press of Virginia.

Day, Abby (2017) *The Religious Lives of Older Laywomen: The Final Active Anglican Generation*. Oxford: Oxford University Press.

Díaz-Stevens, Ana María (1994) 'Analyzing popular religiosity for socio-religious meaning', in Anthony M. Stevens-Arroyo and Ana Maria Díaz-Stevens (eds) *An Enduring Flame: Studies of Latino Popular Religiosity*. New York: PARAL, pp 17–36.

Dodson, Jualynne E., and Gilkes, Cheryl Townsend (1995) '"There's nothing like church food": Food and the U.S. Afro-Christian tradition: Remembering community and feeding the embodied S/spirit(s)', *Journal of the American Academy of Religion*, 63(3): 519–538.

Finke, Roger, and Stark, Rodney (2005) *The Churching of America, 1776–2005: Winners and Losers in Our Religious Economy*. New Brunswick: Rutgers University Press.

Flores, Richard R. (1994) 'Para el Niño Dios: Sociability and commemorative sentiment in popular religious practice', in Anthony M. Stevens-Arroyo and Ana María Díaz-Stevens (eds) *An Enduring Flame: Studies on Latino Popular Religiosity*. New York: PARAL, pp 171–190.

Flores, Richard R. (1995) *Los Pastores: History and Performance in the Mexican Shepherd's Play of South Texas*. Washington, D.C.: Smithsonian Institution Press.

Foucault, Michel (1977) *Discipline and Punish: The Birth of the Prison*. Trans. by Alan Sheridan. New York: Vintage Books.

Giddens, Anthony (1976) 'Classical social theory and the origins of modern sociology', *American Journal of Sociology*, 81(4): 703–729.

Giddens, Anthony (1991) *Modernity and Self-Identity: Self and Society in the Late Modern Age*. Stanford: Stanford University Press.

Gilkes, Cheryl Townsend (2000) *If It Wasn't for the Women ...: Black Women's Experience and Womanist Culture in Church and Community*. Maryknoll, NY: Orbis Books.

Harding, Sandra G. (1995) 'Just add women and stir?', in Gender Working Group (ed) *Missing Links: Gender Equity in Science and Technology Development*. Ottawa: International Development Research Centre, pp 295–307.

Heelas, Paul (1996) *The New Age Movement: The Celebration of the Self and the Sacralization of Modernity*. Oxford: Blackwell.

Hunter, James Davidson (1991) *Culture Wars: The Struggle to Define America*. New York: Basic Books.

Iannaccone, Laurence R. (1994) 'Why strict churches are strong', *American Journal of Sociology*, 99(5): 1180–1211.

Ignatieff, Michael (1993) *Blood and Belonging: Journeys into the New Nationalism*. New York: Farrar, Strauss, and Giroux.

Inkeles, Alex, and David Smith (1974) *Becoming Modern: Individual Change in Six Developing Countries*. Cambridge, MA: Harvard University Press.

Jameson, Fredric (1991) *Postmodernism, or, the Cultural Logic of Late Capitalism*. Durham: Duke University Press.

Khaldūn, Ibn (1377) *The Muqaddimah: An Introduction to History* (2nd edn). Trans. by Franz Rosenthal. Princeton: Princeton University Press, 1967.

Lakos, William (2010) *Chinese Ancestor Worship: A Practice and Ritual Oriented Approach to Understanding Chinese Culture*. Newcastle-upon-Tyne: Cambridge Scholars Press.

Maduro, Otto (1993) 'Theorizing *tecoatlaxope*: For a reassessment of Latino/a religious agency', Presented at the conference *Methodology*, sponsored by PARAL, 15–19 April, Princeton, NJ.

Marler, Penny Long (2008) 'Religious change in the West: Watch the women', in Kristin Aune, Sonya Sharma, and Giselle Vincett (eds) *Women and Religion in the West: Challenging Secularization*. Aldershot: Ashgate, pp 23–56.

Masuzawa, Tomoko (2005) *The Invention of World Religions: Or, How European Universalism Was Preserved in the Language of Pluralism*. Chicago: University of Chicago Press.

McGuire, Meredith B. (1981) *Religion: The Social Context* (1st edn). Belmont, CA: Wadsworth.

McGuire, Meredith B. (2008) *Lived Religion: Faith and Practice in Everyday Life*. New York: Oxford University Press.

Mitchell, Claire (2005) 'Behind the ethnic marker: Religion and social identification in Northern Ireland', *Sociology of Religion*, 66(1): 3–21.

Morris, Aldon (2007) 'Sociology of race and W.E.B. Dubois: The path not taken', in Craig Calhoun (ed) *Sociology in America: A History*. Chicago: University of Chicago Press, pp 503–534.

Morris, Aldon D. (2017) *The Scholar Denied: W.E.B. Du Bois and the Birth of Modern Sociology*. Berkeley: University of California Press.

Mudimbe, V.Y. (1988) *The Invention of Africa: Gnosis, Philosophy, and the Order of Knowledge*. Bloomington: Indiana University Press.

Okyerefo, Michael P.K. (2018) 'Deconstructing and reconstructing: Embracing alternative ways of producing, classifying and disseminating knowledge: An African perspective', *Etnološka tribina: Journal of the Croatian Ethnological Society*, 48: 27–35.

Omi, Michael, and Winant, Howard (2015) *Racial Formation in the United States* (3rd edn). New York: Routledge.

Rosemont, Henry, Jr (1991) *A Chinese Mirror: Moral Reflections on Political Economy and Society*. La Salle, IL: Open Court.

Rostow, Walter W. (1971) *The Stages of Economic Growth: A Non-Communist Manifesto*. Cambridge: Cambridge University Press.

Roy, Olivier (2004) *Globalized Islam: The Search for a New Ummah*. New York: Columbia University Press.

Rubin, Jennifer (2020) 'How White Supremacy Infected Christianity and the Republican Party', *Washington Post*, 3 August. [online] Available from: https://wapo.st/2EMWBmk [accessed 3 August 2020].

Sack, Daniel (2000) *Whitebread Protestants: Food and Religion in American Culture*. New York: St. Martin's.

Sells, Michael A. (2003) 'Crosses of blood: Sacred space, religion, and violence in Bosnia-Hercegovina', *Sociology of Religion*, 64(3): 3009–3331.

Smith, Christian S. (1998) *American Evangelicalism: Embattled and Thriving.* Chicago: University of Chicago Press.

Spickard, James V. (2002) 'Human rights through a religious lens: A programmatic argument', *Social Compass,* 49(2): 227–238.

Spickard, James V. (2017) *Alternative Sociologies of Religion: Through Non-Western Eyes.* New York: New York University Press.

Stevens-Arroyo, Anthony M., and Ana María Díaz-Stevens (eds) (1994) *An Enduring Flame: Studies on Latino Popular Religiosity.* New York: Bildner Center for Western Hemispheric Studies.

Stewart, Kathleen (2019) 'Why Trump reigns as King Cyrus', *New York Times,* 1 January, p A19. [online] Available from: https://nyti.ms/3cFoiu5 [accessed 28 September 2020].

Tambiah, Stanley J. (1992) *Buddhism Betrayed? Religion, Politics, and Violence in Sri Lanka.* Chicago: University of Chicago Press.

Thye, Shane R., and Lawler, Edward J. (2002) *Group Cohesion, Trust, and Solidarity.* Greenwich, CT: JAI Press.

Wallerstein, Immanuel (2004) *World-Systems Analysis: An Introduction.* Durham: Duke University Press.

Wilson, Lydia (2015) 'What I discovered from interviewing imprisoned ISIS fighters', *The Nation,* 21 October. [online] Available from: https://bit.ly/2GfoqEM [accessed 29 September 2020].

Woodhead, Linda (2008) 'Gendering secularization theory', *Social Compass,* 55(2): 187–193.

11

Whom We Cite: A Reflection on the Limits and Potentials of Critical Citation Practices

Januschka Schmidt

Introduction

For most scholars, an academic publication, either in journals or books, is the gold standard for sharing academic ideas and results (Kreienkamp et al, 2020). Once the publication is out there in the world, many judge the impact of an idea, study, or project by the publication's citation numbers. These two focal points of publications and citations have in recent decades also driven a publication- and citation-based understanding of academic excellence for individuals (for example, h-index), publishers (for example, impact factor), and academic institutions (for example, institution rankings). While the intention of emphasizing ideas and outputs over a person's background (for example, race, gender, country of origin, or seniority) is admirable and seemingly progressive, this approach creates challenges similar to many other equality-focused initiatives, namely that it does not necessarily provide equity or justice in a system that seems to favour some over others. Female scientists, scholars of colour, emerging scholars, and researchers from non-Western backgrounds often have less access to the publication process, are published in lower-impact journals, and are less frequently cited. This chapter discusses some of the biased processes that underlie the publication and citation process, introduces some counter-movements, and translates these into practical suggestions for individuals and institutions.

In this chapter, I propose the approach of critical citation practices, which I define as a conscious engagement with the people we cite throughout the academic research process. The chapter and its content are based on a conference I organized on 'Critical Research Approaches and their Methods' in 2018 and a workshop series I presented about critical citation practices[1] at the University of Groningen in 2019. The majority of scholars I talked with during these workshops were well aware of the inequalities baked into academic structures and want to make their research more inclusive and diverse but simply did not know how. The main, reoccurring issues (especially for emerging scholars) were a lack of accessible information and structural education on citation practices as well as difficulties in applying the abstract ideas of critical research approaches in daily practice. The focus of this chapter is, therefore, expressly practical, and it explicitly discusses the role of emerging scholars.

This chapter is divided into four sections. The first discusses why it is important to engage with citation practices. The second introduces past literature on solutions to citation inequalities. In the third, I examine my proposal of critical citation practices within the wider context of critical research methods. In the fourth section, I discuss the difficulties that young, new, emerging, and disadvantaged scholars might encounter when they want to apply critical citation practices and ways of dealing with these challenges. I close the chapter with a short suggestion for institutional approaches.

Before I address the topics in detail, I want to discuss some of the terminologies I frequently use within the chapter. I will often refer to scholars from advantaged or disadvantaged groups. In the chapter, I cluster women, people of colour, disabled scholars, scholars at non-Western universities, non-English speaking scholars, and emerging scholars in the category of disadvantaged groups. With advantaged or privileged groups, I refer to groups that, as a result of historically grown processes, are structurally in positions of power and influence. Structurally, most privileged are white men from Western universities of the global North. Nonetheless, privilege is a layered concept. Even within disadvantaged groups, some scholars are more privileged than others. For example, on average, scholars from non-Western universities are at a disadvantage in the publication process. But because of the layered nature of privilege, a white person working at a non-Western university likely holds more privilege than a woman of colour working at a university in the United States or Europe (and then, again, there are layers between universities within countries).

Readers who want to explore these issues further could consult Mignolo (2009) and Gómez (2020) for more information about inequality in academia; Foo (2013) and Burbules (2015) to read discussions about the impact factor; Ahmed (2017), Nunkoo et al (2019), and and Kubota (2020) concerning citation practices, as well as discussions about inequality in the publishing process in Coleman (2005) and Lee et al (2010).

Why we need to talk about citations

How we cite and whom we cite often has tangible consequences for the people we cite. Citation indices of how often a scholar is cited in other papers are often seen as a determinant of an individual's academic success (for example, Gálvez, 2017). Jobs and working visas can be contingent on it (Burbules, 2015). Unfortunately, as academia generally is struggling with diversity and inclusion, academic publication and citation practices are contributing to the preservation of the status quo (Kreienkamp et al, 2020).

There are two main aspects in current citation practices which are contributing to unequal access to and value of citation numbers among scholars. These aspects can be summarized into two categories: how institutions use citation numbers as a measurement of academic success, and a scholar's individual citation choices.

Contributions of measurement tools to the status quo

How often a scholar publishes and is cited is quantified in the 'h-index', a tool which allows comparison of the citation rates of academics (Hirsch, 2005). While citation indices such as the h-index are useful tools to measure the influence scholars have in their field of study, this focus on citation rates as an indicator for academic success might be a misshaped approach. For example, a study by Symonds and colleagues (2006) highlights that the h-index is strongly biased against female scholars because articles by women are statistically less cited on average (a phenomenon called the gender citation gap, see Maliniak et al, 2013). Similarly, women are less represented in highly influential bibliometric databases such as Web of Science and Scopus (Leahey, 2006; Hall, 2016; Nunkoo et al, 2019).

Another reason why scholars from disadvantaged groups are less often cited is that, to be successful, journals need to maintain their popularity in their field of study. The popularity of journals is measured through the 'impact factor', which reflects the yearly average number of citations to articles published in that journal as a measurement of the impact of the journal (Mason et al, 2005; Foo, 2013; Burbules, 2015). To maintain or increase the journal's impact factor, publishers prefer to publish papers by established scholars with high citation numbers, because they are expected to be read by many scholars. This preference for authors with high citation rates has been shown to occur at the expense of scholars from disadvantaged groups (Mason et al, 2005; Foo, 2013; Burbules, 2015).

The preference for scholars from privileged groups has an impact on the review process as well. Typically, journals invite experts from their field of study to review prospective papers to establish the relevance and quality of submitted papers. Unfortunately, the perceptions persist in academic publishing that scholars from Western universities are more likely to be experts in their fields than scholars from non-Western universities. As a result, the majority of experts invited to judge the quality of submitted papers come from Western universities (Coleman, 2005; Helmer et al, 2017; Kubota, 2020).

As a result, focusing only on the citation numbers (for example, in the form of h-index, Scopus or Web of Science databases, impact factor) as a measurement for academic success gives a distorted picture of academic expertise, and actively excludes many scholars from disadvantaged groups.

Citation practices and citation choices: consequences for the status quo

It is not only the focus on numbers such as impact factors or citation indices that contributes to the preservation of the status quo. Academics' contemporary citation habits – meaning whom we cite and why we make those choices – have an equally great impact on academic structures.

Besides building on the knowledge of other scholars, one main motivation to cite is to establish our own credibility and knowledge. The voices cited as proof for our expertise (and the names looked for by our readership) often are those voices that are cited regularly in other publications (Mott and Cockayne, 2017; Kubota, 2020). That is not necessarily a harmful practice, considering that many widely cited works have made substantial contributions in their fields. Because our current, citation-based measures for expertise and citation practices structurally privilege a small group of scholars (Mott and Cockayne, 2017; Kubota, 2020), I want to argue that we need to engage more consciously and critically with our choices for citations and expertise.

Moreover, within our contemporary citation practices are also a few habits that coercively preserve the status quo. 'Citation pushing' is one of those practices. Citation pushing (sometimes also called coercive citations) refers to the practice of reviewers 'pushing' authors to include the reviewer's publications in their papers, even if they have little relevance for the argument of the manuscript (Kreienkamp et al, 2020). Because of the power reviewers hold over publication acceptances, authors often feel the need to include those references in their manuscripts (Kreienkamp et al, 2020). As a consequence, reviewers can increase their citation numbers, making it appear that their publications are very influential, even though that might not actually be the case.

A similar form of distorting the citation numbers can be the practice of self-citing. While citing one's own publications is often a necessity to build on previous work, excessive self-citing without good reason can contribute to skewing citation numbers (Maliniak et al, 2013; Nunkoo et al, 2019). Additionally, there is a gendered component to the practice of self-citation, as women statistically tend to cite themselves less, contributing further to the gender citation gap (Maliniak et al, 2013; Nunkoo et al, 2019).

Moreover, empirical studies have shown that scholars with anglophone names are more likely to be cited than scholars whose names are non-anglophone (Mason et al, 2005; Nunkoo et al, 2019). In line with a preference for anglophone names, the most influential journals are English-language journals. As a consequence, to participate in major academic discourses, scholars are often required to use the English language. This practice excludes knowledge that is not or cannot be communicated in English, as well as scholars who have no access to English education (Garcia-Ramon, 2003; Mott and Cockayne, 2017). Similarly, biases in the peer-review process, for example concerning non-anglophone names, author's gender, or institutional affiliation, can contribute to the exclusion of scholars from disadvantaged groups (Helmer et al, 2017). As a result, it is harder for scholars from disadvantaged groups to contribute to academic discourses.

Another form of citing, that can offer support for scholars in the process of recognition but can also contribute to inequality in citation practices, are citation groups (Stewart, 2005; Maliniak et al, 2013). In these groups, the members agree to cite each other to boost each other's presence (Stewart, 2005; Maliniak et al, 2013). While collegial support in groups is generally important and many of these groups likely form around similar academic interests where members build on each other's work, these groups are also reflections of unequal structures in academia. Disadvantaged scholars are less likely to be part of these groups. As a consequence, these groups contribute to the maintenance of the status quo (Stewart, 2005; Ahmed, 2017).

These structural disadvantages within current citation practices and the way we measure excellence as a result of it, contribute to the impression that academics from disadvantaged groups are not as good as scholars from privileged groups. Consequently, being successful in academia becomes even more difficult for those who are already at a disadvantage.

Moreover, this way of building valued knowledge in a field also has a significant impact on which research questions are being asked and which papers are being published. We come up with our research questions not only from looking at the world but are heavily influenced by our academic environment (Tarusarira, 2018). Therefore, if we focus only on papers by a specific group of scholars, we might limit the research questions we perceive as worthy of being asked (Mott and Cockayne, 2017).

Active resistance and citation awareness

Different scholars and journals have approached inequality in citation practices and have proposed practical paths. For example, editors have highlighted their role in educating their authors about inequality in citation choices and the need to enforce strict guidelines concerning diverse bibliographies (Murdie, 2018). Others have also highlighted the need for journals to ensure that reviewers are aware of citation inequalities and are educated in ethical citation practices as well (Dion et al, 2018).

I agree with the need for structural and institutional changes from journals and editors, but also argue that academic authors are also able to contribute to changing inequalities in citations. The most radical citation approach has been suggested by Ahmed (2017). Based on the concept of privilege (having it easier because one is conforming to societal standards), Ahmed concludes that it is harder to not reproduce whiteness in academic research than it is to conform to it. Consequentially, Ahmed argues that scholars must actively work to not reproduce whiteness in their citation practices, and adopts a strict citation policy, saying 'I do not cite any white men. … In this book, I cite feminists of color' (Ahmed, 2017, p 15).

Ahmed's book was one of the first books I read in which the author transparently discussed their citation policy and engaged with their citation choices. Ahmed's approach, in its strictness, challenges us to reject everything we know about research and try something completely new. It also highlights that there is knowledge outside the traditional canon that is often overlooked. However, I do not want to argue for us to blindly accept everything a scholar from a disadvantaged group publishes. On the contrary, I want us to engage as critically with publications from disadvantaged scholars as with those from privileged scholars. I want to argue for us to *start* engaging with these publications and to create a writing and publication environment in which those publications by disadvantaged academics receive the same amount of attention as those by academics in privileged positions.

A less radical, feminist approach to citation practices understands citations as a tool for resistance against the reproduction of hierarchies of power in academia. Consequently, this soft approach proposes to carefully read and count citations before submitting a paper, perhaps by using the gender assessment tool (Sumner, 2018), but at least to self-consciously check one's bibliography for diversity (Mott and Cockayne, 2017; Dion et al, 2018; Nunkoo et al, 2019). I believe this to be helpful advice to learn about whom we cite regularly and for us as authors to identify patterns in our citation practices.

However, I take issue with the idea that we should primarily engage consciously with our citations after we have already finished our manuscripts. If we engage with our references only *after* we finished writing and only then aim to diversify our bibliography, we run the risk of regarding knowledge by disadvantaged authors as add-ons, a performative tool that can make our paper look diverse without having us actually challenge the structures of academic writing and publishing.

Other scholars (Gómez, 2020; Kubota, 2020) suggest that we start considering why we cite certain authors and critically reflect on these choices. For example, Kubota offers a set of questions to reflect on when engaging with our citations, such as:

> What does this citation do to my epistemological stance in relation to race, gender, nationality, culture, and so on? How does this citation

influence the overall status of subaltern scholars? How can I reconcile the practical need to get my work accepted with the promotion of antiracist and antisexist causes? (Kubota, 2020, p 727)

Inspired by Kubota, I want to make the argument with critical citation practices, that we need to start thinking consciously about our sources at the stage of idea conceptualization, or maybe even at the stage of inspiration.

Critical citation practices

I want to propose a set of practices in between Ahmed's radical approach (2017) and the soft approach (Mott and Cockayne, 2017; Dion et al, 2018; Nunkoo et al, 2019) – a moderate approach, which I call 'critical citation practices'. I do not want to suggest that we should never cite researchers from Western or privileged universities. Equally, I do not want researchers to see critical considerations as a post hoc add-on. Rather, critical citation practices ask that we are conscious of whom we cite and actively challenge the way we cite throughout the research process in a structural manner. I suggest that researchers approach a literature review and their citations in a three-step, sequential fashion:

1. focus on authors from the community one investigates (this step is less relevant for research in the natural sciences and formal sciences);
2. consult literature by disadvantaged groups; and only then
3. consider the advantaged and established canon.

Each of these steps is drawn from a range of influential theories within the critical research methods literature. I will discuss these theories and their application to citation practices in more detail in the following subsection.

Power to local communities: indigenous methodologies and participatory research

Decolonial theory is concerned with how power structures privilege and normalize Western worldviews, institutions, and forms of governance as a result of their colonial past. Under those circumstances, decolonial theory argues for deconstructing colonial worldviews and hierarchies to achieve equity (Mignolo, 2009; Grosfoguel, 2011).

One methodological approach which applies decolonial concepts is indigenous methodologies. Indigenous scholars created these methodological approaches as a direct response to negative experiences with research conducted on and with them (Kovach, 2009; Tuck and Yang, 2012; Arvin et al, 2013). Every indigenous population has their own guidelines, but the most famous are probably the OCAP principles. OCAP stands for ownership, control, access, and possession by indigenous peoples over data concerning them, as well as access to and possession of research with that data. The OCAP principles emphasize the agency of indigenous communities and communal forms of ownership of cultural knowledge (Kovach, 2009). For researchers, the OCAP principles formulate a clear set of guidelines: the data and knowledge are collectively owned by the indigenous communities and, as a result, researchers need to collaborate with the communities from the start of the project. This also means that academics need to establish together with the indigenous communities whether the research is relevant and potentially beneficial for them (Kovach, 2009).

Another research methodology that is often based on decolonial ideas is participatory research (Tuck, 2009). Similar to indigenous methodologies, participatory research asks researchers to actively include the researched communities in the research process for a bottom-up approach that empowers the participants (Tuck and Fine, 2007; Boog et al, 2008; Elder and Odoyo, 2018). Participatory research practices exist on a spectrum that runs from participatory research to participatory action research. The spectrum moves along the level of involvement of research participants and can take, for example, the form of involving research participants in the construction of theoretical frameworks. Participatory action research at the far end of the spectrum not only includes community members as fully accepted collaboration partners throughout the research but also creates actual output with them that is applied to the lived realities of the research participants, for example in the form of policies (Tuck and Fine, 2007; Boog et al, 2008; Elder and Odoyo, 2018).

Inspired by the ideals laid out in the OCAP principles and participatory research concerning ownership and honouring the expertise of research participants, I propose the first step in critical citation practices. This first step applies mainly to researchers from the social sciences, humanities, and applied sciences.

Step one: Start by reading works of writers from the group you want to research. Identify the research community you are focusing on and look for scholars or other experts from that community (or as closely related to them as possible) who have written about your topic.

To make our citation practices relevant and potentially beneficial to our participants, it is important to immerse ourselves in our participants' environment and experiences. I want to argue that one very important way to do this is by reading literature from scholars or experts from the group of people we are researching. As a consequence, we reaffirm ownership over knowledge through our citations. Additionally, we give agency to the researched communities because it is their perspectives that inform our questions and research design. As a result, our citation choices, from the start, are bottom-up and rooted in the lived realities of those whom we are researching. I believe this to be of particular importance when we engage in research with disadvantaged communities or communities who have been (violently) exploited by researchers.

Step two: As the second step in critical citation practices, I want to encourage us to 'consider the underdog first', through adopting feminist and critical race theory and *looking for scholars from disadvantaged groups who have written about your topic.* (For scholars from the natural sciences and formal sciences, I would suggest starting with this step in the literature search and review.)

But who are disadvantaged groups? Feminist theories, especially intersectional feminism, and critical race theory offer a good starting point to question existing power structures and reflect on layers of privilege.

Feminist theory looks at the intersection of gender, sex, and sexuality in patriarchal systems (Ali, 2007; Ahmed, 2017). It is important to note the diversity of women all around the world depending on class, race, ability, and country of origin, to just mention a few. Thus, intersectional feminist theory encourages us to take the diversity of women into account and to acknowledge the relative privilege of some, particularly white women (Valentine, 2007; Suzack, 2015; Ahmed, 2017).

Critical race theory has its origins in American legal studies (Bergerson, 2003). Critical race theory in higher education and knowledge production is concerned with the dominant discourse on race and racism and how educational theory, policy, and practice exclude certain racial and ethnic groups from these discourses and spaces (Treviño et al, 2008; Savas, 2014; Pérez Huber and Solorzano, 2015).

In general, applying feminist and critical race values and practices in our citations does not necessarily mean that we have to exclude other aspects. Rather, feminist and critical race theories and methods encourage us to break old habits and actively challenge ourselves to look beyond what we are used to. Therefore, I find intersectional feminist and critical race theories to be a very good starting point in reflecting on privilege and disadvantages in citation practices. Moreover, many feminists and critical race theorists from different disciplines have extensively engaged with academia and the power structures that have historically grown within it, giving us a good vantage point to understand inequality in citation practices.

Based on feminist and critical race theories, I want to encourage us to purposefully engage with scholars from disadvantaged groups in our literature review as early as possible. Moreover, I want to highlight the benefits of considering knowledge from experts outside of academia in addition to academic sources. Engaging with non-academic experts challenges definitions of expertise and knowledge and, as such, allows for diversification and expansion of what is considered knowledge.

Step three: As the last step during the literature search, I propose to 'flip it upside down' through considering more closely the scholars from privileged groups who have written about your topic.

As I have discussed extensively in this chapter, I do not want to argue for the exclusion of privileged voices. However, if we move our engagement with those voices to the end of our literature search, we actively turn the power hierarchies in our citation process upside down. As a result, we challenge ourselves to look beyond that which is immediately available and comfortable. We step outside of our comfort zones to not only make our bibliography more inclusive but also engage with epistemologies that are not normally around us, challenging us to think in new ways.

In sum, I propose a set of three sequential steps to actively challenge our citation habits:

- Start by reading works of writers from the group you want to research.
- Look for scholars from disadvantaged groups who have written about your topic.
- Look at scholars from privileged groups who have written about your topic.

As a bonus step, check on the gender and race balance in your bibliography more generally.

What does that mean for scholars in lower power positions?

It is important to talk about the difficulties of going against the status quo with critical citation practices, especially for emerging and disadvantaged scholars. All scholars need to publish regularly, but most especially emerging scholars often need to publish a significant number of papers to launch and progress in their academic careers. Unfortunately, because critical citation practices are often still different from the traditional way of approaching research (and writing), journals may dismiss a paper with critical citation practices or urge the author to change them. Similar to the difficulties when applying participatory action research, especially citing non–academic experts can come with its own set of difficulties. For example, a community's objectives can change independently from a researcher's objective, or a community's time constraints and priorities can change significantly. Therefore, while I want to emphasize the importance of challenging the definition of knowledge, I want to advise scholars interested in these techniques to make an informed choice regarding their time management and other research restrictions.

Emerging scholars can deal with these kinds of setbacks by, for example, publishing their papers in journals supporting critical research methods. However, these decisions can come with their own share of consequences, as these types of journals often have a low impact factor.

Moreover, I want to suggest that disadvantaged scholars should connect with other (disadvantaged) academics and discuss their research and methodologies with them. Networks can often offer safe spaces with people who have experienced similar inequalities and can share ways of dealing with obstacles. Such groups are also a great way to get inspired and receive feedback on ideas.

Another way to deal with restrictions concerning whom we can cite in our papers is to engage with our traditional sources in a critical way. For example, when we are compelled to focus on or include traditional authors, we can reflect in our papers on how and why our results might have been different if we had used theories and approaches by scholars from disadvantaged groups. With this approach, we can normalize a critical engagement with knowledge and highlight different approaches and ideas. This approach also allows for a more balanced citation policy and normalizes the inclusion of voices by scholars from disadvantaged groups, although disadvantaged scholars should not exclusively be put into opposition and criticism roles.

What does that mean for organizations in power?

Lastly, while critical citation practices can broaden our perspectives to achieve sustainable change, institutions in power need to implement adjustments as well. In this last section, I want to introduce suggestions for how institutions can support structural change.

Academic institutions could create more equality in citation practices by making citation practices and the sociology of knowledge part of education programmes (Nunkoo et al, 2019). Additionally, institutions could adopt more diverse forms of measuring expertise in academia – away from citation numbers and towards taking other forms of knowledge production and communication into account. For example, measures of excellence could include teaching expertise, non-academic publications, or presentations at conferences. As a result, our understanding of expertise would be diversified, offering more than one path within academia (Kreienkamp et al, 2020).

Publishing houses hold particular power over privilege in the publication process. Adopting a fully anonymized triple-blind review process could put the focus on a manuscript's content instead of the background of the author (Nunkoo et al, 2019; or reviewer, Kreienkamp et al, 2020). Additionally, journals could invest more in language assistance programmes, both in the form of translators and of support staff. As English-language journals and publishers remain the de facto knowledge and prestige centres in many fields, we will have to find ways of bridging language barriers if we want to give all brilliant ideas the chance to be influential.

Lastly, I want to discuss the contentious issue of building organizational structures that actively promote the excellence of disadvantaged groups in academia and publishing. Disadvantages in academia are based on deep socio-historical injustices, and simply offering equality of opportunities on paper often does not remove disadvantages. While there have been discussions of the drawbacks of affirmative action policies (Schuck, 2002), the minimal improvements in the last two decades suggest that it might be time to take more active steps to repair decades and centuries of oppression and exclusion (see, for example, Logan, 1996; Tierney, 1997). For publishing houses, this could take the form of purposefully giving editor positions, feature, or lead article status to scholars from disadvantaged groups, or calling for special issues on community-embedded topics with disadvantaged scholars.

Conclusion

In this chapter, I have discussed some of the processes that underlie the current inequalities in the publication and citation process, introduced some counter-movements, and proposed practical suggestions for individuals and institutions based on critical research methods. To discuss some of the harmful aspects of current citation practices I have discussed institutional cultural issues (for example, h-index, impact factors) and individual cultural issues (for example, self-citations, citation pushing, citation circles). In response to these issues, I have suggested that primarily focusing on authors from the community one is investigating reaffirms ownership over knowledge and contributes to a relevant bottom-up approach, as suggested by indigenous and participatory research initiatives. Beyond the immediate community of interest, I have proposed actively engaging with topical literature by disadvantaged groups so as to broaden one's base of knowledge and to critically reflect on topics of layered privilege, as suggested by feminist and critical race theorists. I have proposed to only then complement one's literature search and discussion with the works of the privileged and established canon. I have also discussed the challenges of going against the status quo, especially for disadvantaged groups, and highlighted the importance of academic institutions and publishing houses taking an active stance to make academic knowledge dissemination more reflective and just.

Note

1 The conference was organized with Dr. Joram Tarusarira from the Centre for Religion, Conflict, and Globalization and Dr. Monica Lopez Lopez from the Faculty of Behavioral and Social Sciences at the University of Groningen. I also presented the topic at workshops organized by Activism Today, the University Library Services, and the Feminist Network Groningen.

References

Ahmed, Sara (2017) *Living a Feminist Life*. Durham, NC and London: Duke University Press.

Ali, Suki (2007) 'Feminism and postcolonial: Knowledge/politics', *Ethnic and Racial Studies*, 30(2): 191–212.

Arvin, Maile, Tuck, Eve and Morrill, Angie (2013) 'Decolonizing feminism: Challenging connections between settler colonialism and heteropatriarchy', *Feminist Formations*, 25(1): 8–34.

Bergerson, Amy Aldous (2003) 'Critical race theory and white racism: Is there room for white scholars in fighting racism in education?', *International Journal of Qualitative Studies in Education*, 16(1): 51–63.

Boog, Ben, Slagter, Meindert and Zeelen, Jacques (2008) 'Developing ethics and standards in action research', *Journal of Social Intervention: Theory and Practice*, 17(4): 15–28.

Burbules, Nicholas C. (2015) 'The changing functions of citation: From knowledge networking to academic cash-value', *Paedagogica Historica*, 51(6): 716–726.

Coleman, Major G. (2005) 'Racism in academia: The white superiority supposition in the "unbiased" search for knowledge', *European Journal of Political Economy*, 21(3): 762–774.

Dion, Michelle L., Sumner, Jane Lawrence and Mitchell, Sara McLaughlin (2018) 'Gendered citation patterns across political science and social science methodology fields', *Political Analysis*, 26: 312–327.

Elder, Brent C., and Odoyo, Kenneth O. (2018) 'Multiple methodologies: Using community-based participatory research and decolonizing methodologies in Kenya', *International Journal of Qualitative Studies in Education*, 31(4): 293–311. doi: 10.1080/09518398.2017.1422290.

Foo, Jong Yong Abdiel (2013) 'Implications of a single highly cited article on a journal and its citation indexes: A tale of two journals', *Accountability in Research*, 20(2): 93–106.

Gálvez, Ramiro H. (2017) 'Assessing author self-citation as a mechanism of relevant knowledge diffusion', *Scientometrics*, 111: 1801–1812.

Garcia-Ramon, Maria Dolors (2003) 'Globalization and international geography: The questions of languages and scholarly traditions', *Progress in Human Geography*, 27(1): 1–5.

Gómez, Jennifer M. (2020) 'Exposure to discrimination, cultural betrayal, and intoxication as a black female graduate student applying for tenure-track faculty positions', in Yolanda Flores Niemann, Gabriella Gutiérrez y Muhs, and Carmen G. Gonzalez (eds) *Presumed Incompetent II: Race, Class, Power, and Resistance of Women in Academia*. Logan: Utah State University Press, pp 204–214.

Grosfoguel, Ramón (2011) 'Decolonizing post-colonial studies and paradigms of political-economy: Transmodernity, decolonial thinking, and global coloniality', *Transmodernity: Journal of Peripheral Cultural Production of the Luso-Hispanic World*, 1(1): 1–38. [online] Available at: http://bit.ly/2JEsixP [accessed 15 April 2021].

Hall, C. Michael (2016) 'Publishing patterns of highly cited scholars in tourism and hospitality Google Scholar metrics', *Journal of Hospitality and Tourism*, 14(1): 1–17. [online] Available at: https://bit.ly/3ahMQcy [accessed 15 April 2021].

Helmer, Markus, Schottdorf, Manual, Neef, Andreas, and Battaglia, Demian (2017) 'Gender bias in scholarly peer review', *eLife*, 6: 1–18.

Hirsch, Jorge E. (2005) 'An index to quantify an individual's scientific research output', *Proceedings of the National Academy of Sciences of the United States of America*, 102(46): 16569–16572.

Kovach, Margaret Elizabeth (2009) *Indigenous Methodologies: Characteristics, Conversations, and Contexts*. Toronto: University of Toronto Press.

Kreienkamp, Jannis, Agostini, Maximilian, Kunz, Marvin C., and Meyerhuber, Malte Ingo (2020) 'Normative influences in science and their impact on (objective) empirical research', in Alexander M. Bauer and Malte Meyerhuber (eds) *Empirical Research and Normative Theory – Transdisciplinary Perspectives on Two Methodical Traditions Between Separation and Interdependence*. Berlin: De Gruyter, pp 75–104.

Kubota, Ryuko (2020) 'Confronting epistemological racism, decolonizing scholarly knowledge: Race and gender in applied linguistics', *Applied Linguistics*, 41(5): 712–732.

Leahey, Erin (2006) 'Gender differences in productivity: Research specialization as a missing link', *Gender & Society*, 20(6): 754–780.

Lee, Shi Young, Lee, Sanghack and Jun, Sung Hee (2010) 'Author and article characteristics, journal quality and citation in economic research', *Applied Economics Letters*, 17(17): 1697–1701.

Logan, B. (1996) 'A narrative of affirmative action', *Ohio Northern University Law Review*, 22(4): 1337–1342.

Maliniak, Daniel, Powers, Ryan and Walter, Barbara F. (2013) 'The gender citation gap in international relations', *International Organization*, 67(4): 889–922.

Mason, Patrick L., Myers, Samuel L., and Darity, William A. (2005) 'Is there racism in economic research?', *European Journal of Political Economy*, 21(3): 755–761.

Mignolo, Walter D. (2009) 'Epistemic disobedience, independent thought and decolonial freedom', *Theory, Culture & Society*, 26(7–8): 159–181.

Mott, Carrie and Cockayne, Daniel (2017) 'Citation matters: Mobilizing the politics of citation toward a practice of "conscientious engagement"', *Gender, Place and Culture*, 24(7): 954–973.

Murdie, Amanda (2018) 'We need a new international norm: Eradicating the gender citation gap', *Political Analysis*, 26(3): 345–347.

Nunkoo, Robin, Hall, C. Michael, Rughoobur-Seetah, Soujata, and Teeroovengadum, Viraiyan (2019) 'Citation practices in tourism research: Toward a gender conscientious engagement', *Annals of Tourism Research*, 79(102755): 1–13.

Pérez Huber, Lindsay and Solorzano, Daniel G. (2015) 'Racial microaggressions as a tool for critical race research', *Race Ethnicity and Education*, 18(3): 297–320.

Savas, Gokhan (2014) 'Understanding critical race theory as a framework in higher educational research', *British Journal of Sociology of Education*, 35(4): 506–522.

Schuck, Peter H. (2002) 'Affirmative action: Past, present, and future', *Yale Law & Policy Review*, 20(1): 1–96.

Stewart, James B. (2005) 'Is there racism in economic research?', *European Journal of Political Economy*, 21(3): 790–794.

Sumner, Jane Lawrence (2018) 'The Gender Balance Assessment Tool (GBAT): A web-based tool for estimating gender balance in syllabi and bibliographies', *PS: Political Science & Politics*, 51(02): 396–400.

Suzack, Cheryl (2015) 'Indigenous feminisms in Canada', *NORA – Nordic Journal of Feminist and Gender Research*, 23(4): 261–274.

Symonds, Matthew R.E., Gemmell, Neil J., Braisher, Tamsin L., Gorringe, Kylie L., and Elgar, Mark A. (2006) 'Gender differences in publication output: Towards an unbiased metric of research performance', *PLoS ONE*, 1(1): e127.

Tarusarira, Joram (2018) 'Beyond epistemicide: Toward multiple forms of knowledge', *Counterpoint: Navigating Knowledge*. [online] Available at: https://bit.ly/32idOwj [accessed 18 January 2019].

Tierney, William G. (1997) 'The parameters of affirmative action: equity and excellence in the academy', *Review of Educational Research*, 67(2): 165–196.

Treviño, A. Javier, Harris, Michelle A., and Wallace, Derron (2008) 'What's so critical about critical race theory?', *Contemporary Justice Review*, 11(1): 7–10.

Tuck, Eve (2009) 'Re-visioning action: Participatory action research and indigenous theories of change', *The Urban Review*, 41(1): 47–65.

Tuck, Eve and Fine, Michelle (2007) 'Inner angles. A range of ethical responses to/with indigenous and decolonizing theories', in Norman K. Denzin and Michael D. Giardina (eds) *Ethical Futures in Qualitative Research*. Walnut Creek, CA: Left Coast Press, pp 145–168.

Tuck, Eve and Yang, K. Wayne (2012) 'Decolonization is not a metaphor', *Decolonization: Indigeneity, Education, & Society*, 1(1): 1–40.

Valentine, Gill (2007) 'Theorizing and researching intersectionality: A challenge for feminist geography', *The Professional Geographer*, 59(1): 10–21.

12

Scholarship in a Globalized World: The Publishing Ecosystem and Alternatives to the Oligopoly

Paige Mann

As the world reckons with racial and other systemic injustices, so too must academics reckon with publishing injustices. This must start with a recognition that our books, textbooks, and articles are now more commodities than they are intellectual achievements. It also begins with a recognition that scholars' reactions to that statement will depend on their scholarly positions and privileges.

Scholarly publishing is a multibillion-dollar industry run by multinational corporations (Johnson et al, 2018, p 22). This alone should warn scholars of the need to critically examine the parties and practices involved and their impacts on people. The financial strength of scholarly publishing stems from its corporate control of what counts as scholarly excellence. What was once the scholar's domain has become a pawn of commerce and competition. This transfer of responsibility has produced a complex web of economic, social, legal, and cultural dependencies at the center of which sits the publishing oligopoly.

Scholars, devoting surprisingly little attention to this displacement, may be unaware of the ways that various scholar communities are subjected to oligopolistic powers. Even activist scholars and justice-oriented disciplines reinforce power asymmetries with their silence on the matter. Only by confronting these power asymmetries and scholars' relationships with publishing can readers dismantle the oligopoly and rebuild a more just publishing ecosystem.

Publishing as an arm for profit

Scholarly publishing began in the 17th century; however, only in the 20th century did it become massively profitable. After the Second World War, enrollments in higher education grew across the world. Populations rose, families migrated to urban centers, and marginalized communities − including women and those previously under colonial rule − sought opportunities in the growing knowledge economies (Altbach et al, 2009, pp 80–86, 98–104; Fabricant and Brier, 2016, p 45; Fyfe et al, 2017, p 7). As the student bodies grew, so too did the size of the faculty, which prompted more specialization, professionalization, and expectations to publish (Fabricant and Brier, 2016, p 44; Fyfe et al, 2017, p 7). Sustained investments in higher education and growth in publishing revealed the publishing market's potential. This changed both the publishing business and its business strategies (Fyfe et al, 2017).

Toward the end of the 20th century, however, public investments in higher education dwindled. Despite reductions in library budgets, the costs of library acquisitions continued to rise. Library responses to this double threat triggered profound changes to the publishing ecosystem that culminated with large publishers having the upper hand (Torres and Schugerensky, 2002, p 438; Washburn, 2005, p 59; Beverungen et al, 2012, p 930; Peekhaus, 2012, p 582). Libraries cancelled some subscriptions, subsidized others with book funds, and embraced Big Deal packages from large publishers. Like streaming services today, Big Deals provided access to bundled content at deep discounts (Peekhaus, 2012). Smaller publishers − faced with cancelled subscriptions, fewer book orders, and competition from Big Deals − merged with, or otherwise partnered with, larger publishers (Larivière et al, 2015; Fyfe et al, 2017, pp 9–10; Posada and Chen, 2018; Orlandi et al, 2019, p 57). This concentrated publishing into the hands of a few publishers, such that, by 2013, just five publishers were responsible for half of all journals, papers, and citations (Didegah and Gazni, 2011; Larivière et al, 2015).

In fact, high subscription fees continue to plague libraries. Annual increases of 4–8 per cent are common and contribute to profit margins reported to be as high as 26 per cent for Taylor & Francis, 34 per cent for Springer, 36 per cent for Elsevier, and 46 per cent for Wiley (Pirie, 2009, p 38; Beverungen et al, 2012, p 931; Bosch et al, 2020). These profit margins meet or exceed those of Apple, Google, and Amazon, and they far surpass those of the Standard & Poor's 500 Index (S&P 500) companies, which typically post margins of 2–10 per cent (Yardeni and Abbott, 2014, p 3; Buranyi, 2017). Despite persistent austerity, higher education continues to feed the oligopoly. This can largely be explained by the rise of publisher influence in prestige regimes.

The global impacts of prestige regimes

As the academy grew and globalized, scholars found it increasingly difficult to assess scholarly quality and discern who their peers were. The need arose to evaluate research in ways that could be consistently and objectively applied (Hazelkorn, 2014, p 16; Fyfe et al, 2017, pp 7–8). This opened a door for external, supposedly neutral parties to step in. Besieged by audit cultures and the competition for resources, scholars and institutions welcomed publishers to this role and overlooked any conflicts of interest.

The result was a series of ranking instruments, such as Clarivate's Journal Impact Factor and Journal Citation Reports (JCR), Elsevier's CiteScore, and Digital Science's Altmetric. These tools rank publications according to their "impact factor" – that is, according to how much influence they have in the scholarly world. These rankings influence where scholars publish, with whom they collaborate, and who gets hired and promoted.[1] Publishers, libraries, and funders use these scores to benchmark performance, measure prestige, and inform subscription and funding decisions. Senior administrators as well as governments depend on this research "intelligence" to inform strategic plans and allocate budgets (Torres and Schugerensky, 2002; Collins and Park, 2016; Aspesi et al, 2019, p 14). Reducing quality to a calculation, corporate instruments reorganized scholarship into hierarchies and hijacked what used to be scholarly decisions. As appraisers of research, publishers acquired enormous positions of influence. From these positions, corporations engineered ways to generate revenue, foster competition, and manipulate scholars' relationships with scholarship. Yet, rather than trigger an outcry from scholar communities, corporate influence grew in scope.

Such ranking systems proliferated beyond scholarly journals. For example, 2003 ushered in the Academic Ranking of World Universities (ARWU) (Hazelkorn, 2014, p 13). The following year a new ranking system emerged that would later split into the Times Higher Education World University Rankings (THE) and Quacquarelli Symonds (QS) (Hazelkorn, 2014, p 15). Although rankings focus on higher education, arguably more attention is paid to the oligopoly. Twenty per cent of a QS score is based on faculty citation data from Elsevier (QS Quacquarelli Symonds Limited, 2021). At least 60 per cent of an ARWU score is based on Clarivate data (Academic Ranking of World Universities, nd). For a THE score, 38.5 per cent is based on Elsevier data with an additional 33 per cent derived from "academics randomly selected by Elsevier" (Ross, 2020, p 5). Consequently, while global rankings drive frequent assessments, resource allocations, changes to funding formulas, and promotion criteria, the oligopoly is what drives global rankings (Deem et al, 2008; Hazelkorn et al, 2014).

This system gives the big publishers undue influence over research, funding, and career trajectories. Moreover, it exposes a core defect in profit-based regimes. By deliberately designing instruments to be elitist, corporations capitalize on economic wealth at the expense of scholarly wealth. This sacrifices diverse approaches to scholarship. At issue are those who decide what counts as scholarship, what makes it valuable, who benefits from it, who gets to participate and under what terms.

Research reveals that Latin American publications are significantly under-represented in international research tools. Beigel (2014) found that Scopus and Clarivate's Web of Science (WoS) indexed between 8 and 50 per cent of these publications when compared against Latin American indices such as Red de Revistas Científicas de América Latina y El Caribe, España y Portugal (Redalyc), Scientific Electronic Library Online (SciELO), Citas Latinoamericanas en Ciencias Sociales y Humanidades (CLASE), Índice de Revistas Latinoamericanas en Ciencia (PERIODICA), and Latindex. Navas-Fernández et al (2018) found that Scopus indexed only one quarter of Spanish journals, and WoS indexed a mere tenth of Spanish journals. Beigel (2014) also found that social sciences and humanities papers authored by scholars affiliated with sub-Saharan African institutions numbered 20,434 in African Journals Online (AJOL), as compared to 9,823 papers in Scopus and 3,728 in Clarivate's Social Sciences Citation Index.

Conversely, around half of all publications in JCR and Elsevier's Scopus are based in the United States (US) or the United Kingdom (UK) (Didegah and Gazni, 2011).[2] Additionally, global rankings represent fewer than 1 per cent of universities, most of which are located in the US (Deem et al, 2008, pp 85–86; Hazelkorn, 2014, p 23).

These studies underscore how core research tools used by students and researchers around the world valorize Anglo–American models of scholarship and undermine other models of excellence. This creates a split reality for scholars: those in the global North operate largely unaware of, and unencumbered by, global pressures on scholars, while those in the global South may face pressures to conform to foreign standards (Deem et al, 2008, pp 85–86; Jöns and Hoyler, 2013; Paasi, 2015). Even China, which is starting to defy the Anglo–American hegemony, has spent hundreds of millions of dollars to "improve" Chinese journals, many of which are publishing in English (Cyranoski, 2019).

Le Roux (2015) conveys these pressures in more detail and from a South African perspective. Toward the end of the 20th century, when mergers and acquisitions began to create today's publishing oligopoly, foreign publishers approached South African publishers. This raised concerns about "predatory" interests, foreign ownership of local research, loss of access to local research, and a "re-colonization of South African knowledge production" (le Roux, 2015, p 315). Yet, over time, deals were made reaping both benefits and costs. "Whereas previously South African journals had provided a relatively safe platform for local academics to publish, without intense global competition, now they actively sought to improve the quality and range of submissions, and to solicit papers from authors based in other countries" (le Roux, 2015, pp 313–314).

Journals changed their editorial policies and boards, their authors and audiences, their formatting and titular practices. Though accepted overall as positive, le Roux (2015, pp 316–317) laments that these deals make profit a "key driving force behind journal publishing. [This sustains] an ongoing tension between the local and the international, as indigenous knowledge is now being promoted at the same time as the importance of participating in global knowledge production."

Writing from personal experience, Canagarajah (2002, pp 12–13) shares another way that corporate regimes of excellence capitalize on economic wealth at the expense of scholarly wealth. He describes how his global perspectives were cannibalized in scholarly publishing.

> I began to experience the inequalities in publishing most intensely when I returned to Sri Lanka from postgraduate work in the United States. Though I faced a lot of difficulties in conducting research and writing, these matters could not be addressed in the articles I wrote [for Northern audiences]. In a few instances, in order to explain the discursive differences in my work, I mentioned in a paragraph or two the problems of periphery scholars in conducting research and publishing according to center requirements. But eventually, I had to omit these statements in the final drafts as reviewers felt that they were irrelevant to the focus of my paper. ... [S]uch publishing assumptions and practices place hurdles in the way of addressing the concerns relating to different contexts of knowledge production.

Unfortunately, these pressures will likely intensify as surveillance of online behaviors becomes increasingly commonplace within and beyond the publishing industry. Through acquisitions that include social networks, collaborative writing tools, preprint servers, and reference management software, publishers are inserting themselves more broadly into informal and non-traditional scholar spaces.[3] This enables them to observe previously obscure activities. They can, in principle, now see the questions that scholars are asking, who is reading what, and who is talking to whom (Schonfeld, 2017a; Schonfeld, 2017b; Aspesi et al, 2019; Chen et al, 2019; Aspesi et al, 2020). Like Google and Facebook, these corporations are becoming the digital infrastructure that can amass data, exploit user behavior, and breed dependence (Zuboff, 2019). This heralds a new era where Big Data, artificial intelligence, and surveillance capitalism expand what can be analyzed and commercialized in research and education.[4] This will surely affect researcher profiles in Research Information Management Systems (RIMS; also known as Current Research Information Systems: CRIS).

However, perhaps more concerning is that data on past performance can be used to predict and manipulate future performance (Aspesi et al, 2019, p 16). For example, institutions are currently working with Wiley to analyze conversations with prospective students to "form deeper connections with learners" and to understand their decision-making processes (Pearson, 2019, pp 11–12; Wiley, 2021a). Scholars must recognize these mutations in the publishing industry and respond by changing how we operate.

Leveraging intellectual capital to transform scholarly publishing

To transform an ecosystem centered on corporate juggernauts, scholars must act both collectively and in ways that benefit fellow scholar communities. Through economic, social, legal, and cultural mechanisms, scholars can circumscribe the powers of the oligopoly.

Reflect on where and how intellectual capital is invested

First, scholars can reflect on where and how we invest our intellectual capital. As scholars, intellectual capital refers to all that we do through our research, teaching, and service. This includes the scholarship we donate to publishers, the rights and responsibilities associated with that scholarship, the clout we have with publishers, and the labor we donate as editors and peer reviewers. In an era of increasing surveillance, intellectual capital also includes our online activities. Decisions about where and how we invest this capital are not neutral. They either fortify empires or resist them, center dominant players or those on the periphery. To achieve the latter, scholars must dismantle the oligopoly and its competitive regimes of excellence. Scholars must also reclaim control over scholarly excellence and distribute power and resources in ways that prioritize diverse approaches to scholarship.

Reclaim the tenets of excellence and terms of assessment

Second, scholars can reclaim the tenets of excellence and the terms under which we are assessed. Although prestige metrics and data analytics are distinct areas, both collect and analyze data used to measure the value of scholars and scholarship. For this reason, the following principles aim to empower people and mitigate their commercial exploitation. They build upon the HuMetricsHSS Values Framework, the Declaration on Research Assessment (DORA), and the Leiden Manifesto. Scholars are encouraged to engage their communities to embed these principles into policy documents and contracts with providers.

- Scholar communities will own and govern their data and use of that data. Providers shall have temporary access to that data and only by permission.
- Providers will manage a community's data in service to that community. Providers will be accountable to communities whose data they manage.
- The management of data will use CARE and FAIR[5] data principles to maximize community and inter-community benefits.
- The collection of data and how it is used to measure performance will be transparent.
- Assessments will value local priorities, rejecting principles of universalism which promote competition and hegemony.
- Communities will hold ourselves accountable to others in the scholarly publishing ecosystem. This aims to foster equity and minimize harm in the use of data and assessments.

Foster bibliodiversity

Third, scholars can foster bibliodiversity. Bibliodiversity interrupts prestige regimes and instead cherishes a publishing ecosystem with a diversity of thought and actors. It recognizes that "knowledge practices and institutions may be structured and enacted in ways that simultaneously privilege certain epistemic values, while being unjust or dismissive toward particular knowers or ways of knowing" (Shearer et al, 2020, p 4).

Perhaps the biggest challenge to come out of the shift from print to digital has been to traditional gatekeeping. As publishing barriers were eased, more diverse publishers and publishing models entered the scene (Nwagmu, 2016). Exemplars of this are Redalyc and AmeliCA, which were founded primarily to support open access (OA)[6] publishing in Latin America. Facing exclusion from, and assimilation into, Northern publishing circuits, these initiatives have shifted their focus to oppose the oligopoly (Chan, 2018; Debat and Babini, 2019). Guided by the United Nations Sustainable Development Goals, they prioritize local priorities and social good over Northern prestige (Becerril-García and Aguado-López, 2019). Treating scholarship as a public good, they invest in nonprofit, academic-owned discovery platforms and metrics. In fact, their approach to accessibility surpasses that of corporate publishers. Through in-house software development, AmeliCA and Redalyc enable better preservation of scholarship and support for screen readers and language translation.[7] Their work prioritizes non-commercial OA publishing, smaller publishers, and a diversity of readers.

To support bibliodiversity, it is important to recognize that corporations have become the largest OA publishers, and they now sabotage competition through OA co-option and confusion. To protect their investments, they instituted document versions to restrict which versions could be openly shared.[8] To protect their revenues, they hybridized OA. Hybrid OA collects library subscription fees along with article-processing charges (APCs). While this helps to underwrite publishing costs, APC-based publishing models risk amplifying the research of wealthier scholars and hindering the research of the less wealthy (Nabyonga-Orem et al, 2020).

Consequently, scholars must be wary of efforts that advance OA at the expense of equity. Initiatives like Plan S, while noble in intent, are reinforcing pay-to-publish models which prioritize corporatized OA and privilege wealthier scholars (Debat and Babini, 2019). Scholars would also do well to critically examine the definition of predatory publishing. Newer publishers, many from the global South, are disproportionately labeled as predatory for not conforming to mainstream, hegemonic practices (Nwagmu, 2016; Bell, 2017, pp 657–660; Raju, 2018).

To support bibliodiversity, scholars must invest intellectual capital into established and emerging publishing models that are run by, and for, scholars. These include university presses and society publishers, community-controlled OA repositories and preprint servers, and non-existent or very low APCs.[9] Scholars can expand go-to lists of publishers and publications by exploring Redalyc, African Journals Online, Le Grenier des savoirs, the Directory of Open Access Journals (DOAJ),[10] the Radical Open Access Collective, the Library Publishing Directory, and the Open Textbook Network.

Limit publisher monopolies on content

Fourth, scholars can limit publisher monopolies on content. Recognizing OA's potential to decouple profit and exclusion from publishing, the Association of College and Research Libraries (ACRL) put out a bold policy. ACRL "recommends as standard practice that academic librarians publish in open access venues, deposit in open repositories, and make openly accessible all products across the lifecycle of their scholarly and research activity, including articles, research data, monographs, presentations, digital scholarship, grant documentation, and grey literature" (ACRL, 2019). This can only happen when authors "retain rights to these products of scholarship and make them available for reuse under an appropriate license." ACRL's policy recognizes the pivotal role that copyright and licenses play in relations between content creators, users, and providers.

In the print age, copyright laws helped balance the interests of these parties. However, copyright has not kept pace with the shift to digital publishing. As a result, parties must draw heavily on legal contracts to determine costs and the terms of use. With greater access to business and legal expertise, providers sought an advantage. By preserving the print-based practice of copyright transfers from authors to publishers, providers retained a monopoly over content. This puts users, unable to get content elsewhere, at a disadvantage.[11] As a result, libraries must often sign contracts with unfavorable terms that include confidentiality clauses. This hinders libraries' ability to compare costs and terms of use with other libraries.

To limit publisher monopolies, scholars can exercise their legal rights with four actions: they can retain some copyrights, post scholarship to OA repositories, assign open licenses, and reuse openly licensed work. Without government oversight, scholars must use publishing contracts to negotiate terms that are favorable to readers. This means transferring only those copyrights that are essential to online publishing. Scholars may be surprised to learn that this can be relatively easy to do with persistence and grace.[12] Next, scholars can exercise the rights they have retained by lawfully posting their work to OA repositories and assigning open licenses to their work.[13] This enables people to legally access and use scholarship. This is in stark contrast to traditional practices that restrict distribution, require payment, and place limits on use. Instead, openly licensed textbooks and other scholarship can be used in courses and life without reliance on fair use, fees, or university affiliation.

By making scholarship openly available, scholars turn scholarship from private goods into public goods. These actions also prompt changes in the ways that scholarship is financed, and power is distributed. While ResearchGate and SciHub offer extralegal workarounds to monopolies, scholars can use the legal strategies presented here to strengthen the OA movement.

Protest exploitative uses of monopolies

Fifth, scholars can protest exploitative uses of monopolies. Scholars must devote attention to ways that publishers wield their monopoly powers over content (American Library Association, 2019). As advocates for our research and teaching communities, librarians negotiate for the rights to do text and data mining, course packs, course reserves, and interlibrary loans. Librarians also advocate for perpetual access to content in their contracts (ESAC, nd). Though underestimated and often invisible, librarians can be some of scholars' staunchest champions. However, to be successful negotiators, librarians must be able to end negotiations when necessary. This requires scholars' willingness to forego access to scholarship, which has afforded some large university library systems the leverage needed to assert fairer negotiating terms (Bastian, 2018; Kell, 2019; Sanders, 2019).

Scholars must also recognize when providers are disadvantaging users by sidestepping librarians and contracting directly with users. This strategy eliminates collective bargaining powers and increases revenue. Digital, proprietary textbooks and related modules may use this strategy. They are sometimes marketed to faculty and administrators as tools that assess learning and save students money. However, they enable corporate surveillance of learners and undermine cost-saving strategies. Digital restrictions prevent the sharing of textbooks between students, use of library course reserves, and used-book discounts (Nagle and Vitez, 2020, p 5).

For years, only a handful of providers used the direct-to-consumer strategy, but this may be changing (Pearson, 2019, pp 13, 36). When the global pandemic prompted a shift to online learning, librarians saw an uptick in use by a few surprising actors. Publishers like Oxford University Press, Modern Language Association, American Psychological Association, and the American Chemical Society refused to license some of their content to libraries, or did so at exorbitant prices.[14] This business strategy forces users to either pay for content themselves, forego access, or use extralegal workarounds. While this presents financial, academic, and legal burdens for individuals, its effect on libraries cannot be overlooked. By disabling libraries from democratizing access to information, corporations disregard marginalized communities. These communities already face greater economic, educational, and judicial risks, which strategies like direct-to-consumer only exacerbate.

Divest funding from the oligopoly

Lastly, scholars can divest funding from the oligopoly. In what can be described as a toxic relationship, scholars cede undue power and authority to an exploitative oligopoly. At a time when surveillance capitalism is taking root in scholarly publishing, scholars must dismantle the corporate foundations that distort and hegemonize scholarship. The publishing oligopoly is a recent phenomenon and alternatives to the oligopoly are possible. Bold investments are needed to develop and sustain scholar-led publications, technologies, and infrastructures that contribute to a common good. Failure to act will leave initiatives vulnerable to acquisition, but AmeliCA illustrates what is possible (Mallapaty, 2020; Tracz, 2020; Wiley, 2021b).

With the support of scholars, librarians can divert subscription fees away from the oligopoly and into community-led, open initiatives (Lewis, 2017; Bosch et al, 2020). Remaining funds can sustain payments for core titles only available through the oligopoly. These payments should be subject to additional scrutiny as well as an accounting for the ways that these investments impact on the publishing ecosystem. While radical, this approach is possible so long as library divestitures echo broader scholarly efforts.

Publishing as a relational practice

As participants in a commercial ecosystem dominated by an oligopoly, scholars face multiple disadvantages. While publishing previously offered more of a reciprocal relationship, the dynamics have grown more exploitative over time. Rooted in the transfer of scholarly authority to corporations, it is now accurate to describe publishing as a competitive activity that valorizes Anglo-American models of scholarship. This is likely to grow more pronounced as corporate use of surveillance capitalism and Big Data increases.

To reverse these trends, scholars must update our discourse and practices. In our research and teaching spaces, scholars must associate publisher-defined 'scholarship' with hegemony, 'reputation' with profit, and 'excellence' with privilege. By illuminating the many actors, mechanisms, and motivations at play, scholars can correct the systems that facilitate corporate greed and alienate us from one another. By choosing communities over competitions, open access over monopolies, and bibliodiversity over an oligopoly, scholars can co-create an ecosystem that affirms the needs of a diverse world.

Notes

[1] Although Clarivate Analytics is not a publisher, its business goals and strategies increasingly overlap with those of publishers, warranting scrutiny. Digital Science is owned by Holtzbrink Publishing Group and is sibling to Springer Nature.

[2] Data downloaded on 21 April 2019 showed that 27 per cent of Scopus publications came from the US and 21 per cent came from the UK (Elsevier, nd).

[3] Examples include Wiley's acquisition of Authorea and Elsevier's acquisition of the Social Science Research Network (Elsevier, 2016; Pepe, nd.).

[4] In 2006, Elsevier stopped referring to itself as a publisher and emphasized itself as a data analytic company (Reed Elsevier, 2005). In 2018, Kleinman (2018a, 2018b) reported that Elsevier's parent company, RELX, and Clarivate sought to buy THE, underscoring corporate dominance in scholarly prestige and business intelligence.

[5] These acronymns refer to the CARE Principles for Indigenous Data Governance (see https://www.gida-global.org/care) and the FAIR Guiding Principles (see https://www.go-fair.org/fair-principles/).

[6] OA can lead to more equitable publishing by enabling free access to information, and freedom from most restrictions that discourage use.

[7] Marcalyc, developed by Redalyc, automates a process that converts journal content into a flexible machine-readable format. This enables journals in Redalyc to share content in multiple formats including HTML and ePUB. Readers can then translate texts into various languages with assistance from online tools.

[8] To determine which versions of a work can be posted legally, refer to publishing agreements, AmeliCA's AURA, Dulcinea, or SHERPA RoMEO. AURA, Dulcinea and RoMEO document the policies of many publications and outlines the versions that can be legally posted. Open Access Button's *Direct2AAM: Helping Authors Find Author Accepted Manuscripts* instructs authors on locating author-accepted manuscripts within journal-submission systems.

[9] Institutional repositories are typically managed by academic librarians. Scholar-owned repositories include repositories in the Open Science Framework Preprints network, Zenodo, and Hyper Article en Ligne.

[10] Scholars can use DOAJ to find journals that do not charge article processing charges (APCs).

[11] The COVID-19 pandemic shone a spotlight on this issue. While publishers received praise for granting free, temporary access to some content, libraries hit walls trying to provide communities with access to core material (Anderson et al, 2021; Fazackerley, 2021).

12 Authors of articles may be interested in SPARC's Author Addendum. Authors of long-form scholarship may be interested in Emory University and the University of Michigan's Model Publishing Contract for Digital Scholarship. The Authors Alliance also provides excellent resources on retaining and regaining copyrights, understanding and negotiating the terms of publishing contracts.

13 Creative Commons licenses are popular open licenses.

14 A few libraries have publicly drawn attention to these challenges (University of Guelph Library, 2020; Grand Valley State University, University Libraries, 2020). Scholar communities have also raised awareness about access to media (Cagle, 2019).

References

Academic Ranking of World Universities (nd) 'Methodology'. [online] Available from: http://bit.ly/arwu2020 [accessed 6 April 2021].

Altbach, Philip G., Reisberg, Liz, and Rumbley, Laura E. (2009) 'Trends in global higher education: Tracking an academic revolution. A report prepared for the UNESCO 2009 World Conference on Higher Education', *UNESCO*. [online] Available from: https://bit.ly/3cAmfru [accessed 17 March 2021].

American Library Association (2019) 'Competition in digital markets', Testimony before the U.S. House of Representatives Committee on the Judiciary, 15 October. [online] Available from: https://bit.ly/2QVNtSk [accessed 3 April 2021].

Anderson, Johanna, Ayris, Paul, and White, Ben (2021) 'E-textbooks – Scandal or market imperative?', *LSE Impact Blog*, 17 March. [online] Available from: https://bit.ly/3fOLGJo [accessed 6 April 2021].

Aspesi, Claudio, Allen, Nicole, Crow, Raym, Daugherty, Shawn, Joseph, Heather, McArthur, Joseph T.W., and Shockey, Nick (2019) 'SPARC landscape analysis: The changing academic publishing industry – Implications for academic institutions', *Scholarly Publishing and Academic Resources Coalition*. [online] Available from: https://bit.ly/3cM4rd4 [accessed 17 March 2021].

Aspesi, Claudio, Allen, Nicole, Crow, Raym, Joseph, Heather, McArthur, Joseph T.W., and Shockey, Nick (2020) '2020 update: SPARC landscape analysis and roadmap for action', *Scholarly Publishing and Academic Resources Coalition*. [online] Available from https://bit.ly/3cGfHHX [accessed 17 March 2021].

Association of College and Research Libraries (2019) 'ACRL policy statement on open access to scholarship by academic librarians'. [online] Available from: https://bit.ly/3tnt4Ui [accessed 17 March 2021].

Bastian, Hilda (2018) 'Europe expanded the "No Elsevier deal" zone and this could change everything', *Absolutely Maybe*, 30 July. [online] Available from: https://bit.ly/3ePcwAD [accessed 17 March 2021].

Becerril-García, Arianna, and Aguado-López, Eduardo (2019) 'Redalyc – AmeliCA: A non-profit publishing model to preserve the scholarly and open nature of scientific communication', *UNESCO*. [online] Available from: https://bit.ly/3eQi4KY [accessed 17 March 2021].

Beigel, Fernanda (2014) 'Publishing from the periphery: Structural heterogeneity and segmented circuits. The evaluation of scientific publications for tenure in Argentina's CONICET', *Current Sociology*, 62(5): 743–765.

Bell, Kirsten (2017) ' "Predatory" open access journals as parody: Exposing the limitations of "legitimate" academic publishing', *tripleC*, 15(2). [online] Available from https://bit.ly/3cXeJHJ [accessed 17 March 2021].

Beverungen, Armin, Böhm, Steffen, and Land, Christopher (2012) 'The poverty of journal publishing', *Organization*, 19(6): 929–938.

Bosch, Stephen, Albee, Barbara, and Romain, Sion (2020) 'Costs outstrip library budgets: Periodicals Price Survey 2020', *Library Journal*, 14 April. [online] Available from: https://bit.ly/3eMsyLu [accessed 17 March 2021].

Buranyi, Stephen (2017) 'Is the staggeringly profitable business of scientific publishing bad for science?', *The Guardian*, 27 June. [online] Available from: https://bit.ly/3cJef7D [accessed 17 March 2021].

Cagle, Chris (2019) 'Kanopy: Not just like Netflix, and not free', *Film Quarterly*, 3 May. [online] Available from: https://bit.ly/3rQRi8l [accessed 6 April 2021].

Canagarajah, A. Suresh (2002) *A Geopolitics of Academic Writing*. Pittsburgh, PA: University of Pittsburgh Press.

Chan, Leslie (2018) 'SciELO, open infrastructure and independence', *SciELO in Perspective*, 3 September. [online] Available from: https://bit.ly/3cGe Oz7 [accessed 17 March 2021].

Chen, George, Posada, Alejandro, and Chan, Leslie (2019) 'Vertical integration in academic publishing', in Leslie Chan and Pierre Mounier (eds) *Connecting the Knowledge Commons: From Projects to Sustainable Infrastructure*, Marseille: OpenEdition Press.

Collins, Francis L., and Park, Gil-Sung (2016) 'Ranking and the multiplication of reputation: Reflections from the frontier of globalizing higher education', *Higher Education*, 72(1): 115–129.

Cyranoski, David (2019) 'China splashes millions on hundreds of homegrown journals', *Nature*, 11 December. [online] Available from https://go.nature.com/3eVUpcl [accessed 17 March 2021].

Debat, Humberto, and Babini, Dominique (2019) 'Plan S in Latin America: A precautionary note', *PeerJ Preprints Archive*. [online] Available from: https://bit.ly/2QgEivB [accessed 17 March 2021].

Deem, Rosemary, Mok, Ka Ho, and Lucas, Lisa (2008) 'Transforming higher education in whose image? Exploring the concept of the "world-class" university in Europe and Asia', *Higher Education Policy*, 21: 83–97.

Didegah, Fereshteh, and Gazni, Ali (2011) 'The extent of concentration in journal publishing', *Learned Publishing*, 24(4): 303–310.

Elsevier (2016) 'Elsevier acquires the Social Science Research Network (SSRN), the leading social science and humanities repository and online community'. [online] Available from: https://bit.ly/2PEqbAd [accessed 6 April 2021].

Elsevier (nd) 'Source title list [Scopus sources September 2018 tab]'. [online] Available from: https://bit.ly/3fOJgdM [accessed 6 April 2021].

ESAC (nd) 'Negotiation principles internationally', Efficiency and Standards for Article Charges. [online] Available from: https://bit.ly/38RlrgT [accessed 17 March 2021].

Fabricant, Michael, and Brier, Stephen (2016) *Austerity Blues: Fighting for the Soul of Public Higher Education*. Baltimore: Johns Hopkins University Press.

Fazackerley, Anna (2021) '"Price gouging from Covid": student ebooks costing up to 500% more than in print', *The Guardian*, 29 January. [online] Available from: https://bit.ly/3mpKVYh [accessed 6 April 2021].

Fyfe, Aileen, Coate, Kelly, Curry, Stephen, Lawson, Stuart, Moxham, Noah, and Røstvik, Camilla Mørk (2017) 'Untangling academic publishing: A history of the relationship between commercial interests, academic prestige, and the circulation of research', Zenodo/CERN Preprint Archive. [online] Available from: https://bit.ly/3vCPGSw [accessed 17 March 2021].

Grand Valley State University, University Libraries (2020) 'Statement on textbooks in the library collection'. [online] Available from: https://bit.ly/3fRMEEz [accessed 6 April 2021].

Hazelkorn, Ellen (2014) 'Rankings and the global reputation race', *New Directions in Higher Education*, 2014(168): 13–26.

Hazelkorn, Ellen, Loukkola, Tia, and Zhang, Thérèse (2014) 'Rankings in institutional strategies and processes: Impact or illusion?' European University Association. [online] Available from: https://bit.ly/38MVfnx [accessed 17 March 2021].

Johnson, Rob, Watkinson, Anthony, and Mabe, Michael (2018) 'The STM report: An overview of scientific and scholarly publishing', International Association of Scientific, Technical and Medical Publishers. [online] Available from: https://bit.ly/3tv4Szs [accessed 17 March 2021].

Jöns, Heike and Hoyler, Michael (2013) 'Global geographies of higher education: The perspective of world university rankings', *Geoforum*, 46: 45–59.

Kell, Gretchen (2019) 'Why UC split with publishing giant Elsevier', *University of California News*, 6 March. [online] Available from: https://bit.ly/2OAFMQY [accessed 17 March 2021].

Kleinman, Mark (2018a) 'FTSE giant RELX plots £100m bid for Times Higher Education', *Sky News*, 26 November. [online] Available from: https://bit.ly/3cGAlI1 [accessed 17 March 2021].

Kleinman, Mark (2018b) 'Former Thomspon Reuter arm plots bid for universities bible' *Sky News*, 30 November. [online] Available from: https://bit.ly/3eQhOfe [accessed 17 March 2021].

Larivière, Vincent, Hausten, Stephanie, and Mongeon, Philippe (2015) 'The oligopoly of academic publishers in the digital era', *PLoS ONE*, 10(6): e0127502.

Le Roux, Elizabeth (2015) 'Publishing South African scholarship in the global academic community', *Notes and Records*, 69(3): 301–320.

Lewis, David W. (2017) 'The 2.5% commitment', IUPUI ScholarWorks Repository. [online] Available from: http://hdl.handle.net/1805/14063 [accessed 17 March 2021].

Mallapaty, Smriti (2020) 'Popular preprint servers face closure because of money troubles', *Nature*, 13 February. [online] Available from: https://go.nature.com/3eOtSxg [accessed 17 March 2021].

Nabyonga-Orem, Juliet, Asamani, James Avoka, Nyirenda, Thomas, and Abimbola, Seye (2020) 'Article processing charges are stalling the progress of African researchers: A call for urgent reforms', *BMJ Global Health*, 5(9): 1–4, e003650.

Nagle, Cailyn and Vitez, Kaitlyn (2020) 'Fixing the broken textbook market, 2nd edition', Public Interest Research Group. [online] Available from: https://bit.ly/2QgJXli [accessed 17 March 2021].

Navas-Fernández, Miguel, Abadal, Ernest and Rodrigues, Rosângela S. (2018) 'Internationality of Spanish scholarly journals indexed in Web of Science and Scopus', *Revista Española de Documentación Científica*, 41(3): e209.

Nwagmu, W.E. (2016) 'Open access in the developing regions: Situating the altercations about predatory publishing', *The Canadian Journal of Information and Library Science*, 40(1): 58–80.

Orlandi, Ludovico Bullini, Ricciardi, Francesca, Rossignoli, Cecilia and De Marco, Marco (2019) 'Scholarly work in the internet age: Co-evolving technologies, institutions and workflows', *Journal of Innovation & Knowledge*, 4(1): 55–61.

Paasi, Anssi (2015) 'Academic capitalism and the geopolitics of knowledge', in John Agnew, Virginie Mamadouh, Anna J. Secor, and Joanne Sharp (eds) *The Wiley Blackwell Companion to Political Geography*: Chichester, West Sussex, Malden, MA and Oxford: Wiley Blackwell, pp 509–523.

Pearson (2019) 'Annual report and accounts 2019', Pearson Publishing. [online] Available from: https://bit.ly/2Q7akde [accessed 17 March 2021].

Peekhaus, Wilhelm (2012) 'The enclosure and alienation of academic publishing: Lessons for the professoriate', *tripleC*, 10(2): 577–599.

Pepe, Alberto (nd) 'Authorea is acquired by Atypon and joins the Wiley family'. [online] Available from: https://bit.ly/3dFyfIT [accessed 6 April 2021].

Pirie, Iain (2009) 'The political economy of academic publishing', *Historical Materialism*, 17: 31–60.

Posada, Alejandro, and Chen, George (2018) 'Inequality in knowledge production: The integration of academic infrastructure by big publisher', Conference paper presented at ELPUB 2018 in Toronto, Canada, June. [online] Available at https://bit.ly/3vxpB7s [accessed 17 March 2021].

QS Quacquarelli Symonds Limited (2021) 'QS world university rankings – Methodology'. [online] Available from: https://bit.ly/3wmZIYl [accessed 18 March 2021).

Raji, Reggie (2018) 'Predatory publishing from a Global South perspective', *Library Publishing Coalition Blog*, 7 February. [online] Available from: https://bit.ly/3tvgSkh [accessed 17 March 2021].

Reed Elsevier (2005) 'Annual reports and financial statements: 2005', Reed Elsevier Publishing. [online] Available from: https://bit.ly/3tzYdnF [accessed 17 March 2021].

Ross, Duncan (2020) 'Methodology for overall and subject rankings for the Times Higher Education world university rankings 2021'. [online] Available from: http://bit.ly/the2021 [accessed 6 April 2021].

Sanders, Robert (2019) 'UC faculty to Elsevier: Restart negotiations or else', *University of California News*, 8 August. [online] Available from: https://bit.ly/3vxY3yJ [accessed 17 March 2021].

Schearer, Kathleen, Chan, Leslie, Kuchma, Iryna, and Mounier, Pierre (2020) 'Fostering bibliodiversity in scholarly communications: A call to action' Zenodo/CERN Preprint Archive. [online] Available at: https://bit.ly/3vC3AUT [accessed 17 March 2021].

Schonfeld, Roger C. (2017a) 'When is a publisher not a publisher? Cobbling together the pieces to build a workflow business', *The Scholarly Kitchen*, 9 February. [online] Available from: https://bit.ly/2Q79tt2 [accessed 17 March 2021].

Schonfeld, Roger C. (2017b) 'What is researcher workflow?', *Ithaka S+ R Blog*, 13 December. [online] Available from: https://bit.ly/3eR55IT [accessed 17 March 2021].

Torres, Carlos A, and Schugurensky, Daniel (2002) 'The political economy of higher education in the era of neoliberal globalization: Latin America in comparative perspective', *Higher Education*, 43(4): 429–455.

Tracz, Vitek (2020) 'F1000 Research joins Taylor & Francis Group', *F1000 Blog*, 10 January. [online] Available from: https://bit.ly/3cIbNhR [accessed 17 March 2021].

University of Guelph Library (2020) 'Commercial textbooks present challenges in a virtual environment'. [online] Available from: https://bit.ly/3cUTPtE [accessed 6 April 2021].

Washburn, Jennifer (2005) *University, Inc.: The Corporate Corruption of American Higher Education*. New York: Basic Books.

Wiley (2021a) 'Student recruitment and enrollment'. [online] Available from: https://bit.ly/2PwacUV [accessed 6 April 2021].

Wiley (2021b) 'Wiley announces the acquisition of Hindawi'. [online] Available from: https://bit.ly/3cR23TH [accessed 6 April 2021]

Yardeni, Edward, and Abbot, Joe (2014) 'S&P 500 sectors and industries profit margins', Yardeni Research. [online] Available from https://bit.ly/3cDncPY [accessed 17 March 2021].

Zuboff, Shoshana (2019) 'Surveillance capitalism and the challenge of collective action', *New Labor Forum*, 28(1): 10–29.

PART IV

Overcoming Intellectual Colonialism

13

Dealing with the Westernisation of Chinese Higher Education: Evidence from a Social Science Department

Fabio Bolzonar

Introduction

The well-known Chinese social scientist Ambrose King Yeo-chi (1978, p 37) wrote that sociology is 'a Western flower transplanted into Chinese soil' through the translations of Herbert Spencer's *The Study of Sociology* and Franklin Giddings' *Principles of Sociology* at the turn of the 20th century. In consolidating their power in East Asian countries, colonial administrators not only imposed unequal commercial treaties; they also spread Western social theory; this act, among others, relegated Asian social sciences to the margins (Alatas, 2000). This coloniality of knowledge (Mignolo, 2007) was even extended to countries that were not subject to formal colonial domination (Alatas and Sinha, 2001). As a consequence, Asian social sciences have not become sources of universally accepted paradigms and of professionally recognised knowledge translated beyond their countries of origin (Clammer, 2000, p 47).

This theoretical weakness has hindered the development of distinct Asian sociological schools and has also prevented the accumulation of knowledge, as the careless application of Western concepts and methods to Asian societies has often produced poor results (Nakane, 1992, p 4). Within China, Western epistemological hegemony has largely evaded challenge. Even though China and several other East Asian countries now play a major role in the global economy and their universities now attract a growing number of Western students and scholars, social science in most Asian nations is still dominated by Western scholarship disseminated by the leading North American and Western European universities (Qi, 2014).

On a world scale, however, debate on the Westernisation of knowledge has begun to generate its own significant scholarship, as have the efforts to decolonise higher education in general (de Oliveira Andreotti et al, 2015). Most contributions to this subject have come from intellectuals from the global South, feminist scholars, black social scientists, and students from indigenous communities (Keskin, 2014). These scholars have raised strong criticisms against the exclusionary curricula of Western universities (Peters, 2015; Bhambra et al, 2018) and have advocated 'epistemic disobedience' in order to decolonise knowledge (Mignolo, 2009). Although a few scholars have noted the West's intellectual hegemony in Asia at large (Wang, 2011; Alatas and Sinha, 2017), the Westernisation of higher education in China and the Eurocentrism of teaching sociology in that country have been the object of little focused debate.

Against this background, this chapter discusses the Westernisation of social theory in contemporary China. Its aim is to provide insights on the Eurocentrism of Chinese sociology and also, in accordance with the contributions to the volume of which this chapter is part, to indicate some actions that might foster greater epistemic pluralism in academic activities.

The following sections will focus on the teaching of social theory. This discipline, which is overwhelmingly produced in the global North (Go, 2016), has a prominent place in sociology's disciplinary culture (Connell, 2006, p 237). It is thus a good tool for showing the persistent coloniality of knowledge in Chinese social sciences. Pedagogical practices have a central role in reproducing the Eurocentrism of social theory. As a basic unit of the university, the classroom is one of the key places that can highlight the colonial nature of universities. Curricula 'shape how undergraduates, graduate students and academics understand and study the world. This is one of the reasons why curricula have become a popular target of marginalised students and academics seeking to decolonise the university' (Richardson, 2018, p 231).

The observations presented in this chapter draw on my experience as a researcher and lecturer in sociology at Fudan University from 2015 to 2017. Founded in Shanghai in 1905, Fudan is one of China's elite universities, renowned for its international outlook,[1] as several classes are taught in English, roughly 200 exchange programmes have been established with leading Western universities (for example, Columbia University, the University of Toronto, the University of Sydney, KU Leuven, the University of Manchester, Science Po) and 40 per cent of students are likely to spend a part of their education abroad (Times Higher Education, 2022).

The chapter is divided into four sections. The first section discusses some factors that have contributed to the Westernisation of sociology in contemporary China and that currently constrain our effort to promote greater pluralism of epistemology. The second provides some observations, drawn from my teaching, on how to help students become more aware of social theory's Eurocentrism. The third suggests some strategies to combat this Eurocentrism and to promote intellectual diversity in higher education. The final section provides some brief observations on the prospects for de-Westernising Chinese higher education.

Some historical notes on the Westernisation of Chinese sociology

The Westernisation of contemporary Chinese sociology is a result of the historical and political events that have shaped the development of higher education in the country. Three factors, among others, are particularly important. These are the troubled development of the Chinese sociological school, the educational reforms promoted by Chinese authorities, and the increasing international mobility of Chinese students.

Following China's military defeats in the mid-19th century, Chinese intellectuals became increasingly intrigued by the possibility of using Western knowledge to modernise their country. By the early 20th century, debates revolved around one single question: should Chinese people preserve their traditional cultural identity, or should they take on a Western one? (Fei, 2015, p 39). Sociology was enthusiastically received in China by those favouring the latter course. In the eyes of several Chinese scholars, this novel discipline was 'one of the salient features of Western culture and was recognised and accepted as a part of important Western scholarship by modern educational institutions' (King, 1978, p 38). In 1948, when the Communist Party imposed its authority over mainland China, there were 21 universities with sociology departments and roughly 600 undergraduate students enrolled in sociology programmes (Kejing, 1993, p 91). In this light, it is not an overstatement to say that mid-20th-century China seemed to be one of the most flourishing scenes for sociology outside of Western Europe and North America (King, 1978, p 39).

This acceptance should not lead us to assume that Chinese thinkers uncritically assimilated Western concepts and theories (Qi, 2014). Since the beginning of the 1930s, many of them had adopted critical attitudes towards Western social science and advocated 'sinicising' it. As Fei Xiaotong, arguably the founding father of Chinese sociology, noted, 'Western innovations are never precisely appropriate' for China (Fei, quoted in Hamilton and Zheng, 1992, p 15). Chinese scholars tended to understand this 'sinicising' project in two ways. One was to apply the discipline's existing Western theoretical paradigms to empirical facts drawn from Chinese society. The other was to attempt to integrate Western theories with Chinese cultural principles (Gransow, 1993, pp 100–101).

However, the development of a distinct Chinese sociological school was abruptly interrupted in the early 1950s when the Communist regime started to suppress any possible sources of internal dissent. Sociology came under increasing criticism as it was blamed for being a 'bourgeois discipline'. Sociology departments began to be closed, and most Chinese sociologists, including Fei, were accused of being 'rightist' (Pasternak, 1988). Despite various scholars' efforts to convince the regime that sociology could have an ancillary role in promoting Marxism–Leninism, by 1952, the discipline had ceased to exist on the mainland. It was not rehabilitated until 1979, after the end of the Mao era. In this second life, however, Chinese sociology focused on empirical and policy-oriented research, without much interest in theoretical debates (Wu, 2009). Although the rehabilitation helped Chinese scholars to establish closer links with the international academic community, particularly with American Chinese social scientists, Chinese sociology's theoretical weakness contributed to putting it under American sociology's influence (Yuhua et al, 2010, p 305).

In the three decades since the 1990s, Chinese sociologists have broadened their research interests and have shown greater attention to establishing more solid theoretical foundations for a distinct Chinese sociological school (Song, 2016; Fei, 1991). Their attempts have principally taken two directions. Zheng Hangsheng (2009) has proposed a kind of 'theoretical self-awareness': the construction of a distinct theoretical paradigm able to explain the social transformations happening in China. Fei Xiaotong (2015, p 47) has pointed out that the increasing contacts and exchanges with the West call for Chinese people to acquire greater 'cultural self-awareness' of their own society's historical and social foundations. Although both approaches represent novel efforts to indigenise Chinese sociology, they have not yet led to an original theoretical and research programme that could counterbalance the Western influence (Chen, 2017). As a consequence, Western sociology continued to have a remarkable impact on Chinese social science (Qi, 2014).

The reforms of Chinese higher education introduced since the mid-1990s also played a decisive role in strengthening Western influence on Chinese academia. As part of its commitment to modernise higher education, the Ministry of Education launched two overarching plans, Project 211 and Project 985, in 1995 and 1998, respectively. These projects aimed to make Chinese universities world-class universities (Ministry of Education, 2015a, 2015b). To reach this goal, public authorities have emphasised the adoption of globally oriented teaching programmes and publishing in international journals (Ministry of Education, 2015b; Chen, 2017). This put China's universities under the pressure of the current highly competitive international ranking systems (Fry, 2012) and left behind those higher education institutions that did not adopt the prevailing Western university model (Beerkens, 2010). In this sense, Chinese universities have been encouraged to follow the path undertaken by other Asian countries that 'are trying to learn and even copy the Western-based world class model' (Mbembe, 2016, p 38). This emulation of the Western model has also exerted pressure on young scholars, whose evaluations are based on the criteria 'publish internationally or perish'. Even though this development has pushed Chinese social scientists to open their intellectual perspectives, it has also led them, as in other Asian countries, to turn their backs on local scholarly communities and to publish according to the international audience's rules (Keim, 2010; Wang, 2011).

This openness of Chinese higher education to the Western model has also been favoured by the increasing international mobility of Chinese students. Although reliable data on this phenomenon are difficult to obtain, due to different countries' varying measurement criteria, the Organisation for Economic Co-operation and Development (OECD) has shown that China dominates the flow of international scholarly mobility (OECD, 2020). Brooks and Waters trace this to the country's 'substantial and growing unmet domestic demand for higher education, and [its] seemingly insatiable desire for 'Western' experiences' (2011, p 45). While past studies have noted that the majority of these students, who generally belong to the wealthiest families, used to remain abroad after graduating (Xiang and Shen, 2009), the most recent statistics provided by Chinese authorities show a growing trend of students returning to China after completing overseas studies (Ministry of Education, 2018).[2] Western-educated students typically acquire not only the skills that they have learned abroad but also the values and practices of the academic system in which they have been educated (Altbach, 2004, p 12). In this sense, they can become the active agents for the reproduction of the Western influence on Chinese higher education, as these highly qualified students are more likely to obtain prestigious positions in top Chinese universities, academic institutions, and government bodies.

Dealing with the Westernisation of social theory in teaching

These observations could easily encourage pessimism about the possibility of combatting Eurocentrism in social science. However, critical pedagogical practices that sensitise students to the biases of Western theories can open avenues to fostering epistemological diversity. I draw this conclusion from my teaching experience at Fudan University.[3] There, I had the opportunity to teach two classes: sociology of religion and Western social theory. I will focus on the latter course, which I taught in collaboration with a senior faculty member, because I was involved in designing the course syllabus, giving lectures, and managing several tutorials.[4]

My class was composed of roughly 80 students. All of them were Chinese, aged between 18 and 20, from different provinces and social backgrounds. Besides their age, the most common characteristic shared by these students was the fact that more than half of them told me they were members of the Communist Party. However, only a few said they were interested in political questions and none was regularly engaged in party activities. Their decision to adhere to the Communist Party was principally the outcome of family pressure and, often, a strategy to strengthen their professional profile. Being a Party member was thought to increase the likelihood of being admitted to the most selective universities and of obtaining a better job after graduating. Though the great majority of these students nourished a sense of patriotism, their political consciousness did not lead them to pay attention to the issues related to the hegemonic role of Western knowledge and the different kinds of intellectual imperialism that permeated their curriculum. These topics sounded new to them.

I was surprised by the relatively large number of students attending my class, and I was intrigued to know why these young Chinese were interested in Western social theory. My curiosity further increased when my teaching assistant, a Chinese graduate student, told me that the course in Western social theory was one of the toughest for undergraduate students and their chances of getting a good grade were generally lower than for other classes. I asked students about their decision to attend my course and got various answers. Some I expected, others not. Several students told me that the course in Western social theory was one of the few that provided them with theoretical foundations in the social sciences. Most of the other undergraduate courses focused on teaching research methods or merely presented the results of empirical studies. Other students said that getting a good grade in Western social theory was an important asset for being selected for an exchange programme in a foreign university. For them, the possibility to study abroad could also have a positive effect on their career prospects, because Chinese employers tend to place great importance on students having international academic experiences. Even though Fudan had significantly increased the number of exchange programmes, the competition for them was fierce, and several students thought that they needed to highlight their interest in Western knowledge so as to increase their chances of being selected. The most unexpected response I received was from a student who told me that she wanted to attend a class in Western social theory because she enjoyed reading Western sociologists, notably Habermas, as they provided her with the intellectual tools to criticise the Chinese government, which she disliked.

After two lectures, I realised that most students were struggling to relate the course material to contemporary Chinese social reality. They also had a hard time understanding Western social theory's Eurocentric perspective.

To make my lectures more interesting and to help the students acquire a critical approach to the subjects that we were discussing, I thus started to highlight the question of Eurocentrism and the importance of enriching Western theoretical paradigms with alternative perspectives. I did that through a three-step pedagogy. First, I suggested considering the positionality of the various theories that I was teaching. To what extent was a given theory shaped by the political and cultural milieu in which it was elaborated? What were the problems that this theory considered and those that it ignored? Could this theory have the universality that it claimed? I asked these questions and others. In doing so, I hoped to show that Western social theories are historically and socially embedded rather than universal. I also wanted to give the students some insights about the process of radical inclusion and radical exclusion implied in Western systems of knowledge production.

The second step of my pedagogical practice started from the assumption that sociological theory courses should recognise students' historical context if we wish to promote epistemic pluralism (Alatas and Sinha, 2017, p 4). I thus suggested that students should identify the possible parallelisms between the European events that inspired the social theories that we were considering and the historical events in their country. For example, the study of the French Revolution should be meaningful for Asian students because the rise of social consciousness leading to political upheavals, the question of who controls government powers, and the problematic affirmation of human rights are topics that could resonate in contemporary Asian societies (Alatas, 2002, p 153).

Dealing with Eurocentrism seriously asks us to go beyond 'the tendency to keep a northern conceptual framework while putting in more southern content' (Connell, 2018, p 404). In light of that, the third step of my pedagogical approach consisted of encouraging students to cross-fertilise Western social theories with Asian social thought. Max Weber's theory of the Protestant ethic, for example, is a good ground for such an effort because many scholars see Confucianism as having similar compatibility with capitalism (Rošker, 2017).

I developed this approach both in lectures and in tutorials. Composed of between five and seven students, each tutorial was designed to discuss the key theoretical questions considered during the lectures. However, tutorial discussions also provided the opportunity to deal with politically sensitive issues related to contemporary China. During a tutorial on Rousseau, for example, some students raised the question of the limits of government authority, and they debated whether Rousseau's concept of freedom was too Eurocentric to be applied to non-Western societies. A student pointed out that populous countries, like China, which are characterised by great internal diversity, require tighter social control to prevent them falling into anarchy. According to him, this problem was understood by Chinese emperors, and later by the Communist Party, both of which had established a centralised state bureaucracy. In a tutorial in which we spoke about Bourdieu, students questioned whether it was possible to generalise his theory beyond France and whether Bourdieu's idea of social capital had some resemblance with the Chinese concept of *guanxi* (interpersonal networks). The students' arguments were sometimes unclear, and we seldom reached consensual conclusions. However, they led students to greater awareness of the Eurocentric nature of Western social theory and the need to enrich it with cultural elements drawn from local realities.

Student reactions were mixed, as was the case with Alatas and Sinha's (2001) experiences teaching classical social theory to Singapore's students. As I expected, several students showed little interest in the question of Eurocentrism. They considered the problem too abstract and not relevant to their interests. In contrast, other students demonstrated great interest. They enjoyed the critical perspective of our class discussions because it was something new to them and something that other sociology courses did not provide. However, what attracted their attention most were the biases that affected Western knowledge, rather than the economic and political inequalities implied in it. In other words, these students seemed to be conscious that Western social theory does not have the universality that it claims, but they were less aware of the political and economic inequalities from which it sprang. Not surprisingly, none of them was willing or even thought to criticise university authorities because their sociology curricula did not take epistemological diversity into adequate consideration. The student mobilisations to decolonise universities that took place in several countries around the world could hardly be possible in mainland China. The regime does its best to dissuade any kind of student mobilisation, apart from those actions that are formally approved by the Party authorities.

Overall, I suppose that this experience in dealing with Eurocentrism in teaching social theory was positive. Even though I did not attempt to explore all of the multiple facets of European epistemic hegemony, I could help students become more aware of their positionality and could show them the usefulness of alternative approaches to social theory that go beyond the unspoken biases of the discipline.

Further actions to de-Westernise sociology

'Critique is essential but by itself not enough to bring about fundamental changes in the social science domain' (Sinha, 2000, p 99). To combat the biases of Eurocentrism and foster epistemological pluralism in social science, intellectual criticisms should go hand in hand with actions aimed at disrupting, if not reversing, the mechanisms that have sustained colonial knowledge. Teaching activities provide good possibilities for such an endeavour.

This does imply that we should dismiss the difficult economic and political questions entangled with the Westernised knowledge. I strongly agree with Raewyn Connell's claims that decolonising sociology involves considering the redistribution of resources and the composition of sociology's workforce at the global level (2018, p 405). Epistemic inequality is grounded and mutually reinforced by economic inequality. We cannot combat the former unless we address the latter. To these economic questions, we should also add political issues. The unequal flow of knowledge in higher education is often sustained by political authorities that consider Western knowledge to be a tool to project their soft power in the international political arena. In other cases, like China, national governments favoured the Westernisation of their higher education sector to make their universities more able to compete in an international academic context that remains based on Western canons. Although some changes are probably beyond our power, through a focus on teaching, we, as scholars, can become agents of small, bottom-up changes that can play a crucial role in combating Western epistemic hegemony.

Our efforts to oppose Eurocentrism should also not lead to rejecting Western social theory. Even though this discipline is affected by cultural bias and is grounded in the radical exclusion of non-Western knowledge (Connell, 2010), it has been the source of remarkable intellectual achievements. Dismissing Western social theory because of its Eurocentrism would be like throwing the baby out with the bathwater (Alatas, 2011, p 248). Neither would it be appropriate to replace Eurocentrism with another kind of ethnocentrism. Unfortunately, this has been the outcome of several critiques of Eurocentrism that have tended to replace one centrist discourse with another (Karaosmanoğlu and Karaosmanoğlu, 2016, p 197). Instead, the real and most difficult challenge to going beyond Eurocentrism consists in paying more attention to local theories and promoting a cross-fertilisation between Western and non-Western thought. This is probably the most effective way to develop a more inclusive intellectual paradigm (Miike, 2006).

In the last decade, several remarkable studies have laid the foundations for this effort. In *Connected Sociologies* (2015), Guminder Bhambra has proposed a comprehensive critique of the dominant sociological imagination and sought to pave the way for alternative and non-Western perspectives. *Sociological Theory beyond the Canon* (2017) by Syed Farid Alatas and Vineeta Sinha is an insightful textbook that integrates Western social theory with the social thought of non-Western scholars. Concerning Chinese sociology, Xiaoying Qi has indicated in *Globalized Knowledge Flows and Chinese Social Theory* (2014) how some concepts drawn from Chinese culture can enrich Western theory. In other words, the current scholarship that has criticised Eurocentrism, the Westernisation of knowledge, and the various kinds of elite domination has reached a high level of sophistication and awareness of the social embeddedness of narrow epistemic perspectives. This gives us a solid ground on which to redesign our social science curricula.

Can we escape from Eurocentric biases? Can we develop pedagogical practices grounded in more inclusive epistemes? Can these efforts be understood by students and, possibly, supported by academic institutions? It is challenging to answer these questions. However, I would like to propose three suggestions to promote greater epistemological diversity in teaching social theory.

First, we need to acquire greater awareness of our intellectual biases and of Eurocentrism's impact on our intellectual practices. How can we combat Eurocentrism if we do not see it? Even as the efforts to decolonise higher education, combat Westernised knowledge, and support indigenisation are growing, the demands for promoting greater diversity in teaching, writing, and researching have not yet become mainstream. I, myself, came across the problems of Eurocentrism at a relatively late stage of my academic life. Eurocentrism was never debated in the undergraduate and graduate sociology classes I attended, even though I studied in different universities and various countries. In this sense, I think that Western scholars should acquire a stronger awareness of their own cultures' intellectual strengths and limitations, so as to establish a closer dialogue with other cultures, as Zheng (2009) and Fei (2015) suggested for the Chinese.

Second, we need to promote greater awareness among our scholarly colleagues – both Western and non-Western – about the issues related to the unequal flow of knowledge. To do this, we need closer dialogue and stronger collaborative efforts. While Western social scientists should become more aware that a narrow ethnocentric perspective undermines the scientific validity of Western theories, non-Western scholars could provide invaluable insights to revise Western theoretical models, making them more inclusive. They could also help social scientists in the global North to overcome the cultural and linguistic barriers that limit their ability to imagine alternative perspectives. This task is not easy. If Western scholars face problems of academic credibility in approaching non-Western perspectives, scholars from the global South can sometimes overlook the forces that created the West's current domination of knowledge. Some of my Chinese colleagues showed little or no awareness of the issue of Eurocentrism. They knew that social theory was principally European in provenance and they knew that Chinese higher education was emulating the American model, but they did not consider these questions important. Some of them also told me to be glad that Chinese authorities were reshaping the higher education of their country to match North American universities, because this reform improved Chinese universities' standards. This highlights a theoretical weakness of Chinese sociological scholarship: it lacks a programme of postcolonial reflection, such as those developed by Connell in *Southern Theory* (2007) and Bhambra in *Connected Sociologies* (2015) (Chen, 2017). It also casts some doubts on the willingness of some national academic communities to promote epistemic diversity.

Third, student involvement in our efforts to combat the Westernisation of knowledge is of great importance. Through the relational practices of teaching, 'the diverse background and positionality of the students is not suppressed, but, on the contrary, becomes a tool for enriching the learning experience of all' (Richardson, 2018, p 210). Furthermore, the interactions in the classroom can play a decisive role in helping students to become conscious of the limitations of their disciplines' concepts and of the possibilities of expanding them beyond just Western sources. In the end, students are some of the 'final consumers' of the knowledge that they use to understand the world and that will shape their professional practices in the years to come. The fact that Eurocentrism in some countries, like China, has received limited attention from academic bodies makes it even more important to involve students in the debates on Eurocentrism and Westernisation.

Conclusion

This chapter has discussed the Westernisation of higher education and the Eurocentrism of social theory in China. The argument presented here started by introducing some historical and macro-structural factors that have favoured the Westernisation of Chinese sociology, described some strategies to deal with Eurocentrism in teaching social theory, and suggested possible avenues for de-Westernising higher education and promoting greater epistemic pluralism.

As far as possible, the preceding sections have avoided addressing theoretical questions about the Westernisation of knowledge and the Eurocentrism of existing social theory. Although high-profile intellectual discussions on these issues are helpful for understanding the epistemic violence of Western knowledge (and Western scholars), we are more in need of practical strategies to reverse the unequal flow of knowledge that define higher education in Western and non-Western countries. In consideration of that, the observations presented in this chapter have principally drawn from my teaching activities, discussions with Chinese colleagues, and interactions with students at a leading Chinese university from 2015 and 2017. Building on these experiences, this chapter was designed to present first-hand and empirically based observations on possible ways to combat Eurocentric biases in Chinese academia about which Western countries have limited knowledge. This task is important, as China is playing an increasingly important role in higher education through its universities and the growing international flow of Chinese students and scholars.

My staying in China led me to think that historical, institutional, and political factors severely limit the possibilities of opposing Eurocentrism and reversing Westernisation, and this effort is further undermined by Chinese scholarship's limited familiarity with and interest in postcolonial studies. However, the possibilities opened by the increasing involvement of Chinese social scientists with the international academic community, the feasibility of a closer dialogue between Western and non-Western scholars, and the responsiveness of Chinese students to alternative perspectives may lead to some degree of optimism. The struggle to combat Eurocentrism and to de-Westernise higher education is not easy, but it is definitely a struggle worth engaging.

Notes

[1]   The Times Higher Education (2022) ranks Fudan in 60th position worldwide and in third place in China, after Peking University and Tsinghua University.

[2]   In 2017 roughly 600,000 Chinese students left their country to study abroad. These figures were 11.7 per cent higher than in 2016; the numbers returning to China after completing their studies rose to 480,900, up 11.2 per cent from the previous year. Of these returning students, 227,400 had earned a Master's degree or higher (Ministry of Education of the People's Republic of China, 2018).

[3]   I was hired by Fudan University in late 2015, some months after completing my PhD at the University of Cambridge. My academic status in this Chinese university was atypical: I was formally registered as a graduate student, even though I was a post-doctoral fellow. I was, in fact, the first Western fellow at the School of Social Development and Public Policy since the Cultural Revolution. I soon realised that my ambiguous status was motivated by bureaucratic and political reasons. Even though Chinese universities are increasingly willing to invite Western scholars for a short period, the political suspicion of foreign social scientists leads Chinese authorities to burden them with bureaucratic procedures to dissuade them from staying for a medium or long period. Therefore, it was less problematic to register me as a student than as a scholar.

[4]   The course of Western social theory that I taught was aimed at introducing undergraduate students to the basic tenets of Western social thought from its origins to the present.

References

Alatas, Syed F. (2011) 'The definition and types of alternative discourses', in Georgette Wang (ed) De-Westernizing Communication Research: Altering Questions and Changing Frameworks. New York: Routledge, pp 238–253.

Alatas, Syed F. and Sinha, Vineeta (2001) 'Teaching classical sociological theory in Singapore: The context of Eurocentrism', Teaching Sociology, 29(3): 316–331.

Alatas, Syed F. and Sinha, Vineeta (2017) Sociological Theory beyond the Canon. London: Palgrave Macmillan.

Alatas, Syed H. (2000) 'Intellectual imperialism: Definition, traits, and problems', Southeast Asian Journal of Social Science, 28(1): 23–45.

Alatas, Syed H. (2002) 'The development of an autonomous social science tradition in Asia: Problems and prospects', *Asian Journal of Social Science*, 30(1): 150–157.

Altbach, Phillip G. (2004) 'Globalisation and the university: Myths and realities in an unequal world', *Tertiary Education and Management*, 10(1): 3–25.

Beerkens, Eric (2010) 'Global models for the national research university: Adoption and adaptation in Indonesia and Malaysia', *Globalisation, Societies and Education*, 8(3): 369–391.

Bhambra, Gurminder K. (2015) *Connected Sociologies*. London: Bloomsbury.

Bhambra, Gurminder K., Gebrial, Dalia, and Nişancıoğlu, Kerem (2018) (eds) *Decolonising the University*. London: Pluto.

Brooks, Rachel, and Waters, Johanna (2011) *Student Mobilities, Migration and the Internationalisation of Higher Education*. London: Palgrave Macmillan.

Chen, Hon F. (2017) *Chinese Sociology State-Building and the Institutionalisation of Globally Circulated Knowledge*. London: Palgrave Macmillan.

Clammer, John (2000) 'Cultural studies/Asian studies: Alternatives, intersections, and contradictions in Asian social science', *Southeast Asian Journal of Social Science*, 28(1): 47–65.

Connell, Raewyn (2006) 'Northern theory: The political geography of general social theory', *Theory & Society*, 35(2): 237–264.

Connell, Raewyn (2007) *Southern Theory: The Global Dynamics of Knowledge in Social Science*. Cambridge: Polity.

Connell, Raewyn (2010) 'Learning from each other: Sociology on a world scale', in Sujata Patel (ed) *The ISA Handbook of Diverse Sociological Traditions*. London: Sage, pp 40–51.

Connell, Raewyn (2018) 'Decolonizing sociology', *Contemporary Sociology*, 47(4): 399–407.

de Oliveira Andreotti, Vanessa, Stein, Sharon, Ahenakew, Cash, and Hunt, Dallas (2015) 'Mapping interpretations of decolonisation in the context of higher education', *Decolonisation: Indigeneity, Education and Society*, 4(1): 21–40.

Fei, Xiaotong (1991) 'Luetan Zhongguo di Shehuixue', *Shehuixue Yanjiu*, 1: 2–8.

Fei, Xiaotong (2015) *Globalisation and Cultural Self-awareness*. Berlin/Heidelberg: Springer.

Fry, Tony H. (2012) 'Futuring the university', *Journal of Contemporary Educational Studies*, 63(3): 54–66.

Go, Julian (2016) *Postcolonial Thought and Social Theory*. Oxford: Oxford University Press.

Gransow, Bettina (1993) 'Chinese sociology: Sinicisation and globalisation', *International Sociology*, 8(1): 101–112.

Hamilton, Gary G., and Zheng, Wang (1992) 'Introduction: Fei Xiaotong and the beginning of a Chinese sociology', in Fei Xiaotong, *From the Soil: The Foundations of Chinese Society*. Berkeley: University of California Press, 1–36.

Karaosmanoğlu, Defne, and Karaosmanoğlu, Kerem (2016) 'Criticizing Eurocentrism: Limitation and alternatives', in Lutfi Sunar (ed) *Eurocentrism at the Margins. Encounters, Critics and Going Beyond*. New York: Routledge, pp 197–214.

Keim, Wiebke (2010) 'The internationalisation of social sciences: Distortions, dominations and prospects', in *International Social Science Council, World Social Science Report 2010*. Paris: UNESCO Publishing, pp 169–171.

Kejing, Dai (1993) 'The vicissitudes of sociology in China', *International Sociology*, 8(1): 91–99.

Keskin, Tugrul (2014) 'Sociology of Africa: A non-orientalist approach to African, Africana, and Black studies', *Critical Sociology*, 40(2): 187–202.

King, Ambrose Y. with the collaboration of Wang, Tse-Sang (1978) 'The development and death of Chinese academic sociology: A chapter in the sociology of sociology', *Modern Asian Studies*, 12(1): 37–58.

Mbembe, Joseph A. (2016) 'Decolonizing the university: New directions', *Arts and Humanities in Higher Education*, 15(1): 29–41.

Mignolo, Walter D. (2007) 'Introduction: Coloniality of power and de-colonial thinking', *Cultural Studies*, 21(2–3): 155–167.

Mignolo, Walter D. (2009) 'Epistemic disobedience, independent thought and decolonial freedom', *Theory, Culture & Society*, 26 (7–8): 1–23.

Miike, Yoshitaka (2006) 'Non-western theory in western research? An Asiacentric agenda for Asian communication studies', *The Review of Communication*, 6(1–2): 4–31.

Ministry of Education of the People's Republic of China (2015a) *Introduction to 211 Project*. [No longer online; originally accessed 12 August 2020; see https://bit.ly/3eBIMFu for an alternative].

Ministry of Education of the People's Republic of China (2015b) *Introduction to 985 Project*. [online] Available from: https://bit.ly/2PBwR28 [accessed 12 August 2020].

Ministry of Education of the People's Republic of China (2018) *Brief report on Chinese overseas students and international students in China 2017*. [online] Available from: https://bit.ly/3t0sHym [accessed 10 May 2020].

Nakane, Chie (1992) 'Introduction', in Chie Nakane and Chien Chiao (eds) *Home Bound: Studies in East Asian Society*. Tokyo: Centre for East Asian Cultural Studies, pp 1–7.

OECD (2020) *Online Education Database*. [online] Available from: https://bit.ly/3dXQnz2 [accessed 11 May 2020].

Pasternak, Burton (1988) 'A conversation with Fei Xiaotong', *Current Anthropology*, 29(4): 637–662.

Peters, Michael A. (2015) 'Why is my curriculum white?', *Educational Philosophy and Theory*, 47(7): 641–646.

Qi, Xiaoying (2014) *Globalized Knowledge Flows and Chinese Social Theory.* New York: Routledge.

Richardson, William J. (2018) 'Understanding Eurocentrism as a structural problem of undone science', in Gurminder K. Bhambra, Dalia Gebrial, and Kerem Nişancıoğlu (eds) *Decolonising the University.* London: Pluto, pp 231–247.

Rošker, Jana S. (2017) 'Between tradition and modernity: Modern Confucianism as a form of East Asian social knowledge', *Asian Studies*, 5(2): 43–62.

Sinha, Vineeta (2000) 'Moving beyond critique: Practising the social sciences in the context of globalisation, postmodernity and postcoloniality', *Asian Journal of Social Science*, 28(1): 67–104.

Song, Linfei (2016) 'Zengqiang Shehuixue Huayu Tixi di Zhongguo Tese', *Shehuixue Yanjiu*, 5: 10–26.

Times Higher Education (2022) *The World University Rankings.* [online] Available from: https://bit.ly/34nttz0 [accessed 31 January 2022].

Wang, Georgette (2011) 'After the fall of the Tower of Babel: Culture-commensurability as a point of departure', in Georgette Wang (ed) *De-Westernizing Communication Research. Altering Questions and Changing Frameworks.* New York: Routledge, pp 254–275.

Wu, Xiaogang (2009) 'Between public and professional: Chinese sociology and the construction of a harmonious society', *ASA Footnotes*, 37(5). [online] Available from: https://bit.ly/3dW0qES [accessed 26 July 2020].

Xiang, Biao, and Shen, Wei (2009) 'International student migration and social stratification in China', *International Journal of Educational Development*, 29(5): 513–522.

Yuhua, Guo, Yuan, Shen, and Lee, Ching K. (2010) 'A new agenda for the sociology of transformation in China', in Sujata Patel (ed) *The ISA Handbook of Diverse Sociological Traditions.* Los Angeles: Sage, pp 305–312.

Zheng, Hangsheng (2009) 'Cujin Zhongguo Shehuixue di "Lilun Zijue": Women Xuyao Shimeyang di Zhongguo Shehuixue?', *Jiangsu Shehuikexue*, 5: 1–7.

14

Opportunities and Challenges in Integrating Indigenous Peoples and Cultural Diversity in International Studies

Gretchen Abuso

Introduction

A major legacy of Spanish and American colonialism in the Philippines education system is the dominance of Western perspectives in teaching and research practices. Almost 100 years after the American departure, English is still used as the official language across all areas in Philippine society, local schools commonly adopt Western models in instruction and research, and Filipinos themselves generally prefer college degrees that offer international career prospects, most notably in nursing and international studies. In university settings, the most apparent impact of the dominance of the "global North" is the marginalization of academic fields and disciplines that focus on and emphasize the country's ethnic diversity. It can be argued that this neglect in understanding the inherently diverse character of the Philippines has pushed its indigenous peoples (IPs) to the country's impoverished peripheries.

Owing to its archipelagic geography, the Philippines is inherently culturally diverse, with more than 170 ethnolinguistic groups spread over more than 7,000 islands (Alvina et al, 2020, p 5). Remarkably, the country has retained this cultural diversity despite suffering multiple waves of colonial subjugation spanning more than three centuries. However, rather than being a source of national pride, the IPs in the Philippines are the most marginalized groups in the country. The continued exclusion and discrimination against ethnic minorities and the long history of their struggle for basic rights are among the most apparent markers of the colonial legacies in the Philippines.

"Minoritization" (Rodil, 1994) of IPs in the Philippines began with the Spanish colonial policy of distinguishing inhabitants in the islands between those who converted to Christianity and those who resisted conversion (Hardacker, 2012). The latter were referred to as *infieles* or pagans. These distinctions provided a convenient rationale for the "civilizing mission" of the later American colonial regime that took over the islands at the beginning of the 20th century. The Americans established the Bureau of Non-Christian Tribes, which purportedly sought to document the non-Christian inhabitants in the colony. In doing so, it perpetuated the racialized language of tribes that survives in Filipinos' contemporary notions of civilizational hierarchy (Hau and Tinio, 2003). Unsurprisingly, it placed Christian Filipinos on top. Back then, Muslims and other non-Christians in the southern island Mindanao were even described as "uncivilized races" (Abinales and Amoroso, 2005, p 124).

Indigenous groups and their cultures managed to survive these multiple waves of colonial domination by withdrawing to the upland mountains, where they maintained their traditional life-styles, rituals, political structures, and economic activities (Montillo-Burton and Echavez, 2011). Successive colonial policies aimed at assimilating all inhabitants into a monocultural subjugated class, along with later Philippine state policies that institutionalized the status of cultural minority (Rodil, 1994), nearly decimated the ethnic and linguistic diversity in the country. Indigenous groups that survived into the 21st century and continue to practice their distinct culture comprise only 10 to 15 percent of the country's population. As recently as 2017, the Commission on Population of the Philippines acknowledges the "lack of data on the number and distribution of IPs [indigenous persons] in the Philippines"; it estimates that the IP population is between 8 and 14 million (PopCom, 2017, p 16).

American model of education in postcolonial Philippines

While pre-Spanish cultures in the islands did not completely disappear, IPs' resistance to colonial influence led to their historical marginalization and oppression (Ting et al, 2008, p 79). Today, descendants of colonial subjects that assimilated into the Spanish and American imposition belong to the Christian majority, and those who retreated to the hinterlands so that they could continue their indigenous ways constitute the minority. Without discounting the "Hispanicised society" created by the Spaniards, scholars have argued that contemporary social and political conditions in the Philippines are better understood against the backdrop of the "state structures erected and imposed in the course of the American colonial era" (Hedman and Sidel, 2005, p 7). Three of these American colonial legacies that continue to define Philippine society are: (1) the linguistic hierarchy which places English on top, (2) the educational system, and (3) the continued popularity of professions that promise opportunities abroad for Filipinos. These are the subject of this section.

The presence of hierarchy in Philippine languages can be traced to the Spanish period, when Spanish was used by members of the elite class while native vernaculars continued to be used by the masses (Hau and Tinio, 2003). The current privileged status enjoyed by the English language is the result of the 1898 American takeover, which mandated teaching English in Philippine classrooms (Lorente, 2013; Maca, 2017). The Americans saw English as the appropriate language when introducing their progressive ideas about democracy, business, and civil governance (Hau and Tinio, 2003; Lorente, 2013). The emphasis on English proficiency was perpetuated by the Philippine government on its transition to commonwealth status in 1935. English continues to be one of the country's official languages and is the designated mode of instruction in schools. As a result, Filipinos commonly use English in business transactions, industry, academia, and in the international arena. English is a marker of educational achievement and a means of access to an improved way of life and privileged socioeconomic class. This is not to say that English totally wiped out local tongues, but in a country of more than 150 languages it is ironic that Filipinos today are known globally for their competitive edge in speaking English, a foreign and colonizing language.

The current public education system – including higher education – was also introduced by the Americans (Abinales and Amoroso, 2005). While the Spanish supported education in law, medicine, and the priesthood, the Americans were inclined towards engineering, nursing, economics, agriculture, medical technology, and computer science (Gonzalez, 1989). Americans established the Pensionado Program in 1903 to fill key posts in governance and politics by sending Filipinos to study in the United States (Calata, 2002). The Americans also introduced academic institutions built along American lines, including education for women and the masses. These ideals continue to dominate higher education: English continues to be the language of instruction, the fruits of American research and writing are the main sources of learning, and graduate studies in the United States are still a widespread aspiration.

Two unintended consequences of the Americans' system are the overexpansion of private education (Alcala, 1999) and the rapid growth of certain degree programs irrelevant to the Philippine context. As part of liberal freedoms introduced during the period, the Americans allowed private education, mostly run by Catholic orders, to continue operating. To keep tuition fees low, private universities opened degree programs that did not require expensive facilities for training and instruction, eventually leading to the overexpansion of programs in the liberal arts and humanities at the expense of the natural sciences (Gonzalez, 1989). Today, 80 per cent of university-level institutions are privately run. By providing opportunities to those who cannot be accommodated in state universities, private schools have been instrumental in shaping the educational aspirations of young Filipinos (Asis and Battistella, 2013; Ortiga, 2020, p 58).

This brings us to another glaring impact of colonialism in the Philippines: the prominence of international migrant labor in the country's development agenda (Orbeta and Abrigo, 2009; Agbola and Acupan, 2010). This creates disproportionate enrolment in degree programs that promise career opportunities overseas (Ortiga, 2017). Emigration of Filipinos to the United States began with farmers who worked in the Hawaiian and Californian plantations in the first decade of the American occupation. At present, 46 per cent of Filipinos living abroad are in the United States (Tan, 2019). While many immigrants seek better opportunities in any country, the United States remains the top choice of Filipinos for relocation (Absuelo and Hancock, 2018). A national migration survey conducted in 2018 reveals that 13 per cent of households in the Philippines have family members working overseas (PSA and UPPI, 2019). The Philippines is now among the world's top exporters of temporary labor migrants (Eder, 2016).

Many Filipinos actively seek higher education as a vital qualification for emigration. Not only are highly educated Filipinos more inclined to emigrate (OECD and SMC, 2017), but they are also most likely to land permanent migrant status, especially in the United States (Orbeta and Abrigo, 2009). Because of this, the education system in the Philippines has evolved into producing globally employable and competitive graduates (Ortiga, 2015; Eder, 2016). The Commission on Higher Education (CHED), the state agency tasked with regulating higher education in the Philippines, appears to endorse these inclinations by mandating universities to ensure that their "programs are at par with international standards and graduates and professionals are highly competent and recognized in the international arena" (CHED, nd, p 1).

Feeding into the dominant "culture of migration" that portrays overseas work as an ideal life goal (Asis and Battistella, 2013), universities in the country have been eager to expand degree programs that are popular with "student consumers and their future foreign employers" (Ortiga, 2015, p 5). Ortiga's study of the Philippine private education sector revealed that owners and administrators seek "to predict labor gaps in migrant destination countries and develop programs that would be appealing to aspiring migrants" (Ortiga, 2015, p 5). These developments have obviously come at the expense of shortages in occupational degrees that answer local demands; they produce a mismatch between university qualifications and the needs of the domestic labor market (Eder, 2016).

Nursing is one of these degree programs popular in private schools due to its high demand overseas. At one time, this led to the proliferation of private schools offering nursing programs; the resulting oversupply of nurses prompted CHED to impose a moratorium on opening new programs in the profession (OECD and SMC, 2017). Today, the Philippines is widely recognized as top producer and exporter of nurses to the world (Ladrido, 2020; Lopez and Jiao, 2020).

We can trace this back to the American colonial government, which established the first nurse training school in 1907. On one level, this provided an outlet for white American women's urge toward missionary work and their wish for a sense of heroism in the colony (Choy, 2003). On another level, the healthcare profession also served to complement the modernizing agenda of the Americans and contributed to their objectives of disposing of the indigenous knowledge systems still practiced among local inhabitants by painting the treatment of diseases using local beliefs and practices as primitive and backwards (Eder, 2016). Early nursing education taught by Americans created images and reinforced narratives that idealized the American way of life.

Between 1956 and 1973, more than 12,000 Filipino nurses worked in the United States. In the 1970s, a new narrative was developed by the Philippine government which proclaimed nursing as the country's "international specialty," and nurse migrants were hailed as heroes whose remittances greatly contributed to nation building (Brush, 2010). This started the state policy of treating labor migration, not only of nurses but of all overseas work, as a contemporary expression of nationalism. Thus, began the popular trend of inaugurating degree programs that promise opportunities of going "international."

International studies in the Philippines programs

Far from being exclusive to nursing programs, we find the same pattern of high enrollment in training programs for hotel and restaurant service (Ortiga, 2015), seamanship (Galam, 2020), and other fields that offer greater chances of working overseas. To appeal to the migrant aspirations of young Filipinos, private universities in the Philippines have been opening "trendy" college majors that hint at possibilities of going "international" (Ortiga, 2020). At present, there are 28 undergraduate and graduate programs in the country that offer international studies, international relations, diplomacy, foreign service, and global studies (PHISO, 2020). Out of these universities, only four are state subsidized – a fact that suggests private universities are the sites of most program expansion. A foundational text on international studies in the Philippines (Cruz and Adiong, 2020), which sought to critically map the teaching and practice of the discipline in the country, recognized the dominance of Western narratives and theoretical approaches in these programs. While there has been a growing clamor to develop and integrate non-Western thought into the programs and to recenter the discipline of international relations on the Philippine context, these have not translated into including local scholarship in such programs at the undergraduate level. Like the programs and disciplines introduced during the American colonial period, international studies in the Philippines still bears significant traces of "American-based education" and continues to "imitate the Western privileging of positivist-based knowledge claims and industry-oriented pedagogy" (Cruz and Adiong, 2020, pp 2–3). In doing so, these programs overlook the value and contributions of local cultural knowledge in the practice of international relations.

The popularity of majoring in anything "international" is nowhere better exemplified than in my own institution, Xavier University. The Bachelor of Arts in International Studies (or AB IS) consistently posts a high number of enrollees each school year. The extent of its popularity is demonstrated in the enrolment patterns of the program between 2012 and 2016: the program registered *more students* than the rest of the liberal arts programs *combined*. Recent figures show that, as of the school year 2019–20, out of all the liberal arts majors in the university, 49 per cent belong to the International Studies program.

In 2015, I took over teaching the course "Peoples and Cultures of the Philippines" to International Studies majors. I was pleasantly surprised to learn from students that the subject, designed to focus on local cultures and indigenous peoples, is a requisite subject in their program. The inclusion of a subject on IPs among the required courses in the curriculum of international studies is attributed to the professed mission of the university, which proclaims its devotion to "the appreciation, preservation, and enrichment of the Filipino culture and heritage." A Catholic university founded by American Jesuits in 1933, Xavier University exemplifies the institutions built by religious orders to channel their missionary work in the Philippines. Its expansion through the years benefited from the liberal education system installed during the American colonial period. Along with its mission of proclaiming the joy of the Gospel, the university also endeavors to safeguard the cultural heritage in Southern Philippines (Mindanao).

Against the backdrop of a colonially influenced liberal arts program and a mission-driven curriculum, I begin the semester by encouraging students to recognize the relevance of a subject that places the precolonial culture of the Philippines at center stage. Understanding and appreciating IPs and cultural practices give International Studies majors the knowledge they will need to better represent and advocate for their country in their future careers in international relations and diplomacy. Given that many Filipinos look forward to working outside the Philippines, this rationale can be relevant for Filipino teachers and professors looking into integrating the study of IPs into any subject.

Peoples and cultures of the Philippines

In early 2019, CHED directed Philippine universities to ensure the integration of "Indigenous Peoples (IP) Studies" in their curricula. While the move towards mainstreaming the study and teaching of indigenous cultures in higher education is a welcome development, even long overdue, the task can be daunting and challenging. The first challenge a lecturer will encounter is the relative absence of scholarship and research on IPs; this is largely due to the historical marginalization I outlined earlier and to the Westernized higher education model we follow. I have, however, found useful and practical resources for teaching this subject to International Studies students. In the following sections, I discuss the subject "Peoples and Cultures of the Philippines," the relevant literature for the course, and some practical methods for teaching.

The course description for "Peoples and Cultures of the Philippines" states that the subject surveys "the various ethnic communities in the Philippines: lowland, coastal, highland and Muslim" (CAS, 2012). The course further examines the social problems and issues confronting indigenous cultures under the impact of change and development. The course title indicates its classical roots in the 1970s, when the first courses in anthropology were taught at Xavier University and before the concept of IP was mainstreamed through the passage of the Indigenous Peoples Rights Act in 1997.

While the course primarily focuses on indigenous ways of life in the Philippines, I have found it relevant to recognize the contemporary nature of cultural diversity in the country by including in the discussion prominent expatriate groups such as the South Korean community. In other words, keeping the classical title "Peoples and Cultures" offered the opportunity to expand the discussion beyond indigenous cultural communities and recognize the multicultural character of contemporary Philippine society.

Literature and resources on IPs of the Philippines

Certainly, the first order of business for any teacher is to assemble the most useful materials and resources on the subject at hand. Here, I chronologically describe the extant scholarship on precolonial Philippine culture and later efforts to document indigenous peoples and their ways of life.

Unfortunately, the Spanish colonizers had little interest in the natives they ruled, so their record keeping was largely limited to keeping track of tax payments and citizenship. Their most vivid depiction was Antonio de

Morga's *Sucesos de las Islas*, which was published in 1609, 44 years *after* the Spaniards established their colony. While the book is primarily based on personal experiences and documentation from eyewitnesses (Cummins, 1969), it is considered one of the important primary accounts of early Spanish colonial conquest in Asia.

Nor did the indigenous people themselves keep written records. Even today, indigenous societies of the Philippines primarily transmit their histories and customs orally through ritual and performance. This means that documentation of much of the Filipino culture during the Spanish regime exists mainly "within the realm of experience and in the memory of the members of [indigenous] communities" (Punzalan, 2006, p 383).

The Americans, on the other hand, were interested in documenting the islands' diverse "unhispanized" cultures and treated the Philippines as a site for ethnographic exploration among the archipelago's ethnolinguistic groups. One product of these interests was *The Philippine Islands, 1493–1898* by James Alexander Robertson and Emma Helen Blair, a 55-volume compilation of Spanish records in the islands; it has been long considered the key reference on the history of the country in the those years (Cano, 2008).

However, Morga's *Sucesos de las Islas* and Blair–Roberston's *The Philippine Islands* are artifacts of the colonial process. The first supported Spanish colonialism, the second supported the American variety. Thus, the first challenge in teaching a course on IPs is overcoming the colonial perspective.

We can see a similar colonial perspective in early anthropological accounts of the peopling of the islands. When explaining the physical and cultural variations among the Filipino peoples, for example, Henry Otley Beyer proposed a Wave Migration Theory, which attributed the physical differences among Filipinos to genetic commingling among a series of migrations. Further research has since discredited Beyer's theory (Griffin, 2016), and this research, along with archaeological findings provides us today with better understanding of the Filipino ancestors. The discovery of a new species of ancient human, now called *Homo luzonensis*, places the existence of humans in the Philippines as far back as 50,000 to 67,000 years ago (Détroit et al, 2019).

An in-depth discussion of this topic lets the teacher contrast the Spanish and American colonial ideas with contemporary knowledge. It also presents the opportunity for students to recall the creation stories that they might have encountered in their childhood. The Filipino Jesuit folklorist, Francis Demetrio, provides an excellent summary on the common themes that appear in the "Creation Myths among the Early Filipinos." Demetrio's (1968) scholarly analysis of the creation stories gives students a new perspective on their own local folklore and mythology. Demetrio also extols the need to recognize local creation stories because of they let Filipinos "realize that their ancient myths and tales ... colored with their own character and culture are ... part of the more worldwide stream of mythology and folklore" and not just some local legend. Moreover, the rich "body of Philippine myths, against the background of comparative mythology and universal folklore ... create a sense of confidence and pride ... in these living mirrors of his past". For Demetrio: '[the Philippines'] ancient traditions are not something to be ashamed of but something to be cherished and valued because they mirror forth the history of the human spirit as it rises up to higher conquests through the continual struggle with the forces of ignorance, meanness, and irrationality' (Demetrio, 1968, p 79).

An important resource that proved valuable yet convenient is the digitized documentation of Filipino intangible cultural heritage compiled by the National Commission for Culture and the Arts (NCCA) and the International Information and Networking Centre for Intangible Cultural Heritage (ICHCAP) of the Asia–Pacific Region, an office of the United Nations Educational, Scientific and Cultural Organization (UNESCO). The vast collection, aptly titled Pinagmulan (Tagalog for "origin"), edited by Filipino anthropologist Jesus T. Peralta (2013), is accessible through ICHCAP's e-knowledge platform (UNESCO/ICHCAP, nd). The collection classifies the diverse elements of indigenous cultures and the colonial influences within them, if any, into five domains: (1) Oral traditions and expressions; (2) Performing arts; (3) Social practices, rituals, and festive events; (4) Knowledge and practices concerning nature and the universe; and (5) Traditional craftsmanship (UNESCO/ICH, nd). Pinagmulan therefore firmly roots the place of Philippine indigenous traditions in maintaining cultural diversity in the face of growing globalization. The collection is remarkable, as it richly documents and showcases the color and diversity of Filipino culture from the northernmost to the southernmost parts of the country and presents them in a simplified narrative that any student or anyone interested can easily access and understand.

Among notable entries in the collection is the Darangen Epic chant of the Maranao people, one of the major Muslim ethnic groups in the country. Its inclusion in the collection is significant because it provides a way for average readers to learn and appreciate the rich history and culture of Muslim Filipinos, who are among the most marginalized groups in the country. Another ethnic minority featured in the compilation are the Jama Mapun, an ethnic group dwelling at the tip of southwest Philippines. The extensive list of constellations that form part of their knowledge system concerning nature and the universe not only provides an alternate appreciation of the celestial patterns but also demonstrates the strength of indigenous knowledge systems in the Philippines. These two selections and other indigenous cultural knowledge and practices featured in the Pinagmulan collection demonstrate the wealth of knowledge and information that can be gained from the various indigenous groups in the country. The UNESCO/ICHAP Project has created similar digitized collections for the intangible cultural heritage of other countries, available online.

Instructional and classroom activities

Assembling the relevant literature may constitute the crucial start of teaching a course on IPs, but putting together appropriate and meaningful methods of delivering the content is no less challenging. In this section, I describe some of the practical instructional and classroom activities that can be used in teaching the course on IPs, including regional cuisines, role playing, museum tours, and field site visits.

Food and cooking traditions form part of the visible and material elements of culture and are among the most foundational elements of culture. Regional cuisines embody the long tradition of identifying places with their traditional foods; cuisine is now an important part of contemporary cultural heritage of countries and regions within them (Hall and Gössling, 2013). Doreen G. Fernandez (1988), a food writer and cultural historian, summed up Philippine food as the product of its colonial history and cultural adaptation, blending Malay, Chinese, Indian, Spanish, and American flavors. Traces of foreign traditions can be tasted in Philippine dishes, though Filipinos transformed these into what is now considered Philippine cuisines in a process that Fernandez calls "indigenization of Philippine food". Fernandez cites trading, colonization, and global cultural communication as the points of entry of these foreign flavors into the Philippine cuisines. An instructional activity featuring cuisines allows students to experience and enjoy the food and cooking traditions that embody the country's colonial history and cultural diversity. An enjoyable but meaningful activity I often organize in class is having students prepare selected regional cuisines which they then present to the entire class along with information on the history and story behind the cuisine.

Role play may already seem out of place in university classrooms, but, given the right context and meaning (Jordan, 2016), this time-tested technique lets students appreciate indigenous social practices and rituals. When possible, I connect the students to a member of an indigenous group in the campus who can provide first-hand information about their social practices and rituals. Alternatively, I let the students make use of the Pinagmulan material to choose an indigenous social practice or ritual that they feel they can re-enact in the classroom. Another way this assignment can be done is through digital documentation of the social practice or rituals in forms of digital media such as a photo series and short videos. While this activity runs the risk of what might be considered cultural appropriation, this does not necessarily have to be the case. The assignment itself can become an opportunity to introduce the risks of adopting or using elements of another culture without consent or without fully understanding the meaning/s behind the element (Young and Brunk, 2012). Hence, while this suggested assignment might be fun and instructive, it must be performed with much consideration and respect for the indigenous culture it chooses to represent in the classroom.

The value of visiting a museum on ethnic cultures and/or the indigenous community cannot be overstated. One place we start is at the National Museum of the Philippines. This contains the National Museum of Anthropology, which houses extensive collections on the cultural heritage of the Filipino people and the natural history of the Philippines. While the National Museum is in Metro Manila, regional branches have been established in 14 locations outside the capital region, allowing greater accessibility to the general public. It is worth noting, though, that even this repository of the country's cultural heritage traces its roots to the colonial past: the Museum was founded in 1901 under the American administration (National Museum, 2010). The study of indigenous cultures does not have to entail organizing long-distance travel to the National Museum and its branches, however. A lot of universities today have established their own repositories of local history and cultural heritage. Xavier itself has an extensive and well-curated collection on the ethnohistory of Northern Mindanao and the ethnology of Mindanao. In the same city, Capitol University established its own repository, Museum of Three Cultures, which houses collections on the three dominant cultures of Northern Mindanao. Another museum on campus grounds is the Aga Khan Museum of Islamic Arts at the Mindanao State University; it displays Maranao and other Moro artifacts. The class can be an opportunity to discover and explore the local public museums, and even private collections opened to the public.

Finally, the subject of IPs should be taken as a fitting opportunity to engage with local and nearby indigenous communities. This may be as simple as asking university students who hail from an indigenous group to discuss their culture and the issues they face. Or one can visit a local "protected homeland" or "ancestral domain"; the National Commission of Indigenous Peoples (NCIP), the primary government agency responsible for protecting and promoting the rights of IPs, has declared these at several places in the country. Northern Mindanao, for example, has successfully obtained declaration of 14 ancestral domains covering more than 8,000 hectares that belong to the indigenous group Higaonon. Engaging with indigenous cultural communities allows for students and professors alike to learn about the requirements that such indigenous communities set for granting entry to outsiders. For instance, the Talaandig people in the province of Bukidnon require non-Talaandig to perform a ritual asking permission to enter their territory (Burton and Canoy, 1991).

Conclusion

Vestiges of the Philippines' colonial history are conspicuously apparent in our Westernized education system, in our use of the English language, and in the aspirations of most Filipinos to work abroad. The popularity of degree programs that promise careers overseas can be traced to the structures, policies, and curricula introduced during the colonial era. The continued dominance of elitist perspectives and global North interests in education and work in the Philippines has greatly contributed to the marginalization of the country's ethnic minority groups.

In the preceding discussion, I have illustrated some of the meaningful opportunities available for teaching the subject of IPs at university level. This, in itself, provides the space and moment to interject cultural diversity into the classroom and beyond. Through this chapter, I have presented the subject and issues concerning IPs as a relevant and consequential university course even in degree specializations dominated by Western perspectives and internationalized motives. My objective here has been to identify a place and space for the study and discussion of the issues of IPs not only in the curricula for international studies, nursing, and any program training young Filipinos to work overseas, but in all degree programs in the country. By mainstreaming discussions on IPs in the classroom format, universities are forming a generation of citizens who will be aware of the issues and struggles confronting ethnic minorities; this should contribute to a greater recognition of the merits of cultural diversity in Philippine society.

References

Abinales, Patricio N., and Amoroso, Donna J. (2005) *State and Society in the Philippines*. Lanham, MD: Rowman & Littlefield.

Absuelo, Ruby, and Hancock, Peter (2018) 'The inefficacy of strong ties networks in migration employment outcomes: Underemployment of Philippine graduates in the United States', *Asian Journal of Social Science*, 46(3): 235–259.

Agbola, Frank W., and Acupan, Angelito B. (2010) 'An empirical analysis of international labour migration in the Philippines', *Economic systems*, 34(4): 386–396.

Alcala, Angel C. (1999) 'Higher education in the Philippines', *Philippine Studies*, 47(1): 114–128.

Alvina, Corazon S., Roces, Marian P., Subido, Kristina T., and Tiongson, Emilie V. (2020) *The Philippines: Cultural Policy Profile*. Singapore: Asia-Europe Foundation. [online] Available from: https://bit.ly/3bVkKVR [accessed 5 October 2020].

Asis, Maruja M.B., and Battistella, Graziano (2013) *Country Migration Report: The Philippines*. [online] Available from: https://bit.ly/2Ns6XNb [accessed 17 March 2021].

Brush, Barbara L. (2010) 'The potent lever of toil: Nursing development and exportation in the postcolonial Philippines', *American Journal of Public Health*, 100(9): 1572–1581.

Burton, Erlinda M., and Canoy, Easterluna S. (1991) *The Concept of Justice Among the Indigenous Communities of Northeastern Mindanao: A Comparative Study of Customary Laws and Resolution of Conflicts*. Cagayan de Oro City: Xavier University.

Calata, Alexander A. (2002) 'The role of education in Americanizing Filipinos', in Hazel McFerson (ed) *Mixed Blessing: The Impact of the American Colonial Experience on Politics and Society in the Philippines*, Westport, CT: Greenwood Press, pp 89–98.

Cano, Gloria (2008) 'Blair and Robertson's *The Philippine Islands, 1493–1898*: Scholarship or imperialist propaganda?' *Philippine Studies* 50(1): 3–46.

CAS (2012) *College of Arts and Sciences Bulletin of Information*. Cagayan de Oro City: Xavier University.

CHED (nd) *Strategic Plan for 2011–2016*. Commission on Higher Education. [online] Available from: https://bit.ly/3cFNSQ4 [accessed 6 December 2020].

Choy, Catherine, C. (2003) *Empire of Care: Nursing and Migration in Filipino American History*. Durham: Duke University Press.

Cruz, Frances Antoinette, and Adiong, Nassef Manabilang (eds) (2020) *International Studies in the Philippines: Mapping New Frontiers in Theory and Practice*. New York: Routledge.

Cummins, J.S. (1969) 'Antonio de Morga and his *Sucesos de las Islas Filipinas*', *Journal of Southeast Asian History*, 10(3): 560–581.

Demetrio, Francis (1968) 'Creation myths among the early Filipinos', *Asian Folklore Studies*, 27(1): 41–79.

Détroit, Florent, Mijares, Armand S., Corny, Julie, Daver, Guillaume, Zanolli, Clément, Dizon, Eusebio, Robles, Emil, Grün, Rainer, and Piper, Philip J. (2019) 'A new species of Homo from the Late Pleistocene of the Philippines', *Nature*, 568(7751): 181.

Eder, Rosalyn (2016) 'I am where I think I will work: Higher education and labor migration regime in the Philippines', *Educational Studies*, 52(5): 452–468.

Fernandez, Doreen G. (1988) 'Culture ingested: notes on the indigenization of Philippine food', *Philippine Studies*, 36(2): 219–232.

Galam, Roderick (2020) 'Futures on hold: The Covid-19 pandemic, international seafaring and the immobility of aspiring Filipino seafarers', *LSE Southeast Asia Blog*. [online] Available from: https://bit.ly/3lr69EO [accessed 3 October 2020].

Gonzalez, Andrew (1989) 'The Western impact on Philippine higher education', in Philip Altbach and Viswanathan Selvaratnam (eds) *From Dependence to Autonomy: The Development of Asian Universities*. Dordrecht: Springer, pp 117–141

Griffin, P. Bion (2016) 'A tale of two giants: Wilhelm G. Solheim II (1924–2014) and William A. Longacre Jr (1937–2015)', *Asian Perspectives*, 55(2): 240–247.

Hall, C. Michael, and Gössling, Stefan (eds) (2013) *Sustainable Culinary Systems: Local Foods, Innovation, and Tourism and Hospitality*. London: Routledge.

Hardacker, Erin P. (2012) 'The impact of Spain's 1863 educational decree on the spread of Philippine public schools and language acquisition', *European Education*, 44(4): 8–30.

Hau, Caroline S., and Tinio, Victoria L. (2003) 'Language policy and ethnic relations in the Philippines,' in Sumit Ganguly and Michael E. Brown (eds) *Fighting Words: Language Policy and Ethnic Relations in Asia*. Cambridge, MA: MIT Press, pp 319–352.

Hedman, Eva-Lotta, and Sidel, John (2005) *Philippine Politics and Society in the Twentieth Century: Colonial Legacies, Post-Colonial Trajectories*. London: Routledge.

Jordan, Josh T. (2016) 'Simulation and character ownership in secondary dramatic literature education', *International Journal of Role-Playing*, 6: 46–50.

Ladrido, Portia (2020) 'How the Philippines became the biggest supplier of nurses worldwide', *CNN Philippines*. [online] Available from: https://bit.ly/38PXtm9 [accessed 3 October 2020].

Lopez, Ditas B., and Jiao, Claire (2020) 'Supplier of world's nurses struggles to fight virus at home', *Bloomberg.com*, 23 April. [online] Available from: https://bloom.bg/2OzXBQ9 [accessed 3 October 2020].

Lorente, Beatriz (2013) 'The grip of English and Philippine language policy', in Lionel Wee, Lisa Lim, and Robbie B. H. Goh (eds) *The Politics of English: South Asia, Southeast Asia and the Asia Pacific*. Amsterdam: John Benjamins Publishing, pp 187–201.

Maca, Mark (2017) 'American colonial education policy and Filipino labour migration to the US (1900–1935)', *Asia Pacific Journal of Education*, 37(3): 310–328.

Montillo-Burton, Erlinda, and Echavez, Chona R. (2011) *Exclusion of and Discrimination against the Indigenous Communities: Case Study of the Philippines*. Indian Institute of Dalit Studies, 5(1). [online] Available from: https://bit.ly/2P6bULO [accessed 16 March 2021].

National Museum (2010) *Annual Report 2010*. [online] Available from: https://bit.ly/2Q6oL18 [accessed 3 October 2020].

OECD and SMC (2017) *Interrelations between Public Policies, Migration, and Development in the Philippines*. London: Organisation for Economic Co-operation and Development and Scalabrini Migration Center

Orbeta, Aniceto Jr, and Abrigo, Michael R.M. (2009) 'Philippine international labor migration in the past 30 years: Trends and prospects', *Philippine Institute for Development Studies Discussion Paper Series No. 2009–33*. [online] Available from: https://bit.ly/2NrK0cR [accessed 17 March 2021]

Ortiga, Yasmin Y. (2015) 'Educating for export: Producing Filipino migrant workers for the global market'. PhD dissertation, Department of Sociology, Syracuse University.

Ortiga, Yasmin Y. (2017) *Emigration, Employability and Higher Education in the Philippines*. New York: Routledge.

Ortiga, Yasmin Y. (2020) 'Shifting employabilities: Skilling migrants in the nation of emigration', *Journal of Ethnic and Migration Studies*. doi: 10.1080/1369183X.2020.1731985.

Peralta, Jesus T. (ed) (2013) '*Pinagmulan*: Enumeration from the Philippine inventory of intangible cultural heritage'. UNESCO: NCCA and ICHCAP. [online] Available from: https://bit.ly/3bTuPCA [accessed 16 March 2021].

PHISO (2020) 'Degree programs that are relevant to the study of the "International" in the Philippines', Philippine International Studies Organization. [online] Available from: https://bit.ly/3rYDV6H [accessed 3 October 2020].

PopCom (2017) *The Philippine Population Management Program: Directional Plan 2017–2022*. [online] Philippine Commission on Population. [online] Available from: https://bit.ly/3tuWhga [accessed 3 October 2020].

PSA and UPPI (2019) 2018 National Migration Survey, Quezon City, Philippines: Philippines Statistics Authority and University of the Philippines Population Institute. [online] Available from: https://bit.ly/2P0owUT [accessed 6 October 2020].

Punzalan, Ricardo L. (2006) 'Archives of the new possession: Spanish colonial records and the American creation of a "national" archives for the Philippines', *Archival Science*, 6(3–4): 381–392.

Rodil, Rudy B. (1994) *The Minoritization of the Indigenous Communities of Mindanao and the Sulu Archipelago*. Davao City: Alternate Forum for Research in Mindanao.

Tan, Edita A. (2019) 'Prospects of Philippine migration', *University of the Philippines School of Economics Discussion Paper No. 2019–02*. [online] Available from: https://bit.ly/3lp2K9o [accessed 17 March 2021].

Ting, Michael Teodoro G. Jr, Bagsic, Augencio C., Eguilos, Mylene M., Jaen, Ryan, Respicio, Maria Lourdes P., and Tan, Christopher Ryan (2008) 'Modernity vs. culture: Protecting the indigenous peoples of the Philippines', *European Journal of Economic and Political Studies*, 1(1): 77–98.

UNESCO/ICH (nd) 'What is intangible cultural heritage?'. [online] Available from: https://bit.ly/3GZxyqN [accessed 12 November 2019].

UNESCO/ICHCAP (nd) 'E-Knowledge Center: ICHAP project resources'. [online] Available from: https://bit.ly/33GoSat [accessed 16 March 2021].

Young, James O., and Brunk, Conrad G. (eds) (2012) *The Ethics of Cultural Appropriation*. New York: John Wiley & Sons.

15

Decolonial Praxis beyond the Classroom: Reflecting on Race and Violence

Federico Settler

Introduction

In the aftermath of the 2020 Black Lives Matter protests in the US, a US-based colleague and I discussed the implications of anti-racism protest for classroom practices in human and social sciences. As two scholars of colour, we recognised our shared deep desire to make space and to honour the embodied experience of our students as they shared an experience of racialised violence that stretched across the Atlantic. We also noted our shared despair and pessimism that this had happened before and would happen again. For us, it raised questions about how to teach our students to be alert to the seriousness of this moment – this violence, directed at their bodies and their sense of belonging in the world – while also teaching them to arm themselves for the stubborn persistence of white supremacy.

For me as a scholar of colour, it often feels that I conduct my teaching in a context of violence. As Katherine McKittrick reminds us, 'learning and teaching and classrooms are, already, sites of pain. ... [T]he site where we begin to teach is already white supremacist' (Hudson and McKittrick, 2014, p 238). While faculty of colour understand that teaching in such spaces is physically taxing and emotionally draining, students of colour don't always recognise this as violence but, rather, consider their sense of bewilderment and disorientation as natural, and expect that it will be soothed by institutional mechanisms of incorporation such as O-week (student orientation) or Freshers' Week. In the opening pages of *On Being Included*, Sarah Ahmed asserts that we need to think 'more concretely about institutional spaces, about how some more than others will be at home in institutions that assume certain bodies as their norm' (Ahmed, 2012, p 3). In this Ahmed calls us to a simultaneous examination of the institutional cultures as well as the embodied experiences of those persons not considered the norm.

At the university where I teach (University of KwaZulu-Natal [UKZN]), this period of orientation at the beginning of the academic year is often followed by periods of disruption and student protests as another cohort of students questions the purpose of the university and the white normative culture that is associated with higher education. In South Africa, these critiques about access and institutional culture found echoes nationally as students from across the country called for a change. These campaigns were known as the #Rhodesmustfall and #Feesmustfall campaigns, as students sought to decolonise the institutional cultures of universities and for improved access for poorer students to higher education. There are excellent accounts of the student campaigns during this period in South Africa, but that is not the focus of this chapter (Booysen, 2016; Ndlovu, 2017; Habib, 2019). This period between 2015 and 2016 saw persistent and widespread protests at university campuses in South Africa, which were often met with institutional dismissal or police suppression and violence.

The discontent among South African university students across the country soon gave birth to one of the largest public interest campaigns in the country's democratic era. The protest actions by university students assumed a wide range of subversive formats. For example, at institutions like the University of Cape Town and the University of Witwatersrand (in Johannesburg), students occupied administrative buildings through sit-ins reminiscent of the Occupy Movement. Students used the occupied spaces as campus campaign centres, where they would invite regular speakers, hold workshops, and invite the university administration for meetings during the months of occupation. As part of their decolonial efforts, students at the University of Cape Town did more than just occupy the vice-chancellor's office; they also renamed it Azania House. Similarly, at the University of Witwatersrand, the occupied student union building was popularly renamed after anti-apartheid martyr Solomon Mahlangu (Liphosa and Dennis, 2017). At these and other schools, students engaged in discussions about the coloniality of apartheid-era art, sculptures, and portraits on campuses. In some places these symbols were defaced, damaged, and removed, while elsewhere students erected makeshift shanty homes, to symbolically highlight the socioeconomic disparities between many students (Evans, 2016).

On provincial university campuses, where we generally find a higher proportion of students from areas ruled over by traditional authorities, students incorporated indigenous religious rituals into their protest actions. For example, burning *mphepho* (an indigenous herb burned as incense) had become common as a protective measure against police violence; it also incorporated the ancestors into the campaigns for decolonising the university. These kinds of disruptive practices not only offered an accessible and tangible register for marking out the sacred, but they also introduced alternative registers of knowledge and authority that decentred both their privileged peers and us, the university teachers who served as allies. I recall that on another such occasion, when we met with some students in the protest hall in the morning following a furious debate the previous evening, one student announced: 'last night, our ancestor, Steven Bantu Biko came to me in a dream, and he instructed me to bring fire to this struggle'. This announcement was met with both laughter and delight from his fellow students. The laughter offered relief in a context of tension, and it also marked a moment of recognition among the students of colour that an element of the indigenous had been introduced into the university context. In her examination of critical pedagogy, where she reflects on the role of laughter and the place of affect in the racialised classroom, Esther Ohito suggests that: 'By "cracking up", both pedagogue and students perforated White supremacy, and created cracks through which gratifying, healing, and ultimately liberating feelings could slide into the space and seep into their bodies' (2019, p 139). So, when this student introduced his dream as a call to arms, none of the student leaders questioned the legitimacy of dreamscape as a knowledge register. During this period, it became increasingly evident that the invocation of the ancestors or indigenous rituals, having been incorporated into the student campaigns, produced local articulations of what constitutes a decolonial protest action. In doing this, students used indigenous religious frames as a mechanism not just through which to resist coloniality but also through which to mediate and introduce new indigenous registers of knowing and being.

BlackSundaysSalon: learning together outside the classroom

In one of the many efforts to fashion scholarly rationale for their actions, I was invited by the students to facilitate a seminar series on 'Fanon, Race, and Violence'. However, through our discussion, it became evident that a seminar format was too formal and centred on a single academic's expert knowledge. The students' disquiet and suspicion of anyone formally associated with or employed by the university ran so deep that deliberation was not possible until we agreed on the nature of our conversations. A small group of student leaders from across various disciplines and academics agreed to establish an experimental space that came to be known as BlackSundaysSalon.

BlackSundaysSalon emerged out of a promissory effort to facilitate a space where black students, academics, activists, and artists would talk and think together about our collective experience of being 'space invaders' – a way of framing our sense of being out of place in the university.[1] By the spring of 2015, an online presence was established that announced:

> Black Sundays Salon is a social, cultural, and intellectual platform created jointly by a collective of students, staff, and activists associated with UKZN. The platform provides a space for exchange and interaction for young black thinkers, performers, and artists to think through and talk through ideas about identity, race and decolonization in postcolonial Africa.

The Salon was exclusively for people of colour, variously attached to the university community. We agreed to meet for two to three hours on the third Sunday of every month, in the afternoon. We would meet on the university campus or in the neighbourhood around campus. The idea was to ensure that students would have ready access to the meetings. During the next six months, we held regular meetings at which we discussed topics suggested or requested by the students, so long as they dealt with 'identity, race, and decolonization'. Every meeting included two or three academics, who would co-facilitate the meeting with a student leader. We would variously read together, watch a documentary, or have a speaker on a specific topic. Unlike classrooms, our deliberations followed a flat structure with a mixed format of contributions. Anyone could choose to submit a piece of art, poetry, or music, or to speak – in English or the vernacular.

The Salon also included eating together, because many of our university students lived in precarious situations and often with food insecurity. Midway through the meetings, we would break and get food and something to drink; this often marked the beginning of more relaxed exchanges between the members. For the first six months, we engaged with a wide range of topics including 'Frantz Fanon', 'The Black Body in Performance', 'Being Black on Campus'. In the subsequent years, we also discussed the topics 'Music and Resistance' and 'Poetics of Protest'.

During this period, we established a community of care and exchange, intended to introduce a decolonial or border pedagogy that seemed possible only beyond the university classroom. The salon provided a space where we shared our ideas about decolonising the curriculum and our anxieties about allies. It was also a space where we found our ideas about solidarity tested. But, most significantly, we developed a shared language about what it means to be black on a colonially established university campus, along with analytical tools for detecting and critiquing white normativity. And we established possibilities for resisting coloniality that centred both black embodiment and a respect for the indigenous. The salon provided a space where students' lived experiences and indigenous ways of knowing could be expressed without having to translate themselves into colonially intelligible frames. It let participants speak freely, without the need to justify or qualify the veracity of their claims about how they experience the university space or university classroom.

BlackSundaysSalon offered a space for reflection about the violence and alienation students experienced on the university campus. Thus, during a period when academic programmes were suspended and students were deprived of their learning community, we sought to fashion a decolonial praxis. In this regard, we invited a critical understanding of history, we privileged emancipatory and critical teaching practices, and we sought to decentre colonial epistemological approaches. To give expression to this ambition, we produced several curatorial moments that not only disrupted the relationship between academic facilitators and students but opened new registers for thinking and speaking about race and violence in the context of the university.

While the salon emerged as a response to a particular set of circumstances, it also gave expression to an emerging set of decolonial pedagogical ambitions. These ambitions are, in part shaped by Cervantes-Soon and Carrillo's (2016) notion that a decolonial or border pedagogy privileges the epistemologies and ways of being in the world of those who find themselves in the colonial, social, and institutional borderlands. As they sought to explore the alienation that their students experienced within mainstream educational institutions, Cervantes-Soon and Carrillo argued that border thinking 'instead constitutes a potentially radical way of re-imagining knowledge and educational practices for oppositional social transformation' (2016, p 282). Drawing on the idea that students already know things about the social world that frustrates their ambitions or grants them opportunities, these efforts encourage students' development as agents of social change; doing so is best understood as a mode of decolonial praxis.

In reflecting on decolonial praxis in the South African context, the work of Maria Lugones (2007) and Gloria Anzaldua (1987) offers a useful conception of border or decolonial thinking. Lugones argued that border thinking is critical for mobilising these various synergies between the academic and the activist, while Anzaldua, through a blend of socio-biographical narratives and poetics, offered a four-fold conception of borderland as at once physical, geopolitical, geo-economic, and emotional or shamanistic. The South African university context demanded a border thinking and pedagogy because, for many black students, the university emerged as a borderland where physical cultures edged each other and where tensions over race and class also come into sharp contrast. For Anzaldua, the borderland produces emotional and material effects in the lives of those who occupy that space. As she notes in the preface to *Borderland/La Frontera*, it is 'not a comfortable territory to live in, this place of contradictions'; yet later she reminds her readers that '[l]iving in a state of psychic unrest, in a Borderland, is what makes poets write and artists create' (1987, p 73). It is precisely by imagining the university space as a borderland and as a site of struggle, where students of colour are both at home and strangers (Anzaldua, 1987, p 216), and where the emotional, spiritual, and cognitive converge to reconstitute subaltern knowledge (Lugones, 2010, p 753), that a decolonial praxis emerges as a mode of trespassing, negotiating, and sustaining.

Curating race and violence

During the periods of unrest discussed earlier, BlackSundaysSalon met regularly to reflect on experiences of alienation in the university and on the violence used to contain student action. While students sought to draw attention to the epistemic violence reproduced at the university, their critics drew attention to the acts of arson and damage done to buildings and statues by students. All the while, the presence of police and security services became a fixed feature on and around most university campuses.

As educators, we were faced with the issues of how to assist students with the completion of the curriculum, as well as how to meaningfully incorporate their embodied experiences into our teaching and learning. While some colleagues found these two issues to be mutually exclusive, several academics from drama, media studies, education, politics, and religion saw this as an invitation for creative, decolonial engagement with our students. Our work with students in the monthly salon motivated us to help our students to reflect on the idea of the university as a colonial institution and to think constructively about the violent defence of that idea. We were moved to collaborate with students on several curatorial events that might give expression to our pedagogical ambitions.

Prisoners' Memorial

The first curated event was erected in response to the arrest and imprisonment of 21 students from the Pietermaritzburg campus of UKZN between late September and early October 2016. These students were charged with public disorder. A court interdict against further protests prevented students from meeting as a community in groups larger than four people, and so some staff offered their classes as deliberative spaces (Grassow and le Bruyns, 2017). While some colleagues hosted learning seminars in a central hall to provide students with a space for reflection, others of us sought to make visible the trauma and absence of those students who had been imprisoned. With colleagues, we erected a pop-up memorial on the site where students used to gather at the start of a protest (see Figure 15.1). Twenty-one flattened black refuse bags were placed on the main campus lawn, with the memorial mimicking a cemetery. A sheet of white paper detailing the name of the

Figure 15.1: Photos of the Prisoners' Memorial

Source: Federico Settler

student was placed on the plastic sheet, and it also showed where students were imprisoned and the number of days they had been incarcerated.

As a curated artistic event, it was not prohibited under the court interdict, and soon students who were drawn to the site began to read and stand in silence to remember the events of the preceding weeks. While some students wept, others expressed dismay at the fact that students had then been imprisoned at a regional high-security prison for more than ten days. The members of the BlackSundaysSalon who erected the memorial left students to linger in the space, without intervening or directing the exchanges between students who visited the site. Even though the popular sacrality of the memorial evoked a serious and sombre mood, the memorial provided a space for critical recollection and exchange between students and faculty invested in the outcome of the #Rhodesmustfall and #Feesmustfall campaigns. For students who were sceptical about the protests and worried about the violence, the memorial brought the political and material implications of students' campaigns into sharp focus. For those students who had been active in the student protests, the memorial offered relief and an opportunity to gather in the same space as their peers to signal an embodied critique on the issues of alienation in higher education.

Curating this memorial made it possible for us to draw on public memorials as 'vehicles of memory' through which martyrs and victims are remembered (Jelin, 2007; Duncan, 2009). It also provided a space for learning and reflection. By moving into and through this space, students were able to reflect on the predicament of those students removed from the university to prison – bringing this into conversation with the current lived realities of those standing in the pop-up memorial. Thus was a participatory learning space created.

Public Sculpture

After months of conflicts between students and security services, we sought to produce a moment or event that would invite students to reflect on and speak about the violence. With this curated public sculpture, we wanted to think more intentionally about our pedagogy. We noted that erecting a sculpture provided an alternate way through which to memorialise people's lived histories on campus. It simultaneously invited students to write themselves into the institutional history of the university while also offering a counter-narrative to the stone statues of colonial benefactors erected on the campus during the previous century. On the other hand, curating this public sculpture was a commentary on violence, incidents of fire, and fear of incarceration, as well as an effort to make visible the students' collective rejection of coloniality.

In collaboration with several members of the BlackSundaysSalon, including four staff members, we developed a sculpture, which was made up of steel frames of desks, barbed wire, with slogan-printed T-shirts, a mirror, and burned textbooks on a bed of salt (see Figure 15.2). All the elements were everyday materials collected from around campus, but they variously reflected the recent history of violence. Using charred textbooks and twisted metal, in particular, depicted the twisted and strained relationship of students to the university. The use of barbed wire represented the repression of student protests. We placed the sculpture in a busy intersection on campus, and to

Figure 15.2: Photos of the Public Sculpture

Source: Federico Settler

incorporate student-viewers' participation into the sculpture, we placed a mirror in the centre of the sculpture and a chalkboard on the ground. No explanation or commentary accompanied the sculpture. It was thus up to each student to interpret the sculpture and write on the chalkboard or leave their mark in the salt. Most students paused at the evocative sculpture and sat or stood close by while discussing the meaning with their friends. The paradox and provocation of curating violence and fire on campus during a period of increased securitisation were not lost on the students, and many cheered while others just laughed. But other students were anxious that this sculpture would invite a new cycle of trouble and repression.

In our initial ambition, we had hoped that the installation would culminate with a final act where the sculpture would be set alight, but the university would not give us permission to do this. Thus, as a commentary on the violence that characterised conflicts across several campuses, we curated the sculpture to produce a public classroom as we sought to disrupt ideas about where learning might take place. This space also afforded us the chance to incorporate into the tertiary learning space students' experiences of violence. Pedagogically, this event allowed us to ask questions about what knowledge is valued, as well as whose lived experiences are centred in university classroom deliberations. While both the Prisoners' Memorial and the Public Sculpture opened a deliberative space where students' lived experiences were at the centre of our learning encounter, these curated moments, literally born out of fire, introduced a decolonial praxis with an effect beyond what we as creators could have initially imagined.

What was striking about these initial efforts was the impulse to attend to both the indigenous, as an ontological disruption, and the privileging of students' current lived experience as knowledge archives that should shape our efforts to decolonise the university. While the #Rhodesmustfall and #Feesmustfall campaigns were necessary protests that aligned a wide range of interests, they served largely as a call for the institutional and learning culture of the university to be a less alienating space for black students. Similarly, the deliberation within BlackSundaysSalon was premised on the belief that decolonising the university had to be about more than changing the curriculum, but also about how to significantly change the institutional cultures of universities and the focus of our pedagogical efforts. Heidi Mirza reminds us that in higher education contexts where women, black students, people of colour (POC), and indigenous scholars are treated as strangers, or intruders, transformative strategies will inevitably emerge.

> In their space on the margin, with their quiet and subversive acts of care and 'other ways of knowing,' these women [and black students, POC, and indigenous scholars] operate within, between, under, and alongside the mainstream educational and labor market structures,

subverting, renaming and reclaiming opportunities ... through the transformative pedagogy of 'raising the race'. (Mirza, 2015, p 8)

We were confident that our curatorial events provided a kind of transformative pedagogical encounter that emerged out of and responded to black students' experiences of exclusion. Although student protests and academic disruptions ceased after an agreement was reached between student leaders, university administrators, and government in late 2016, it had become evident that this long effort of teaching, learning, speaking, and curating violence would continue well beyond the formal end of the #Rhodesmustfall and #Feesmustfall campaigns.

Decolonial love and eating as decolonial praxis

We found that most students continued to live with a sense of anxiety and ambivalence with respect to belonging at university. We learned from our BlackSundaysSalon deliberations that although the #Rhodesmustfall and #Feesmustfall campaigns were characterised by unrest and violence, our students had deep and intimate archives of knowledge that predated their entry into university. We learned that our students possessed reservoirs of knowledge about racialised violence and that this knowledge determined how they moved in the social space of the university campus. Students were alert to being subjects of particular regimes of surveillance, which in turn provoked their sense of alienation, of being out of place. This reality resonates with Cervantes-Soon and Carrillo's argument that 'By recognising these subaltern knowledges of border thinking, border pedagogy repositions people on the margins as creators, thinkers, and knowers. This constitutes the very condition of possibility as youth are given the opportunity to reclaim their agency and challenge dominant and Eurocentric intellectual thought in creative ways' (2016, p 286).

Long after the formal end of the protest campaigns, BlackSundaysSalon provided space for continued conversations about psychic unrest, epistemic and other violence, and how to decolonise campus, in terms of learning, teaching, and living. The group sought to cultivate a mode of praxis that simultaneously disrupts coloniality, but it also sought to make space for imaginatively crafting ideas about the university and about ourselves, born out of our collective lived experience.

One year after the end of the protest campaign, BlackSundaysSalon invited well-known artist, feminist, and activist, Ukhona Mlandu, to spend a few days with our members on campus. Her visit involved a one-day public art event titled #100AfricanReads (see Figure 15.3) and a discussion. She is the founder of makwande.republic, an African artist retreat in the rural Eastern Cape province of South Africa, where practitioners can come to 'make sense of the erasure and dispossession' with a view to grow, expand, and become the artist/activist they wish to be.[2]

For the public art event on campus, Mlandu invited students from the Drama Department together with members of the BlackSundaysSalon to participate in an event that mimicked and mocked the colonial representations memorialised on our campuses. In a 2015 public lecture she asserted that

> I find that highly problematic, unless we were to decommission all colonial statues that exist. It is disingenuous and dangerous to ask the public to skip the important step of producing a counter narrative to what already stands. And then #RhodesMustFall happened. This showed us the fault in the reasoning that these colonial structures are a nonissue. (Fikeni, 2015)

In a context where colonial statues remained an emotive issue for many, she called for us to develop decolonial ways of imagining the university space. Through an uncanny ability to destabilise and dismantle unnecessary hierarchies (hooks, 2010), she drew on her own work as a queer activist as well as an indigenous feminist to curate this event. Each student had to select one text from 100 African-authored books and then meditate on its meaning. Then students were to select a costume from a wardrobe presented to them, with the view to fashion themselves as figures that would depict, mimic, or mock their views, feelings, and perspective on the text. This afforded students as well as us as staff the opportunity to imagine ways of being on campus that were transgressive and playful, while engaging in a decolonial space of learning-with. The event produced a series of dynamic and colourful disruptions that celebrated and privileged the students' imaginaries of belonging and being. Juxtaposed against the colonial and apartheid architecture, the students' performance reinscribed the campus space with new meaning(s).

With each stage of the procession and through performative reading from their selected text, such as Sol Plaatje's *Mhudi* (1978) and James Baldwin's *I am not your Negro* (2017), other students were drawn into the meditation. Mlandu offered no direction to the performers as to how much they needed to interact with the audience, except to offer moments of spatial and epistemic rupture through whimsical, colourful, embodied performances and readings. The selection and curation of costumes echoed the work of Yinka Shinobare, the British Nigerian artist who uses colourful wax batik prints, widely used in West Africa, to recreate and sculpt bodies (or mannequins) in colonial tableaus as a way to trouble colonial symbols and historical moments.[3] Mlandu, in curating this event with our students, allowed them/ us to transform not just our bodies through adorning and decorating in the 'wrong' colours, but also to reimagine and ruin the white normative space

Figure 15.3: Photos of #100AfricanReads

Source: Federico Settler

of the colonial university. Through whimsical performance and juxtaposed dress, the performance made the everyday epistemic violence of being in a white supremacist space visible and, momentarily, tolerable.

Through these various curatorial moments, we sought not simply to nurture students' knowledges and experiences, but also to examine the relationship between knowledge and power in the context of institutional, representational, and physical violence against black students. While Lucy Lippard (1997) argues that the landscape and vernacular of the art object are best understood in terms of the space or context within which we live, Anzaldua (1987) reminds us that it is precisely out of contexts of psychic unrest that creative resistance emerges to help forge something new. These curatorial moments allowed us to make visible and to reflect on the students' mediations of violence. At the same time, the university emerged as a contested space where black students' experiences of being out of place became part of the institutional history.

Two days later, as we prepared for the regular BlackSundaysSalon meeting, Mlandu insisted that instead of providing the usual store-bought food, salads, and drinks, she would cook for the students. She cooked an aromatic stew, with *amaqwinyas* (fat cakes), and, through introducing home meal, a staple in many black households, she introduced a sensory and affective layer that extended the performative disruption of the previous days. Reminiscent of most black homes, where eating is social and relational, this introduction of *amaqwinyas* into the salon meeting emerged as a moment where the teacher-curator became the auntie, sister, mother, elder. In this moment, the feeling of being loved enabled 'members of the learning community ... to see the intersections between power, oppression, and pedagogy. Identify their complicity in the status quo and embrace their responsibility to act' (Douglas and Nganga, 2015, p 61). Thus, BlackSundaysSalon emerged as a space where we did not just disrupt institutional hierarchies but also centred African indigenous ways of being in the university learning context. Mlandu's final act of cooking, caring, teaching, and love seems like a strikingly tangible answer to Esther Ohito's question: 'how does the pedagogue invite love and pleasure into the pain-filled field of urban teacher education' (2019, p 123).

Conclusion: curating violence

Through curating violence, we hoped to place indigenous ways of knowing and knowledge registers about violence at the centre of our pedagogical deliberations. We did this to privilege our students' experiences of violence and racism and to incorporate the indigenous as a counter-narrative to the supposedly universal Western ways of knowing and being. In this regard, we sought to produce a decolonial pedagogy. The pedagogical ambition pursued in the development of the three curatorial moments elaborated in the foregoing was made possible by converging registers of meaning-making from the artistic and the indigenous.

In our efforts to help our students reflect on their experience of violence during the period of unrest and student campaigns, #Rhodesmustfall and #Feesmustfall, we sought to create a decolonial learning space through facilitating curatorial moments to interrogate the relations between power, dominance, and knowledge. Doing this in a context where students were denied opportunities to register their discontent through public protest, and where their regular classroom spaces seldom recognise their own pre-existing social and indigenous knowledge, these curatorial moments were opportunities for deliberation. They provided students with the opportunity to think through their experiences of violence, to reflect on the impact of violence, and to freely discuss alternatives, or resistances, to the normal order of university culture.

While the Prisoners' Memorial and the Public Sculpture invoked the necropolitical threat of death, they also humanised the absent and imprisoned students. This border pedagogy made possible the connection of students' immediate struggle within a longer struggle for recognition, while at the same time letting the curatorial meditations on violence be a continuous deliberative process. Curating these experiences of violence was an ongoing participatory process that invited a reflection on the intersection of knowledge and power that was premised on embodied participation or presence. Likewise, Mlandu's #100AfricanReads disrupted the seemingly normal order of campus by inviting the larger student community to move into and through a curatorial event that overtly referenced institutional, epistemic, or physical violence against students.

Finally, all three curatorial moments engaged registers of the indigenous and the artistic to make possible deliberations about violence and race otherwise not possible. This decolonial praxis allowed students to reflect on violence and to develop literacies of violence that drew on their experience of racialised violence as registers of knowledge not ordinarily accessed in the university classroom.

Notes

[1] For details about the establishment of the salon, see https://blacksundayssalon.wordpress.com/; for an account of the salon's activities, events and interests, see https://facebook.com/BlackSundaysSalon.

[2] For details for the event, see https://bit.ly/3cN75iS; for more information about Ukhona Mlandu, see Sarafina Magazine (2018).

[3] This is most evocatively presented in his 'Post-Colonial Globe Man' (2018) https://bit.ly/313mx4Q and his 'End of Empire' (2016) https://bit.ly/3s6ucLM. Many of his sculptures are notable for their spectacular reconfiguring of characters in period costume made from striking batik prints. http://yinkashonibare.com/.

References

Ahmed, Sara (2012) *On Being Included: Racism and Diversity in Institutional Life*. Durham, NC: Duke University Press.

Anzaldua, Gloria E. (1987) *Borderlands: The New Mestiza = La frontera*. San Francisco, Spinsters/Aunt Lute.

Baldwin, James (2017) *I Am Not Your Negro*. New York: Vintage Books,

Booysen, Susan (ed) (2016) *Fees Must Fall: Student Revolt, Decolonisation and Governance in South Africa*. Johannesburg: Wits University Press.

Cervantes-Soon, Claudia G., and Carillo, Juan F. (2016) 'Toward a pedagogy of border thinking: Building on Latin@ students' subaltern knowledge', *The High School Journal*, 99(4): 282–301.

Douglas, T., and C. Nganga (2015) 'What's radical love got to do with it: Navigating identity, pedagogy, and positionality in pre-service education', *International Journal of Critical Pedagogy*, 6(1): 58–82.

Duncan, Christopher (2009) 'Monuments and martyrdom: Memorializing the dead in post-conflict North Maluku', *Bijdragen tot de Taal-, Land- en Volkenkunde*, 165(4): 429–458.

Evans, Jenni (2016) '#Shacksville: UCT Protesters Braai on Jammie Steps', 15 February. [online] Available from: https://www.news24.com/SouthAfrica/News/uct-protesters-set-up-shack-on-varsity-steps-0160215 [accessed 18 March 2021].

Fikeni, Lwandile (2015) 'Public power and the art of placemaking', Smart Cities Dive. [online] Available from: https://bit.ly/3cOqEre [accessed 20 March 2021].

Grassow, Lisa, and Le Bruyns, Clint (2017) 'Embodying human rights in #FeesMustFall? Contributions from an indecent theology', *HTS Teologiese Studies/Theological Studies*, 73(3): a4799.

Habib, Adam (2019) *Rebels and Rage: Reflecting on #FeesMustFall*. Johannesburg: Jonathan Ball Publishers.

hooks, bell (2010) *Teaching Critical Thinking: Practical Wisdom*. New York: Routledge.

Hudson, Peter James, and McKittrick, Kathrine (2014) 'The geographies of Blackness and Anti-Blackness: An interview with Katherine McKittrick', *The CLR James Journal*, 20(1/2): 233–240.

Jelin, Elizabeth (2007) 'Public memorialization in perspective; Truth, justice and memory of past repression in the southern cone of South America', *The International Journal of Transitional Justice*, 1: 138–156.

Liphosa, Pandeani, and Dennis, Nolan Oswald (2017) 'Solomon Mahlangu House: Self-assertion and humanisation through claiming black space', *CLARA*, 1(4): 49–70.

Lippard, Lucy R. (1997) *The Lure of the Local: Senses of Place in a Multicentered Society*. New York: New Press.

Lugones, María (2007) 'Heterosexualism and the colonial/modern gender system', *Hypatia*, 22(1) 186–209.

Lugones, María (2010) 'Towards a decolonial feminism', *Hypatia*, 25(4): 742–759.

Mirza, Heidi S. (2015) 'Decolonizing higher education: Black feminism and the intersectionality of race and gender', *Journal of Feminist Scholarship*, 7/8: 1–12.

Ndlovu, Musawenkosi (2017) *#FeesMustFall and Youth Mobilisation in South Africa*. London: Routledge.

Ohito, Esther O. (2019) '"I just love Black people!": Love, pleasure, and critical pedagogy in urban teacher education', *Urban Review*, 51: 123–145.

Plaatje, Sol T. (1978) *Mhudi*. Oxford: Heinemann.

Sarafina Magazine (2018) 'A conversation with Ukhona Ntsali Mlandu', *Sarafina Magazine*, 2 May. [online] Available from: https://bit.ly/3f1ciXc [accessed 19 March 2021].

Shinobare, Yinka (2018) 'The post-colonial Globe Man' Yinkashobare.com 2018 [online] Available from: https://bit.ly/313mx4Q [accessed 18 March 2021].

Shinobare, Yinka (2016) 'End of Empire' Yinkashinobare.com 2016 [online] Available from: https://bit.ly/3s6ucLM [accessed 18 March 2018].

Epilogue: What We Have Learned

Abby Day, Lois Lee, Dave S.P. Thomas, and James Spickard

We began this project about a year before the COVID-19 pandemic shut down the world. We sent the publisher our final manuscript just as the wealthy democracies began to reap the benefit of the vaccines that they had both developed and hoarded. Poorer countries need those vaccines but cannot get them. COVID-19 highlights the same lines of inequality that afflict higher education: elites benefit while others fall behind.

Here are two other pandemic/education parallels:

- The virus hit working-class and minority communities harder than others because they lack equal access to advanced medicine and because their jobs do not typically give them the freedom of working safely from home. This parallels those communities' lack of equal educational opportunities, including access to the libraries, the technological tools, and the time away from paid work that elite students take for granted. This structural discrimination is in addition to the personal prejudice along ethnic, gender, and other lines that has dogged higher education for decades.
- The virus spread along the same globally connected trade routes that once brought sugar, spices, and slaves to benefit European and American upper classes. Those routes have more recently brought refugees and voluntary migrants, who have increased Western democracies' ethnic, religious, and cultural diversity without, however, having gained equal respect. We find it telling that one of the first vaccines for COVID-19 was developed by a pair of German scientists of Turkish descent, a group long excluded from German intellectual life (Sauerbrey, 2020). What other good ideas might be percolating among those whom our universities traditionally ignore?

Yet the COVID pandemic highlights more than our inequalities; it highlights a transformation in universities' economic role. The fact that university-based research contributed so much to the anti-COVID fight tells us that higher education is no longer an ivory tower, nor (just) a repository of cultural tradition. It is a chief prop for the new 'knowledge economy'.

Cutting-edge technology is no longer born in garages and tinkerers' workshops; it emerges from university laboratories and from the tech giants' research centres built nearby. The American computer industry began as an offshoot of Stanford's, Massachusetts Institute of Technology's, and Caltech's engineering programmes. 'Big Pharma' began in the late 19th century with industrial applications of German universities' chemical research, but its greatest rise came from post-Second World War government support for biomedical research at British, French, German, and United States (US) universities (Daemmrich and Bowden, 2005; Tobbell, 2009). Other industries have similar stories. University-generated knowledge makes the modern economy possible.

Universities also train the personnel who staff the industries that result. As economist David Harvey (2014, p 187) put it, the knowledge economy

> depends on having at [its] disposal a well-educated and scientifically qualified labour force which must be either trained at home (hence the immense significance of the research universities in countries such as the USA) or imported from abroad. ... [This] puts the whole educational system in the cross-hairs of capital's concerns, although, as usual, capital is inclined not to pay for any of it if it can possibly help it.

The result is a push for more 'economically relevant' university curricula and an emphasis on institutional efficiency that pits scholar against scholar and university against university in a fierce competition for funding. Thorp and Goldstein (2018, p 3) write:

> In this approach, the university has a transactional relationship with its students, who pay tuition in exchange for a good job and a good life; an employer–employee relationship with its faculty, who are paid to teach a prescribed number of students and, in some cases, compete for and secure a certain amount of grant funding; and a corporate relationship with its governing board. Student success in this model is measured by postgraduate employment rates and graduate starting salaries. New knowledge is valued for its potential to generate a profit for the inventor and the institution.

This neoliberal university (Seal, 2018) favours diversity initiatives to the extent that they train graduates to work with whatever kind of people best serve the neoliberal system (Harvey, 2005). At most, that requires accepting diverse types of students, faculty, and staff while also including them as full participants in university life. Thus, US universities set up 'Offices of

Diversity and Inclusion', which are designed to make universities 'work better'. The United Kingdom (UK) did something similar (see Stringer, Chapter 1), though its government recently dropped its insistence that universities comply with two major programmes that address gender and racial inequalities, possibly as part of its aggressive turn against Critical Race Studies and what it dismisses as 'woke' culture. Notably, the UK government's Commission on Race and Ethnic Disparities (CRED) claims that the UK should be seen as a model of racial equality, further hailing education as the 'single most emphatic success story of British ethnic minority experience' (CRED, 2021, p 55).

Neoliberalism loves efficiency. It sees no point in decolonization, unless honouring people's societies of origin makes them better workers. And it absolutely does not want its future employees to study the colonial systems that propelled the European and US economies forward, much less the neocolonial ones that keep them there (Dutt, 1904; Clark, 1936; Williams, 1944; Rodney, 1974; Thurow and Kilman, 2009; Patnaik, 2017).

Yet decolonization is important on two levels. One is the level of justice. As Suketu Mehta (2019, p 3) writes in his 'immigrant's manifesto', 'We are the creditors. ... You took all our wealth, our diamonds. Now we have come to collect.' This level drives most of the efforts to decolonize university curricula. They see diversity and inclusion not as charity but as reparations. This decolonization wants to change the power relations that have kept various minorities out. Yet doing so requires that university curricula draw the connection between the West's current dominance and its political and intellectual suppression of other civilizations and of women, minorities, and others at home. Showing the intellectual, scientific, and artistic worth of those who had been misrepresented, or left out of previous curricula – and reconciling with those actions – rebalances the moral world.

The second level is about knowledge. It is not just that the four 16th-century epistemicides laid the ideological groundwork for Europe's colonial expropriation (Grosfoguel, 2013; Thomas, Chapter 7). They also diminished the store of human knowledge. This is more than just the fact that Fibonacci learned his mathematics from Central Asian Muslims or that Europe's early maritime dominance of the Indian Ocean was due in part to the withdrawal of the Chinese 'treasure fleets' 60 years before. It also involves a recognition that the pre-Columbian inhabitants of the Amazon had developed highly efficient ways of farming the (supposedly) 'infertile' jungle and that North America's Amerindians practised a form of agriculture that was able to support large city populations far more sustainably than do our present heavy-ploughing techniques (Mann, 2005; Elbein, 2021). More recently, Western medical researchers have learned from societies in the South Caucasus about the effectiveness of bacteriophage medicine against antibiotic-resistant infections (Thiel, 2004; Parfitt, 2005). Who knows what we would find, were the knowledge in the long-neglected libraries of Timbuktu, Samarkand, and other scholarly centres (Hammer, 2016) part of the canon? Euro-American scholarship covers only part of the human heritage. We have been misled.

Fortunately, active social movements for racial, sexual, gender, economic, epistemic, disability, and other forms of justice are pressing universities to include such missing knowledge. More than just changing the canons or increasing 'body count', they seek diversity, inclusion, and decolonization in many forms. History tells us that institutions respond when there is outside pressure. The Black Lives Matter movement confirms this pattern. To be effective, however, we need to know what to change and how to do it. We shall identify some places to begin.

What needs to change?

Change needs to happen at three levels: to universities and their curricula, to scholarship, and to the institutions that both support and structure academic life. We will summarize each in turn.

Calls to diversify university campus environments and curricula have attracted global attention to 'bottom up' student-led activism agitating for change. Universities need to create more culturally engaging campus environments that help racially and ethnically diverse student and staff populations thrive. Harmful elements of hostile campus environments negatively affect students' achievement (Harper et al, 2018; UUK, 2019), sense of belonging (Gray et al, 2018; Strayhorn, 2019), and interest in their major (Renninger and Hidi, 2020; Quinlan, 2021).

Samuel Museus (2014) outlined nine essential aspects of a university environment that are needed to maximize success among diverse populations. He recommended that campus environments need to engage and reflect cultural relevance by promoting culturally familiar activities, culturally relevant knowledge, cultural community service, meaningful cross-cultural engagement, and activities that promote cultural validation. He further recommended that culturally engaging campus environments should examine the extent to which campus learning and support systems are responsive to the cultural norms and needs of diverse communities. This might include providing holistic support, practising proaction rather than simply reacting to events and demands, creating humanized educational environments, and promoting collectivist cultural orientations that are characterized by teamwork and the pursuit of mutual success.

In their current state, university curricula 'erase and mute' the experiences of ethnic minorities, women, persons with disabilities, and other marginalized groups; this leads to distortions, omissions, and the promotion of stereotypes. If universities are to break this chain and reimagine their pedagogy and curricula (Arday et al, 2020), they need to do more than change their campus environments and build on the traditions of culturally relevant pedagogy (Ladson-Billings, 1995) and culturally responsive education (Bryan-Gooden et al, 2019). They also need to create more culturally sensitive curricula. A culturally sensitive curriculum is one in which attitudes, teaching methods and practice, teaching materials, curriculum, and theories relate directly to students' diverse cultures, identities, histories, and contexts (Thomas and Quinlan, 2021).

A culturally sensitive curriculum goes beyond representing diversity, as this alone is simply performative. Instead, such a curriculum presents positive portrayals of diversity. As Michelle Grue (2021) writes:

> scholars often use diversity and inclusion terms interchangeably, or use them in ways that do not reflect the intent ... [true diversity work] drives academia toward a reality in which people of colour [and otherwise excluded and disadvantaged groups] have equitable access and achievement, their identities are not merely accepted but valued as integral to building knowledge in the disciplines, and their whole selves have power while at university and beyond. (pp 164 and 167)

In addition, such a curriculum needs to equip learners with the sociopolitical and critical awareness to challenge hegemonic power structures. In parallel with Museu's (2014) 'humanised educational environments', a culturally sensitive curriculum needs to promote inclusive classroom interactions – between students and peers and between students and teachers. 'The owl of Minerva has flown, the university [as we know it] is dead' (Thomas and Arday, 2021). Doing equity and diversity for success in higher education is more important than ever.

Besides changing universities, we need to change scholarship. This involves changing the systems that elevate a narrow set of approaches to knowledge over the rest. It involves changing the taken-for-granted canons that have shaped current academic disciplines. And it involves affirming plural approaches to posing and solving intellectual problems. Each of these has implications for both scholarly content and the structures by which that content is produced.

Let us start with the narrow approaches. These go beyond the long-standing fights that pit 'science' against 'the humanities' (Snow, 1959; Pinker, 2013; Pinker and Wieseltier, 2013; Wieseltier, 2013). Each academic discipline has a favoured set of ways to generate knowledge and a favoured set of claims for the knowledge it produces. These shift over time, but at any given point they are heavily institutionalized. American sociology, for example, has for decades become increasingly quantitative (Schwemmer and Wieczorek, 2020), though the 1970s computer revolution shifted its quantitative focus from neighbourhood to survey research (Anderson and Massey, 2001, pp 4–5), and the much later growth of text- and internet-search capabilities facilitated the rise of sometimes questionable content analysis (for example, Perry and Whitehead, 2021). Sociological ethnographers have had to write books, or publish in anthropological journals which have their own favoured and sometimes trendy emphases.[1] Other disciplines have had their own fights (for example, Gage, 1989; Bryman, 2008), and quantitative work is not always ascendant. The point is, however, that such rigidities narrow what counts as scholarship in any one time and place. Work that falls outside these boundaries remains unseen.

Non-Western scholarship and ideas usually fall outside these boundaries. Several of our contributors have described aspects of this, especially Bolzonar's report of Chinese universities' use of Western curricula and structures in their efforts to become 'world class' (Chapter 15), Spickard's exploration of non-Western ideas that could expand the sociology of religion's intellectual toolkit (Chapter 10), and Mann's account of how hegemonic Euro-American publishers distort journal scholarship across the entire world (Chapter 15). Numerous works by Connell (2007), Alatas and Sinha (2017), de Sousa Santos and Meneses (2020), and others show other facets of the problem. The fact is, our universities have embraced a Euro-American standard of what counts as 'excellence', thus setting themselves up as the 'world-class' institutions for other universities to follow. As Hanne Adriansen points out, even global scholarly collaboration has colonial overtones to the extent that Euro-American university 'experts' see themselves as transferring knowledge to others rather than as full partners with those who know different things than they do. She notes that even 'capacity building projects risk creating [what Vananda] Shiva [(2013) has called] "monocultures of the mind". But they can also have the opposite effect: they can empower African [and other] researchers and help them to become more independent' (Adriansen, 2016). The issue is not the programmes themselves; it is the use to which they are consciously or unconsciously put.

This is, after all, the point. At the end of our Introduction, we cited Achele Mbembe's (2016, p 37) statement that decolonizing the university is not to abandon the quest for universal knowledge but 'to reform it with the aim of creating a less provincial and more open critical cosmopolitan pluriversalism'. Decolonizing scholarship promises intellectual progress.

Yet diversifying curricula and personnel and including non-Western ideas in our scholarship are not enough to change our present academic situation. Scholars and teachers still need to make careers, and it is increasingly difficult for new and emerging scholars to gain, through publishing, the recognition that can bring them institutional and economic stability. This is even more difficult for scholars from non-Western or non-elite backgrounds.

The publishing problem is two-fold. First, there are the entry costs. Good scholarship requires access to the literature, but the publishing oligopoly (Mann, Chapter 12) means fewer and fewer universities can afford to give their students and staff the full access they need. Although Open Access initiatives promised change, commercial publishers still impose a monetary barrier. Currently, the favoured approach is to make authors pay a submission or publication fee; this merely transfers the cost from readers to authors. Non-elite authors lack institutional support to pay those fees, so their articles lock out people much like themselves.

A second barrier is more insidious. It results from the current hegemony of English as the international language of scholarship and from the publishers' policy of soliciting most academic reviewers and copy-editors from the global North. These reviewers and editors ensure that prospective authors not only cite the 'correct' people in their papers but follow arcane and otherwise unnecessary house-style rules, right down to the acceptable placement of a semi-colon or en-dash. A further price of entry is to pay the correct level of homage to the Northern, predominantly White male scholarly elite. This often takes the form of 'disciplinary standards' that can be a barrier to interdisciplinary conversations. This is particularly true when the language style of a discipline is excessively opaque (Kornei, 2021).

This barrier recalls Ngũgĩ wa Thiong'o's (1986, p 11) description of how children educated in colonial schools in Kenya were forced to speak English rather than their native languages (in his case, Gĩkũyũ) both inside and outside the school. Were they caught, they would be subjected to humiliating and often physical punishment. Ngũgĩ describes this humiliation regime as a core part of the colonial process. Editors and reviewers who insist that scholars cite only the global North literature impose a similar humiliation regime on scholars from the global South, though they probably think they are helping these Southern scholars 'learn how scholarship works'. They also cut themselves off from learning anything new (Stevens-Arroyo, 1995).

This situation is likely to worsen, as the COVID-19 global pandemic has damaged economies worldwide and will likely reduce money and opportunities for research and training for all but those from elite global North schools. Scholars and institutions need to open more spaces – on editorial boards, review panels, and departmental and institutional committees – to diverse scholars, accepting that non-diverse populations do not understand the experiences, pasts, and futures of those outside their domains of privilege.

How can change happen?

Universities and other knowledge-industry structures need to change; that much is obvious. But how can that be accomplished? We asked our contributors to focus on practical matters: on steps that faculty, staff, and administrators can take to increase diversity, inclusion, and decolonization in academic life. Yet, over the individual course modules, programmes, and departments sit university-wide and sector-wide policies and practices that affect teaching, research, and writing.

Educators and philosophers have written about change for centuries, probably since the ancient Greek philosopher Heraclitus observed that everything is in a state of flux. More recently, highly paid management consultants have advised organizations on how to implement change programmes across their businesses. Those consultants' first task is often to work with organizations to create 'a theory of change'. More practical than theoretical, this refers to creating plans that list objectives and the steps that must be taken to achieve results, usually expressed as 'outcomes'. Most people from the age of ten can create those charts. But, as anyone who has failed at a diet, dropped out of a gym schedule, or missed a publication deadline knows, the problem is usually not one of intention, but of will.

Consultants can help institutions to approach large-scale changes, but often find that the objectives and goals are usually modest, as senior managers urge caution against trying too much too soon. The consultants will nod sagely and mutter as they collect their large fees: they have seen this before. It is yet another example of how people resist change. And that is where they are wrong: people do not resist change. They resist loss.

To test that assumption, we need only to ask ourselves if we would resist a change to our annual salaries – upwards. Or a change to our paid holiday entitlement – increasing. Or a change to the colour of our hair to one we find more flattering, and so on. It is not change people that resist, but loss. When those same management consultants recommend a change to a university's size, or number of staff, or number of programmes, the advice tends to be to reduce, not to increase. That means some people will lose jobs, students will lose a variety of choice, and a department may lose national or international standing.

In creating space for more diversity at senior management level, some people will lose their place at those tables. To increase the number of voices and intellectual diversity in courses and publications, some authors and academics will be edited out. As the elites who have enjoyed their power and unearned privileges see their status being threatened, they will likely resist.

Because no one individual can successfully counter such resistance, we recommend collective action: form or join initiatives that are increasingly mobilizing on campuses worldwide; sign letters and petitions; turn up to rallies and protests; speak up at committee meetings; mentor emerging scholars; join editorial and funding boards and work for changes to strategies; be active in professional organizations. We also recommend collective inaction. Refuse to join editorial or review boards or committees that are not diverse, and say why. Do not, if you are a member of an elite, speak on behalf of those who are not; let them speak for themselves. But do not stay silent in rooms where diverse voices are suppressed; call out their silencing, then get out of the way so they can speak.

It is crucial to note that this effort is not just about helping others; it is about helping everyone – including the elites. As editors, we support what Jodi O'Brien (2021, p 1) calls 'radical inclusion'. Universities and our other elite institutions need to embrace diversity, inclusion, and decolonization for the sake of others, but also for the sake of themselves:

> Radical inclusion is not about giving those who have been historically marginalized the 'gift' of inclusion. Rather, radical inclusion is an opportunity for liberation extended [by those on the margins] *to* those whose experiences are primarily centrist and hegemonic; [it offers elites] an opportunity to practice humility, open-hearted engagement, and a broader humanity. In short, radical inclusion is an invitation to walk with and to be grateful to those whose experiences throw into relief all that is taken-for-granted in everyday status quo experience.

And learn from them.

Change happens. Let's do it well.

Note

[1] See Parkin's (1988) famous send-up of the latter.

References

Adriansen, Hanne Kirstine (2016) 'Global academic collaboration: A new form of colonisation?', *The Conversation*, 8 July. [online] Available from: https://bit.ly/3gYVmS3 [accessed 3 May 2021].

Alatas, Syed Farid, and Sinha, Vineeta (2017) *Sociological Theory beyond the Canon*. London: Palgrave Macmillan.

Allen, Jean M., and Webber, Melinda (2019) 'Stereotypes of minorities and education', in Steven Ratuva (ed) *The Palgrave Handbook of Ethnicity*. Singapore: Palgrave Macmillan, pp 1407–1426.

Anderson, Elijah, and Massey, Douglas S. (2001) 'The sociology of race in the United States', in Elijah Anderson and Douglas S. Massey (eds) *Problem of the Century: Racial Stratification in the United State*. New York: Russell Sage, pp 3–12.

Arday, Jason, Belluigi, Dina Zoe, and Thomas, Dave (2020) 'Attempting to break the chain: Reimagining inclusive pedagogy and decolonising the curriculum within the academy', *Educational Philosophy and Theory*, 53(3): 298–313.

Bryan-Gooden, Jahque, Hester, Megan, and Peoples, Leah Q. (2019) 'Culturally responsive curriculum scorecard', *Metropolitan Centre for Research on Equity and the Transformation of Schools*, New York University. [online] Available from: https://bit.ly/3nRjrM9 [accessed 6 May 2020].

Bryman, Alan (2008) 'The end of the paradigm wars?', in Pertti Alasuutari, Leonard Bickman, and Julia Brannen (eds) *The Sage Handbook of Social Research Methods*. London: Sage, pp 13–25.

Clark, Grover (1936) *The Balance Sheets of Imperialism: Facts and Figures on Colonies*. New York: Columbia University Press.

Connell, Raewyn (2007) *Southern Theory: The Global Dynamics of Knowledge in Social Science*. Cambridge: Polity Press.

CRED (2021) 'The Report', *UK Commission on Race and Ethnic Disparities*. [online] Available from: https://bit.ly/3el2W7Q [accessed 6 May 2021].

Daemmrich, Arthur, and Bowden, Mary Ellen (2005) 'Emergence of pharmaceutical science and industry', *Chemical and Engineering News*, 20 June, 83(25). [online] Available from: https://bit.ly/3gyHxJQ [accessed 22 April 2021].

de Sousa Santos, Boaventura, and Meneses, Maria Paula (eds) (2020) *Knowledges Born in the Struggle: Constructing the Epistemologies of the Global South*. New York: Routledge.

Dutt, Romesh Chundar (1904) *The Economic History of India in the Victorian Age* (1950 edn). London: Routledge and Kegan Paul.

Elbein, Asher (2021) 'What doomed the great city of Cahokia? Not ecological hubris, study says', *New York Times*, 24 April. [online] Available from: https://nyti.ms/2S0szlH [accessed 24 April 2021].

Gage, Nathaniel L. (1989) 'The paradigm wars and their aftermath: A "historical" sketch of research on teaching since 1989', *Educational Researcher*, 18(7): 4–10.

Gray, DeLeon L., Hope, Elan C., and Matthews, Jamall S. (2018) 'Black and belonging at school: A case for interpersonal, instructional, and institutional opportunity structures', *Educational Psychologist*, 53(2): 97–113.

Grosfoguel, Ramón (2013) 'The structure of knowledge in westernized universities: Epistemic racism/sexism and the four genocides/epistemicides of the long 16th century', *Human Architecture: Journal of the Sociology of Self-Knowledge*, 11(1): 73–90.

Grue, Michelle (2021) 'Diversify or decolonise? What you can do right now and how to get started', in Dave S.P. Thomas and Jason Arday (eds) *Doing Equity and Diversity for Success in Higher Education: Redressing Structural Inequalities in the Academy*. London: Palgrave Macmillan, pp 163–174.

Hammer, Joshua (2016) *The Bad-Ass Librarians of Timbuktu and Their Race to Save the World's Most Precious Manuscripts*. New York: Simon & Schuster.

Harper, Shaun R., Smit, Edward J., and Davis, Charles H.F. (2018) 'A critical race case analysis of black undergraduate student success at an urban university', *Urban Education*, 53(1): 3–25.

Harvey, David (2005) *A Brief History of Neoliberalism*. Oxford: Oxford University Press.

Harvey, David (2014) *Seventeen Contradictions and the End of Capitalism*. Oxford: Oxford University Press.

Howansky, Kristina, Maimon, Melanie, and Sanchez, Diana (2021) 'Identity safety cues predict instructor impressions, belonging, and absences in the psychology classroom', *Teaching of Psychology*, 1(6). [online first] Available from: https://bit.ly/3tjXjet [accessed 15 December 2021].

Kornei, Katherine (2021) 'Are you confused by scientific jargon? So are scientists', *New York Times*, 13 April, p D2. [online] Available from: https://nyti.ms/2PnIpFV [accessed 26 April 2021].

Ladson-Billings, Gloria (1995) 'Towards a theory of culturally relevant pedagogy', *American Education Research Journal*, 32(3): 465–491.

Mann, Charles C. (2005) *1491: New Revelations of the Americas before Columbus*. New York: Random House.

Mbembe, Achille Joseph (2016) 'Decolonizing the university: New directions', *Arts and Humanities in Higher Education*, 15(1): 29–45.

Mehta, Suketu (2019) *This Land Is Our Land: An Immigrant's Manifesto*. New York: Farrar, Straus, and Giroux.

Museus, Samuel D. (2014) 'The culturally engaging campus environments (CECE) model: A new theory of college success among racially diverse student populations', *Higher Education: Handbook of Theory and Research* 29, pp 189–227.

Ngũgĩ wa Thiong'o (1986) *Decolonizing the Mind: The Politics of Language in African Literature*. Melton, Woodbridge: James Currey.

O'Brien, Jodi (2021) 'Thought piece', Presented at *Spring Symposium, Project on Gratitude, Injury and Restoration in a Pandemic Age*, sponsored by Center for Religious Wisdom and World Affairs, 7–9 April, Seattle University.

Parfitt, Tom (2005) 'Georgia: An unlikely stronghold for bacteriophage therapy', *The Lancet*, 365(9478): 2166–2167.

Parkin, Frank (1988) *Krippendorf's Tribe* (1998 edn). New York: Bantam Books.

Patnaik, Utsa (2017) 'Revisiting the "drain", or transfer from India to Britain in the context of global diffusion of capitalism', in Shubhra Chakrabarti and Utsa Patnaik (eds) *Agrarian and Other Histories: Essays for Binay Bhushan Chaudhuri*. New Delhi: Tulika Books, pp 278–317.

Perry, Samuel L., and Whitehead, Andrew L. (2021) 'Linking evangelical subculture and phallically insecure masculinity using Google searches for male enhancement', *Journal for the Scientific Study of Religion*, 60(2): 442–453.

Pinker, Steven (2013) 'Science is not your enemy', *The New Republic*, 6 August. [online] Available from: https://bit.ly/3tlp7iE [accessed 3 May 2021].

Pinker, Steven, and Wieseltier, Leon (2013) 'Science vs. the humanities, round III', *The New Republic*, 26 September. [online] Available from: https://bit.ly/3ebv2SX [accessed 3 May 2021].

Quinlan, Kathleen M. (2021) 'Do higher education students really seek "value for money"? Debunking the myth', *London Review of Education*, 19(1): 1–12.

Renninger, K. Ann, and Hidi, Suzanne E. (2020) 'To level the playing field, develop interest', *Policy Insights from the Behavioral and Brain Sciences*, 7(1): 10–18.

Rodney, Walter (1974) *How Europe Underdeveloped Africa*. Washington: Howard University Press.

Sauerbrey, Anna (2020) 'A Turkish-German couple may save us from the virus. So why is Germany uneasy?', *New York Times*, 4 December, p A27. [online] Available from: https://nyti.ms/2VPH3U7 [accessed 7 December 2020].

Schwemmer, Carsten, and Wieczorek, Oliver (2020) 'The methodological divide of sociology: Evidence from two decades of journal publications', *Sociology*, 54(1): 3–21.

Seal, Andrew (2018) 'How the university became neoliberal', *Chronicle of Higher Education*, 3 August, 64(39). [online] Available from: https://bit.ly/3dSoaZh [accessed 15 December 2021].

Shiva, Vandana (2013) 'Tackling "monocultures of the mind"', *The Asian Age*, 24 April. [online] Available from: https://bit.ly/3xFRETg [accessed 3 May 2021].

Snow, C.P. (1959) *The Two Cultures and the Scientific Revolution*. Cambridge: Cambridge University Press.

Stevens-Arroyo, Anthony M. (1995) 'Pluralism in Latino religion today', Presented at *Annual Meeting of the Religious Research Association*, sponsored by Religious Research Association, 28 October, St Louis, Missouri.

Strayhorn, Terrell Lamont (2019) *College Students' Sense of Belonging: A Key to Educational Success for All Students* (2nd edn). London: Routledge.

Thiel, Karl (2004) 'Old dogma, new tricks – 21st century phage therapy', *Nature Biotechnology*, 22(1): 31–36.

Thomas, Dave S.P., and Arday, Jason (eds) (2021) *Doing Equity and Diversity for Success in Higher Education: Redressing Structural Inequalities in the Academy*. London: Palgrave Macmillan.

Thomas, Dave S.P., and Quinlan, Kathleen M. (2021) 'Reimagining the curricula in higher education: Increasing students' interaction with teachers and interest through culturally sensitive curricula', Paper presented at the 6th Biennial International Conference on Access, Participation, and Success, (online) 15–18 March 2021.

Thorp, Holden, and Goldstein, Buck (2018) *Our Higher Calling: Rebuilding the Partnership between America and Its College and Universities.* Chapel Hill: University of North Carolina Press.

Thurow, Roger, and Kilman, Scott (2009) *Enough: Why the World's Poorest Starve in an Age of Plenty.* New York: PublicAffairs.

Tobbell, Dominique A. (2009) 'Pharmaceutical networks: The political economy of drug development in the United States, 1945–1980', *Enterprise & Society,* 10(4): 675–686.

UUK (2019) 'Black, Asian and minority ethnic student attainment at UK universities: #CLOSINGTHEGAP', *UK Universities.* [online] Available from: https://bit.ly/3rr010A [accessed 6 May 2021].

Wieseltier, Leon (2013) 'Crimes against humanities', *The New Republic,* 3 September. [online] Available from: https://bit.ly/3tnSr8d [accessed 3 May 2021].

Williams, Eric (1944) *Capitalism and Slavery.* Chapel Hill: University of North Carolina Press.

Index

References to figures and photographs appear in *italic* type; those in **bold** type refer to tables.